D0375878

THE

DETOX

REVOLUTION

A Powerful New Program for
Boosting Your Body's Ability to
Fight Cancer and Other Diseases

THOMAS J. SLAGA, Ph.D.

SCIENTIFIC DIRECTOR, AMC CANCER RESEARCH CENTER

with ROBIN KEUNEKE

McGraw·Hill

New York   Chicago   San Francisco   Lisbon   London   Madrid   Mexico City
Milan   New Delhi   San Juan   Seoul   Singapore   Sydney   Toronto

Library of Congress Cataloging-in-Publication Data

Slaga, Thomas J.
   The detox revolution / Thomas J. Slaga with Robin Keuneke.
      p.   cm.
   Includes bibliographical references and index.
   ISBN 0-8092-9976-3 (hardcover) — ISBN 0-07-143313-9 (paperback)
   1. Detoxification (Health)   I. Keuneke, Robin.   II. Title.

   RA784.5 .S58   2002
   613—dc21   2002073684

3 4 5 6 7 8 9 10 11   FGR/FGR   3 2 1 0 9 8 7 6 5 4

ISBN 0-8092-9976-3 (hardcover)
ISBN 0-07-143313-9 (paperback)

Interior design by Think Design Group
Interior illustrations by Katie Lambert

McGraw-Hill books are available at special quantity discounts to use as premiums and sales promotions, or for use in corporate training programs. For more information, please write to the Director of Special Sales, Professional Publishing, McGraw-Hill, Two Penn Plaza, New York, NY 10121-2298. Or contact your local bookstore.

This book is printed on acid-free paper.

C O N T E N T S

PART TWO
Detox Recipes

We are living in an amazingly fertile period of scientific discovery. Technology-driven advances in electronics, telecommunications, and medicine have given us the ability to lead longer, more comfortable, more diverse lives. Breakthroughs in molecular genetics and particularly in mapping the human genome promise to revolutionize our understanding of disease, especially in terms of early detection, treatment, and prevention.

I have specialized in cancer research and nutrition for thirty-five years. Early on, I had a glimpse into the powerfully protective world of phytochemicals; it was all the reinforcement I needed to make it my life's work. Over the years, I have held a number of important posts in cancer research organizations up to and including my present position as scientific director of the AMC Cancer Research Center, a Denver-based research and educational institution studying cancer since 1954, and deputy director of the University of Colorado Cancer Center. I have conducted seminars and review panels at the National Cancer Institute and the Environmental Protection Agency among others. (Incidentally, on September 11, 2001, I was across the street from the White House at a meeting of the FDA- and industry-supported Cosmetic Ingredient Review Board when tragedy struck the Pentagon.)

I have cataloged the results of my research in hundreds of papers published by the most prestigious scientific journals. My work on green tea and red grapes, for example, both of which are at the forefront of research today, helped to forge our understanding of the health benefits of the plant compounds they contain.

Despite the mounting evidence, most of us still pay little attention to how diet, lifestyle, environmental factors, and the complex interactions of our genes can affect our health and well-being. Many risk factors have been identified that increase the chance of developing various known diseases. Approximately 80 to 90 percent of all cancers, for example, are related to (a) the use of tobacco products, (b) what we eat and drink, (c) exposure to sunlight and ionizing radiation, and (d) exposure to cancer-causing agents in our environment and workplace. Because of each person's unique genetic makeup, there is no doubt that some are more sensitive to these factors than others. Healthy detoxification systems are critical in counteracting many of these risk factors.

Combining a sensible lifestyle with foods and supplements known to enhance detoxification will not only protect us from many known risk factors, but can also have a profound effect on how our genes behave. This is true even if we inherit faulty genes. Because of the scientific revolution, we now have a better understanding of how nutrients and micronutrients communicate and influence the expression of our healthy or unhealthy genes.

We can't change our genetic structure. We can, however, modify the expression of our genes. For example, if you have inherited genes that predispose you to a life of good health, by following a healthy diet and lifestyle, you will increase the effectiveness of these good genes. Even if you inherited bad genes, good diet and lifestyle habits can decrease your genes' negative expression and help to prevent disease. Of course it also follows that if you live an unhealthy lifestyle, you certainly risk counteracting the good genes and aiding the bad genes.

As an example of the benefits of sensible lifestyle, healthy diet, and detoxification supplementation, imagine two beautiful, gleaming new cars, seemingly identical in every way. The cars are the same age, manufactured the same day and at the same plant. At first glance, they seem perfect; both are fragrant with the aroma of new leather, and in fact they run well and have no apparent problems. However, each car has imperceptible manufacturing defects fundamental to its future performance, although the two were built with identical raw materials, identical strengths, and identical weaknesses.

Now imagine that one car is sensibly driven on a regular basis, not too much and not too little. It is regularly maintained, it is garaged, the oil is changed every three thousand miles, and good-quality gasoline and oil are used. The second car receives inferior care. It is left outside on the street, affected by the elements. A lower octane gas is used and the oil is seldom changed. The driving schedule is erratic. The car sits unused for weeks on end and when it is finally driven, it is driven hard. Which car will manifest the latent manufacturing defects first? Which car do you think will rust and have engine failure first? Which car do you think will last the longest?

Our genetic makeup is similar to the raw materials in a new car in that it contains both strengths and weaknesses. If we take care of the raw material—our body—with a healthy diet and supplements for detoxification, a moderate amount of exercise, and careful stress control, we will stand a much better chance of overcoming genetic weaknesses and improving our genetic strengths.

For better or worse, our genetic makeup is handed down to us from our parents. Whether we have inherited genes programmed for health or for illness, the specific superfoods and supplements discussed in this book can help our bodies to perform at optimum levels of health, to build energy, and to greatly reduce the risk of disease.

The earlier you start a program of the healthy lifestyle described in *The Detox Revolution*, the better your potential results. An expectant woman in the early stages of pregnancy can influence the genes of a fetus by maintaining a healthy lifestyle throughout the pregnancy. In this way the newborn is provided a healthy start. Some benefits can even occur at an older age. It is never too late to begin. A good diet, supplements, exercise, and stress control will do wonders for your health. And of course if you smoke, you should quit as soon as possible.

The Detox Revolution advocates building a rational food pyramid based on strong scientific research. It especially emphasizes the superfoods, including fruits, vegetables, whole grains, legumes, lean meats, and essential fats. Practicing healthy eating habits strongly supports healthy detoxification and immune systems. People who practice this approach live longer, healthier lives. On the other hand, people who eat unhealthy foods, are physically inactive, and do nothing to decrease stress are at greater risk of cancer, heart disease, inflammatory disease, neurological degeneration, diabetes, obesity, and premature aging.

As *The Detox Revolution* explains, it is very difficult to obtain sufficient amounts of important vitamins, minerals, and phytochemicals from even a healthy diet. That's why supporting our detoxification and immune systems with scientifically based supplements is so important. I describe the key supplements as soft drugs because they yield the same benefits as pharmaceuticals, or hard drugs, but without the many side effects. For example, the statin drugs that very effectively lower cholesterol often do so with a number of undesirable side effects. Alternatively, the phytochemicals, D-glucarate and silymarin, can lower cholesterol gradually with essentially no side effects and at the same time have positive effects on our detoxification systems.

This book emphasizes the importance of a healthy detoxification system in preventing many diseases including cancer. Your body's overall detoxification system is made up of several protective systems. The antioxidant system actively protects us from free radicals. The xenobiotic detoxification system converts environmental toxins and cancer-causing agents to nontoxic compounds and/or actively eliminates them from the body. This system also detoxifies substances produced by our bodies such as steroid hormones. We have a DNA repair system that protects the integrity of our genes from permanent damage. The immune system is important in destroying bacteria, viruses, and cancer cells. All these systems work together to protect us from invaders from our environment as well as enemies within our bodies. This book recommends specific dietary and breakthrough supplements to increase the effectiveness of the detoxification systems. After all, the process of detoxification is important to everyone, not just people with cancer or other degenerative diseases.

In these difficult times, with the threat of chemical and biological attacks looming over us, the maintenance of a healthy body becomes more and more important. Proper nutrition and the supplements in this book work together as a team to enhance detoxification; strengthen the immune system; and inhibit the growth of bad bacteria, viruses, and other microorganisms in the body. This is critical for people with inadequate or suppressed immune and detoxification systems; they are the first to succumb to these harmful agents.

The message of *The Detox Revolution* is simple: we don't have to wait for cancer or other degenerative diseases to manifest—or for the pharmaceutical industry to find an ever-elusive cure (which will no doubt arrive with plenty of side effects). Nor do we have to wait for environmental chemicals or chemicals produced by our bodies to trigger the process of cancer or other diseases as we age. By incorporating the strategies presented in this book, you can initiate a lifelong plan of aggressive nutritional practices, exercise, and stress control to support your detoxification system and stay healthy. After all, what's the point of living longer, more comfortable, and more diverse lives through advances in technology if we don't have our health?

—Thomas J. Slaga, Ph.D.

PART ONE

The Detox Revolution

CHAPTER ONE

Detoxification: The Key to Wellness

The human body has two major detoxification systems for the elimination of damaging toxins, xenobiotic detoxification and antioxidant detoxification. Since my early years as a cancer and nutrition researcher, I have been fascinated by the crucial role of these systems in preventing cancer and other degenerative diseases. All of us are exposed daily to health-threatening substances that increasingly permeate our air, food, and water. Why is it then that some people with clearly unhealthy lifestyles—such as smokers—can maintain health while others with healthier lifestyles—such as nonsmokers—develop cancer? There are many variables in each person's life that impact his or her health, but this question is best answered by taking a look at the body's ability to detoxify potential cancer-causing agents and other harmful substances.

Detoxification and Your Health

It's always amazed me—and my colleagues at the University of Texas M.D. Anderson Cancer Center and my research team at the AMC Cancer Research Center—that some people can be exposed for an entire lifetime to radiation, tobacco smoke, or other cancer-causing agents and never get sick. We now know that those people are protected by elevated levels of especially protective detoxification genes. They are truly the lucky ones. For those of us with average to weak inherited genetic protection, such lifestyles appear ill advised if not downright suicidal. We all must play the hand we're dealt, and as there is not a single unpolluted spot left on this earth, we can only control our environment up to a very limited point. We can minimize exposure to toxic conditions present in the air we breathe, the water we drink, and the foods we eat. Those people who live in excessively toxic environments, whether at home or at work; who smoke and/or drink excessive amounts of alcohol; or who have bad diets are clearly putting themselves in harm's way. However they may rationalize it, what they are really doing is banking on having inherited strong detoxification systems. If they are right, they may avoid health problems for a long time. But if they are wrong, they will unfortunately become statistics in the mounting evidence that such reckless living leads to a higher probability of developing cancer, heart disease, arthritis, and other degenerative diseases. Since it is a statistical fact that most of us aren't lucky enough to inherit such strong detoxification systems, doesn't it make sense to reduce as much as possible the health risks from controllable external factors?

Despite great variations in individual genetic makeup, each of us can protect, strengthen, and enhance what we have with sensible lifestyle choices. To eliminate more than 70 percent of the risk factors that can lead to cancer formation and other degenerative diseases, we need only make two such choices: eat a healthy diet and don't smoke. Such a proactive mind-set would go a long way to help our detoxification systems help themselves.

ENHANCING GENETIC FUNCTION

Everyone is born with detoxification genes. These genes work best when supported by good nutrition and key supplements. Optimal genetic function allows the body to effectively absorb nutrients and to cleanse itself.

A healthy diet containing lots of fruits, vegetables, whole grains, and legumes is key to countering the negative health effects of our increasingly polluted environment. Eating a variety of these foods provides access to vital sources of nutrients that support the body's ability to detoxify. As my early studies from the 1970s proved, flavonoids—plant chemicals or phytochemicals found in green tea, flaxseed, soy, and blueberries—provide a jump start for the body's cleansing mechanisms, which helps to prevent cancer. Hundreds of scientific studies support the role of flavonoids in counteracting the effects of many different known and potential cancer-causing agents.

> ## FLAVONOIDS ARE STRONG DETOXIFICATION AGENTS
>
> Experimental studies of both humans and animals have shown many types of flavonoids to be very effective in detoxifying even the most dangerous toxic compounds.

Many people still do not understand the importance of diet and supplements that help the body's detoxification enzymes to perform at optimal levels. As a result, these people lack the necessary amounts of nutrients, vitamins, minerals, and beneficial phytochemicals to deal with toxic conditions created both externally and within the body itself.

There are more than two hundred published studies that suggest a diet high in fruits, vegetables, whole grains, and legumes leads to a decrease in cancer incidence. Also notable, 35 percent of all cancers are directly affected by diet and nutrition. In addition to the key nutrients—proteins, carbohydrates, and fats—a healthy diet supplies important phytochemicals that supercharge the body's detoxification system. Examples of such phytochemicals include flavonoids; D-glucarate, a potent detoxification compound found in fruits and vegetables, which has been of particular interest to me in my research; many sulfur compounds found in cruciferous vegetables, onions, and garlic; diterpenoids and triterpenoids found in rosemary and other herbs and spices; and phenolic and polyphenolic compounds, such as those in tea and, more surprisingly, coffee. These important phytochemicals will be discussed in detail in Chapters 3 and 4.

> ## DIET AFFECTS GENES PROGRAMMED TO ELIMINATE TOXINS
>
> Inadequate nutrition can lead to poor performance of important detoxification genes and in turn lower detoxification-enzyme activity. This weakens the body, which can easily be overwhelmed by pollutants. Cancer, heart disease, arthritis, and other degenerative diseases may result.

People who smoke and/or eat a lot of junk foods give their bodies even more to break down and eliminate. When these factors are taken into consideration, it's surprising that far more people don't get sick.

Mrs. and Mr. Smart Lifestyle

Mrs. and Mr. Not-So-Smart Lifestyle

Detoxification is a key bodily process designed to deal with health-threatening toxic conditions posed by our environment, our diets, and even our bodies themselves. There are many chemical processes taking place in the body all the time, and some of these require a detoxification process after completing their work. For example, steroid hormones such as estrogens and androgens perform vital cellular functions within our bodies, but once a particular function has been performed, these chemicals can cause problems such as overstimulating breast and prostate tissues. Consequently they must be detoxified or removed.

PROTECT YOURSELF FROM HARMFUL SUBSTANCES

Try to avoid overcooking red meat, poultry, or fish; heterocyclic amines are formed in overcooked meats. Don't cook meat over charcoal briquettes; polycyclic aromatic hydrocarbons are produced during the charcoal-burning process. Don't smoke cigarettes or use other tobacco products, which produce polycyclic aromatic hydrocarbons, nitrosamines, free radicals, and aromatic amines. Decrease the amount of junk food you consume; nitrosamines and carcinogens are common in processed foods, particularly in preserved meats.

The Main Organ of Detoxification: The Liver

The liver is the major organ involved in many processes of detoxification including the removal of toxins from the blood. Liver cells filter and destroy large amounts of chemicals, bacteria, and other harmful substances, whether those substances are created inside or outside of the body.

The liver also produces bile, which is needed for absorption and proper digestion of fats and excretion of detoxification waste products. It destroys and processes old red blood cells. The liver prepares the nutrients for other tissues of the body. It converts fats and proteins into fuel. It stores excess blood glucose as glycogen to be broken down and released back into general circulation when blood glucose is low. In addition, it serves as a storage site for vitamins B_{12}, E, K, and D, and iron.

Excessive exposure to certain toxins or poisons can lead to liver damage. Alcohol, acetaminophen, cleaning fluids, industrial chemicals, mushroom toxins, and other chemicals can cause extensive damage if exposure is intense and/or long term. Certain viruses can also damage the liver. But this organ has a remarkable ability to regenerate itself under damaging conditions. In later chapters, I will discuss some breakthrough supplements that help to protect the liver from the damaging effects of chemicals and viruses.

Although the liver is the main organ for dealing with toxic bodily conditions, it is by no means the only one. The body's line of defense against external threats is shared among the three major portals through which harmful agents gain entry into our tissues.

The first portal is the respiratory system where life-supporting oxygen enters the body, is converted to energy for the cells, and then exits in the form of carbon dioxide, a waste product.

The second portal is the digestive system. This system processes food we've eaten, then absorbs it into the circulatory system to be used as fuel and to provide building blocks for tissues and nutrients and other chemical components for critical bodily processes and reactions. The digestive system also determines whether ingested material is useless or dangerous to the body, and, if so, breaks it down and eliminates it through the intestines or absorbs it into the circulatory system to be eliminated via the liver.

The third portal is the skin, which is the body's largest organ. The skin provides a barrier against external environmental pollutants.

DETOXIFICATION OCCURS THROUGHOUT THE BODY

Enzymes essential for the detoxification of environmental chemicals and metals, as well as chemicals produced by our bodies such as steroid hormones, are not just found in the liver, where the bulk of the cleanup process takes place. They are also found in oral and nasal passages, the respiratory and digestive systems, the skin, and most organs and tissues of the body.

The Body's Two Major Detoxification Systems

Humans—in fact, all mammals—have two major systems for eliminating harmful substances from the body: xenobiotic detoxification and antioxidant detoxification. It is important to understand both systems because, for good health, each must function at an extremely high level.

The Xenobiotic Detoxification System

The first system, known as xenobiotic detoxification, disarms health-threatening chemicals and metals from food, water, and air.

It also neutralizes dangerous substances produced within the body. During this process of detoxification, which consists of many different types of complex enzymatic reactions, the body metabolizes or changes these substances to a less dangerous form (Phase I) and converts them if necessary to a water-soluble state (Phase II), something the body requires before it can effectively eliminate them.

TOXINS MIX WITH OIL OR WATER

Toxic agents, whether environmental air and water pollutants, food additives, or internally produced steroidal hormones such as estrogens, are either water based or oil based.

Scientists have a very good idea of how the processes of detoxification work. Cytochrome P-450 is an important class of Phase I enzymes. These enzymes add oxygen to various chemicals such as steroid hormones produced by the ovaries, testes, and adrenal glands, and polycyclic aromatic hydrocarbons, a combustion by-product, to make them less toxic. Then, because these toxins are highly fat soluble, Phase II has to bind them to other molecules (a process known as conjugation) to make them sufficiently water soluble for elimination through urination. Other toxic agents go through a similar process but are eliminated through the feces. Toxins are made water soluble through enzymatic processes involving glucuronide, glutathione, and sulfate, which is used in the enzymatic process to conjugate the steroid hormones in our illustration. Glutathione is employed in modifying particularly reactive toxins. But the majority of toxins, approximately 80 percent, are made water soluble by enzymatic processes involving glucuronide or glucuronic acid. These processes are called glucuronidation. Carcinogens such as polycyclic aromatic hydrocarbons, nitrosamines, heterocyclic amines, aromatic amines, and many other toxins are conjugated by this process. Glucuronidation is the key Phase II detoxification process. It takes place in every tissue of our bodies.

In some cases, Phase I enzymes can actually increase the cancer-causing activity of environmental compounds such as polycyclic aromatic hydrocarbons if there is insufficient Phase II detoxification. Other enzymes involved in the metabolism of carcinogens, such as peroxides and transferase, can also lead to greater carcinogenic activity under certain conditions.

Phase I and II Reactions

Oxidations, reductions, and acetylations are the Phase I enzymatic reactions necessary to decrease the toxic effect of chemicals, to make them more water soluble, and in some cases to facilitate subsequent conjugation reactions and excretion. Here is an example of Phase I and Phase II reactions followed by excretion:

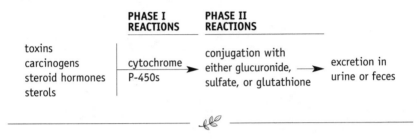

	PHASE I REACTIONS	PHASE II REACTIONS	
toxins carcinogens steroid hormones sterols	cytochrome P-450s	conjugation with either glucuronide, sulfate, or glutathione	excretion in urine or feces

Perhaps by now you are beginning to feel a bit of the awe I have for this marvelously elegant protective system of the body. But at this stage of the discussion, awe gives way to drama, because through an apparent perversity of nature, an enzyme called β-glucuronidase acts to reverse the work of glucuronidation, thereby reintroducing toxins—including steroid hormones such as estrogens and androgens—back into the body.

It has been suggested that β-glucuronidase, which is found in many tissues throughout the body, is intended to work as a salvage enzyme, recycling important compounds made within the body for further work. But something obviously went wrong because when it is applied to toxins, cancer-causing agents, and steroid hormones, it appears that rather than serving the body well, β-glucuronidase does damage. What we know about β-glucuronidase is that it exists in all of us in different concentrations. High levels of this enzyme in the body have been associated with an increased risk for cancer development, whereas low levels indicate a decreased risk. Elevated levels have been observed in people following exposure to tobacco smoke, industrial chemicals, and other cancer-causing agents such as polycyclic aromatic hydrocarbons and nitrosamines. I have already mentioned my interest in the compound D-glucarate, which is found naturally in fruits and vegetables. Here's why it's so important: D-glucarate has been found to be a potent inhibitor of β-glucuronidase. People who eat a diet high in fruits and

Sources of Toxins Controlled by the Xenobiotic Detoxification System

Exposure to certain substances found in our own bodies as well as substances in our environment can have destructive effects on health. Xenobiotic detoxification helps to eliminate toxic compounds from many sources.

IN THE ENVIRONMENT	WITHIN THE BODY
cigarette smoke	androgens
tobacco products	estrogens
certain drugs	other steroids
combustion by-products	bile acids
charcoal-cooked meats	other cellular chemicals
overcooked meats	
herbicides and pesticides	
organic solvents	
toxins in food	

vegetables and who supplement with D-glucarate often have low levels of β-glucuronidase. This is because an active constituent of D-glucarate actually and very effectively halts the reversing affect of β-glucuronidase on the glucuronidation and preserves its good work in eliminating toxins from the body.

D-GLUCARATE IS A POTENT DETOXIFICATION AGENT

Significant levels of the beneficial compound D-glucarate are found in cruciferous vegetables including cabbage, broccoli, brussels sprouts, watercress, alfalfa, and bean sprouts. Apples, grapefruits, cherries, and apricots also contain high levels of D-glucarate.

In this inhibiting role, D-glucarate has been found to have a protective effect against cancers of the breast, prostate, lung, colon, bladder, and skin. It has been observed in research studies of the detoxification process to safely regulate bile acids and steroid hormones to levels that are not likely to progress to cancer. In other scientific studies, D-glucarate has been shown to inhibit the growth of cancer cells. Not surprisingly then, high levels of D-glucarate in the blood are associated with a decreased risk of cancer and low levels with increased risk. D-glucarate has also been shown to lower triglycerides, total cholesterol, LDL, and vLDL (the so-called bad cholesterols), while not affecting HDL (the so-called good cholesterol). And in studies of both humans and animals, no toxicity has been associated with the consumption of D-glucarate.

The significant role D-glucarate and other phytochemicals appear to play in the xenobiotic detoxification will be discussed throughout this book.

The Antioxidant Detoxification System

Antioxidant detoxification involves deactivating or destroying what are known as oxygen reactive species, the most significant category of which is free radicals. At the risk of oversimplification, free radicals can be thought of as very unstable electric charges—sparks—that if not properly controlled can set up extremely serious toxic conditions within the body. Free radicals can be generated by environmental factors such as exposure to cigarette smoke and other pollutants or created from internal reactions such as mitochondrial respiration (the use of oxygen to generate energy), by-products of chemical metabolism, inflammation from strenuous exercise or physical work, and the intake of too many calories. Excessive free radicals rob electrons from normal, healthy tissue creating potentially serious damage at the cellular level. Even more profound, we have recently realized that unchecked free radicals can modify DNA structure, possibly leading to mutations and altered gene programming that can initiate the cancer process. Parkinson's disease, cataracts, artherosclerosis, sperm abnormalities, emphysema, sickle cell anemia, abnormal aging, and stroke are all significantly linked to excessive free radicals in the body.

Fortunately, free radicals can be destroyed by these elements:

- specific antioxidant enzymatic reactions

- antioxidants, which are found in a wide variety of foods and are even produced by the body itself

- certain phytochemicals with antioxidant properties, including flavonoids, sulfur-containing compounds such as those in onions, terpenoids from herbs and spices, and certain vitamins and minerals

---

FREE RADICALS ARE NOT ALWAYS BAD

Researchers at Ohio University have found that certain free radicals, also known as oxidants, play a key role in repairing blood vessels damaged by the buildup of cholesterol. Dr. Goldschmidt, director of the university's Heart and Lung Institute, told the *Journal of Circulation Research* that oxidants often have a highly positive effect on the process. In addition, protective immune cells called macrophages use free radicals to kill bacteria and viruses. Only in excess are free radicals dangerous. It is now possible to determine the level of free radical damage in an individual by taking a blood or urine sample. This will be discussed further in Chapter 9.

In the enzymatic processes, a group of important antioxidant enzymes work together systematically to destroy various free radicals and other reactive oxygen species. All of us inherit these enzymes to some degree. Those with high levels won't have much trouble with free radicals, but those with low levels need to take special care. Most of us fall somewhere in between. Here again, I must risk becoming overly technical in order to explain how these processes work.

The antioxidant enzymes important to the enzymatic processes include several superoxide dismutases (SODs), catalase, glutathione peroxidase, glutathione reductase, thioredoxin reductase, and ascorbic acid reductase. How they are employed depends on the task at hand. Take, for example, superoxide, a highly reactive oxygen molecule. The formation of superoxide is a normal physiological process, but excessive amounts can lead to damage and must be detoxified. There are three different SODs that enzymatically convert the dangerous superoxide molecule to hydrogen peroxide, and then the antioxidant enzyme catalase finishes the job by converting hydrogen peroxide to harmless water and normal oxygen. These SODs need manganese, copper, and/or zinc for their important antioxidant function.

Another family of antioxidant enzymes, ones that contain the important mineral selenium, is called glutathione peroxidases. These enzymes are capable of neutralizing other types of peroxides, such as lipid peroxides, which can give rise to free radicals and alter important lipids in the body's cellular and nuclear membranes leading to a chain reaction called lipid peroxidation. This process is definitely not good for cells and can be a factor in many degenerative diseases.

For antioxidants to be effective in destroying all types of free radicals, they must be in what we call a reduced state. The antioxidant enzymes glutathione reductase and thioredoxin reductase (another selenium-containing enzyme) play an important role in this. Finally, ascorbic acid reductase keeps ascorbic acid (vitamin C), an important dietary antioxidant from fruits and vegetables, in a reduced state so that it can effectively neutralize certain free radicals and in turn help to keep vitamin E, another antioxidant, in a reduced state as well.

The cells of our body produce many chemicals with antioxidizing activity against free radicals. Important examples include glutathione, which is probably the best known, as well as coenzyme Q_{10} (CoQ_{10}), alpha lipoic acid, L-methionine, L-glutamine, taurine, bilirubin, cysteine, and uric acid. These antioxidants help protect important DNA, proteins, and lipids from free radical damage.

Fruits, vegetables, whole grains, and legumes contain many dietary antioxidants to help fight against free radicals including vitamin E, vitamin C (ascorbic acid), and several carotenoids including β-carotene, lutein, and lycopene. These foods also contain many different phytochemicals with antioxidant properties including flavonoids, isoflavones, polyphenols, sulfur-containing compounds, and terpenoids.

In addition to the direct effect that antioxidant activity has on keeping free radicals in check, it also gives support to xenobiotic Phase I and II enzymes further improving the overall detoxification process. The xenobiotic and the antioxidant detoxification systems work together to decrease the burdens imposed by toxins and free radicals, allowing individuals to live longer and healthier lives.

Sources of Free Radicals Handled by the Antioxidant Detoxification System

IN THE ENVIRONMENT	CREATED WITHIN THE BODY
cigarette smoke	respiration for energy
radiation	overeating
ultraviolet light	inflammation
ozone	reactions to iron and other metals
combustion by-products	overexercising
certain drugs, pesticides, and industrial solvents	
other environmental pollutants	

Detoxification of Heavy Metals

Detoxification of heavy metals such as lead, mercury, cadmium, and nickel is a complex function. The body processes metals through a particular metabolic pathway, depending on whether they appear as organic or inorganic compounds or as the elemental metals. Characteristically, heavy metals accumulate slowly in the body and have half-lives that may span many years. This causes a disruption of homeostatis or normal cellular and organ function, which can lead to a disease state. Heavy metals can alter normal mineral balance, suppress the immune system, and do damage to the brain, heart, kidneys, and liver. Heavy metals are more absorbable on an empty stomach, so it is always advisable to eat regularly and avoid skipping meals. Not surprisingly, fruits and vegetables are at the top of my list of foods I recommend be eaten with great frequency because we know that many phytochemicals contained in them, including polyphenols and silymarin, are able to bind (chelate) heavy metals and help prevent absorption. Even if heavy metals are absorbed, sulfur- and sulfhydryl-containing amino acids, such as L-methionine and cysteine, are very effective components in their detoxification. Glutathione, a sulfur-containing molecule, is one of the key agents in the body for the detoxification of heavy metals. Methylsulfonyl-methane (MSM), which occurs naturally in the body, in addition to being an effective free radical scavenger, is an excellent source of sulfur for this purpose.

HEAVY METAL DETOXIFICATION

MSM and N-acetylcysteine (NAC) are both very effective antioxidants and detoxifiers of heavy metals.

Methylation: At the Forefront of Nutrition Research

Methylation is a biochemical process that is crucial for life. It is the initiator of many protective activities, such as transcribing genes, creating or converting critical compounds, and detoxifying harmful chemicals, including homocysteine. The liver, the major detoxification organ, depends on methylation to perform many enzymatic reactions required to detoxify drugs and foreign chemicals. Recent breakthroughs in the study of this process have propelled it to the forefront of scientific interest.

The primary methylating substance, s-adenosylmethionine (SAMe) is formed when methionine, an amino acid, reacts with adenosine triphosphate (ATP), an energy molecule. Although not an antioxidant, SAMe reverses DNA damage by free radicals. Levels of SAMe have been shown to decrease with age.

Methylation deficiencies can bring on cancer and other chronic diseases such as heart disease, depression, and accelerated aging. Elevated homocysteine levels can be a sign of a methylation deficiency throughout the body. High levels of homocysteine can cause lipid peroxidation and sticky platelets and can promote the oxidation of low-density lipoprotein (LDL) cholesterol. In general when cholesterol is elevated, so is homocysteine; both situations are known indicators for heart disease and stroke. To maintain a low level of homocysteine, it has to be methylated by SAMe and converted back to methionine or cysteine, which is further converted to glutathione. Natural detoxification of homocysteine can only occur when enough B vitamins are present. The conversion to methionine requires sufficient folate and vitamin B_{12}; the conversion to glutathione requires sufficient vitamin B_6. These vitamins plus trimethylglycine (TMG) are effective in lowering homocysteine. Most Americans eat plenty of meat so they get large amounts of methionine. Unfortunately, however, the majority of Americans do not eat enough fresh vegetables and whole grains to get sufficient B vitamins. B vitamins are essential in keeping elevated homocysteine from becoming a health problem.

With new breakthroughs in the study of methylation, we now have an answer for why free radicals damage DNA and in turn cause cancer, a question that has eluded scientists for decades. Researchers at Northwestern University found that when a small area of DNA is oxidized, the result is that methylation is altered. As soon as this occurs, protective genetic function is eliminated and cancer genes are free to activate. Scientists now realize that free radical damage occurs through abnormal methylation and that normal methylation keeps cancer genes at bay.

Calorie Intake Management

As sound scientific animal research has demonstrated many times, decreasing caloric intake can positively increase the capabilities of the detoxification system. Studies involving rodents, for example, have shown that decreasing caloric intake by one-third increased their life span and protected them against cancer, immunological dysfunction, and heart disease, and delayed the onset of other degenerative diseases.

*The combined caloric amount of all these fruits and vegetables
is less than that of a single hamburger.*

It appears that the major health benefit of caloric restriction is a decrease in free radical damage and enhanced xenobiotic detoxification. Caloric restriction has been shown to prevent the overproduction of estrogens, androgens, and other hormones; to decrease the potency of cancer-causing agents; to slow cell proliferation (cell proliferation is a requirement for cancer growth); and to normalize respiratory function, which is important to prevent energy formation from throwing off free radicals. When all of these factors are taken together the evidence shows a reduction in the burden on our detoxification systems.

Experiments using mice have demonstrated the significant positive effects of calorie restriction. In one experiment, two groups of one hundred mice each were fed a healthy diet of scientifically blended proteins, carbohydrates, essential fats, and important vitamins and minerals— generally speaking a diet as good as if not better than what most people consume. The control group was allowed unrestricted access to the food. The experimental group was denied the food one-third of the time— effectively a one-third reduction in calories. The control group lived approximately two years; the experimental group lived approximately eight months longer. Eight months may not seem like a long time in human terms, but for mice it represents a significant increase in life span. In another study with mice, using a similar protocol, both groups were given a potent cancer-causing agent. The results revealed that the experimental group living on the restricted diet displayed greater xenobiotic detoxification of the agent than the control group enjoying unrestricted access to food. One more example involves a study of transgenic mice, mice with known genetic mutations that under normal conditions usually develop cancer and die within three to four months. This study showed that when the mice with the bad genes were placed on restricted diets, a much longer period of time elapsed—almost eighteen months— before the cancer even developed. And it was specifically noted in the study of these mice that calorie restriction significantly decreased free radical damage and increased xenobiotic detoxification capabilities.

CHAPTER TWO

Decreasing the Burden on Your Detoxification Systems

As noted in Chapter 1, the body has an elegant natural process of detoxification. However, that process can sometimes be overwhelmed. In this chapter we will take a look at what we can do to support the body's detoxification system. How can we reduce our toxic load? How can we minimize our exposure to harmful chemicals so that the two major processes of detoxification will work effectively? I will address these questions and show you how you can optimize the performance of your body's detoxification systems.

Every day we are exposed to things that threaten our health. Since most of the time we don't see the consequences until far into the future, it is human nature to shrug them off until we are faced with poor health. It's important to understand the dangers posed by a lifestyle that most of us simply take for granted, so that we can gain the conviction required for necessary change.

Our lifestyle decisions have a direct relationship to the toxins and cancer-causing agents that our bodies have to deal with, including both substances that come from outside our bodies and the chemicals and free radicals produced by our bodies. Where and how we eat, breathe, and exercise may seem innocent enough, but in today's world we need to evaluate these choices for the toxins and cancer-causing agents they deliver to our doorstep. In order to protect our good health, the fewer toxins confronting our detoxification systems, the better. We are all exposed to thousands of chemicals every day, of which less than 2 percent has been adequately evaluated for health effects. And that 2 percent has largely been examined in isolation, rather than in *combination*, which is how we experience them in the real world. Given that most scientists believe that a significant number of all cancers are the result of the long-term effects of harmful chemicals, metals, radiation, and free radicals, it's easy to see that there is real cause for concern.

GENETIC DAMAGE FROM CHEMICAL COMBINATIONS

Environmental chemicals frequently combine to form more highly reactive chemicals and free radicals. These toxins can bind strongly with our DNA, modify it, and overwhelm its repair systems, resulting in extensive genetic damage and cancer.

The typical North American is exposed to a large amount, possibly a pound or two, of dangerous chemicals each year. A total of at least twenty toxic compounds were found in 70 to 100 percent of all samples taken in the ongoing EPA project known as the National Human Adipose Tissue Survey. Many of these harmful substances bind easily with the DNA in the human body, producing harmful effects on it and overwhelming its repair systems. Cell mutation and cancer may result.

THE AGENCY FOR TOXIC SUBSTANCES

Find out about toxic chemicals and metals in your area by investigating the Agency for Toxic Substances, part of the Centers for Disease Control and Prevention, at www.atsdr.cdc.gov.

Twenty Lifesaving Recommendations to Boost Your Body's Ability to Detoxify

Healthy lifestyle habits will ensure the peak performance of our detoxification systems. Here are some key recommendations that will help reduce your exposure to harmful chemicals and minimize the production of free radicals. For each recommendation, risk factors will vary

from person to person. Although most of our genetic makeup is identical, those pieces that are not give each of us a unique profile—and a different predisposition to disease. For instance, not everyone who eats a diet high in fried foods, which can lead to exposure to highly carcinogenic chemicals, will get cancer. However, people with a low level of xenobiotic detoxification capability, a genetic factor, may be at increased risk. Even if you are not at a high risk for cancer, avoiding fried foods will reduce the burden on your detoxification system, which is important for staying healthy. The same is true for other recommendations. The positive effects of following them will vary according to the person's unique genetic makeup, but they will greatly help anyone's natural detoxification processes.

1. Don't Smoke

Do not smoke or allow others to smoke in your home or car. Cigarette smoke, even secondhand smoke, is a serious contributor to lung cancer. Smoking and tobacco products are factors in about 30 percent of all cancers, and the risk of developing lung cancer is ten times greater for smokers than for nonsmokers. The degree of risk from smoking depends on the number and type of cigarettes smoked, the length of time an individual has smoked, and how deeply the smoke is inhaled. Cigarette smoking and the use of other tobacco products are a major cause of cancers of the lung, oral cavity, larynx, esophagus, bladder, kidney, and pancreas. Studies have also found an association between tobacco use and leukemia and breast and prostate cancers. This is an area of research in which I have had strong personal involvement; the conclusions were convincing enough to make me quit smoking more than thirty years ago.

Some of the better-known cancer-causing agents in tobacco products, including polycyclic aromatic hydrocarbons (PAHs), heterocyclic amines, benzene, and nitrosamines, are present in cigarette smoke at significant levels. And these dangerous chemicals have a tendency to stay around for a long time. Even after a smoker quits for good, it takes five to ten years to eliminate these chemicals from the body. But there is good news. An enhanced program of detoxification can significantly accelerate elimination. In California, where strict tobacco control legislation has been passed, lung cancer rates dropped almost 15 percent in ten years, twice as fast as other areas in the country. Studies show that women seem to be more susceptible to lung cancer from smoking than men. Cigar smokers, however—mostly men—are seven to eight times more at risk than nonsmokers for developing lung cancer.

The dangers of smoking increase dramatically when it is combined with alcohol. Epidemiologists have estimated that people who are both heavy smokers (one pack or more a day) and drinkers (four or more alcoholic drinks a day) have as much as a ten-times-higher risk of cancer, mainly cancer of the oral cavity, larynx, and esophagus.

TOXINS IN TOBACCO

The smoke from cigarettes and other tobacco products contains more than four thousand dangerous chemicals and gases, including polycyclic aromatic hydrocarbons, benzene, heterocyclic amines, nitrosamines, radioactive elements, carbon monoxide, and many other known cocarcinogens and tumor promoters.

Dr. Steve Hecht and coworkers at the University of Minnesota Cancer Center regularly investigate the role of nitrosamines in cigarette smoke on human cancer. They have found that cruciferous vegetables such as watercress, which contains large amounts of isothiocyanates, are very effective in counteracting tobacco-specific nitrosamine-induced cancer in experimental animals. Along with this phytochemical, D-glucarate, silymarin, flavonoids from grape seed and skin extract, and green tea, rosemary extract, N-acetylcysteine, and alpha lipoic acid all help to detoxify the many cancer-causing agents in cigarette smoke.

If you smoke, stop now! It is never too late to quit. The American Cancer Society has published some good news about the benefits of quitting, which begin almost immediately after the last cigarette is put out. Within twenty minutes, blood pressure, pulse, and body temperature return to normal. After eight hours, that odor known as smoker's breath will disappear; carbon monoxide drops and oxygen rises to normal levels in the blood. The risk of heart attack begins to decrease after only twenty-four hours. Within a couple of days, the ability to taste and smell improves significantly as does breathing capacity. Within two to three months, circulation improves and lung function increases up to 30 percent. Within one to nine months, sinus congestion, coughing, fatigue, and shortness of breath decrease. The cilia that clean debris from the lungs grow back. Within one year, excess risk of coronary heart disease is half that of a smoker. Within two years, heart attack risk drops to near normal. Within five years, lung cancer death rate and stroke risk decrease by half. Within ten years, lung cancer death rate is half that of a continuing smoker and the risk of cancer of the mouth, throat, esophagus, bladder, kidney, and pancreas decreases. Within fifteen years, the risk of coronary heart disease is the same as a person who has never smoked.

So as you can see there are compelling reasons to quit smoking as soon as possible. Get your spouse or friend to quit with you because this makes it much easier. In addition, if necessary, use a nicotine substitute; several studies suggest that this also helps.

HELP FOR SMOKING CESSATION

The American Cancer Society has information and tips on quitting smoking. For information call 1-800-ACS-2345 or visit www.cancer.org. You may also contact the American Heart Association at 1-800-242-1793 or at www.amhrt.org; the American Lung Association at 1-800-586-4872 or at www.lungusa.org; or the National Cancer Institute at 1-800-4-CANCER or at www.nci.nih.gov.

2. Avoid Overexposure to Radiation from Sunlight and X-Rays

Radiation from the sun, especially between 10 A.M. and 3 P.M., is a serious source of DNA-damaging free radicals, which can lead to skin cancer (basal and squamous cell carcinomas and melanoma) and rapid aging of the skin. Limit sun exposure before and after these times and always wear protective clothing and sunscreen. A study in the *International Journal of Cancer* (July 2000) found that people who were at high risk for skin cancer and stayed out in the sun for extended periods of time with limited application of sunscreen were not protected against malignant melanoma. The scientists who conducted the study also warned against long periods of sun exposure and to select sunscreen with an SPF of 16 or higher. The sunscreen should be applied every hour or two. Tanning salons and sunlamps are also to be avoided. In the year 2000, there were more than a million cases of skin cancer in the United States. Proper protection (protective clothing plus frequently applied sunscreen) together with a healthy diet could prevent most of these cancers. Have x-rays taken only if recommended by a dentist or physician; never ask for them. When x-rays are required, make sure the rest of your body is properly shielded.

Dr. Mukhtar and coworkers from Case Western Reserve Cancer Center, as well as researchers at AMC Cancer Research Center, have found that many different flavonoids, green tea polyphenolic antioxidants, and

silymarin are potent inhibitors of ultraviolet light–induced skin cancer in mice. Recently, we at AMC have found that coffee extract, which contains many phenolic and polyphenolic antioxidants, is a very potent inhibitor of skin cancer induced by ultraviolet light or chemical carcinogens.

SUN PROTECTION

Wear protective clothing and use sunscreens that absorb both ultraviolet A and B with an SPF of 16 or greater and that contain zinc oxide or titanium dioxide. Many of the new sunscreens contain antioxidants, which offer additional protection. Apply sunscreen frequently.

3. Avoid Overcooked, Smoked, Burned, and Charred Meats

Charred or fried fat-rich meats (including chicken and fish) contain dangerous PAHs and nitrosamines. A third class of chemicals of great concern to scientists is called heterocyclic amines, which are formed when certain amino acids, the building blocks of protein, become altered after being heated for long periods. Extensive damage to genetic material can result in people who metabolize heterocyclic amines easily.

I've had firsthand experience with many studies of PAHs, nitrosamines, and heterocyclic amines, and I can tell you that exposure to these potent carcinogenic agents in experimental animals leads to cancer very quickly. The risk of cancer from these agents increases when meat goes from overcooked to burned or charred, or when the cooking method involves charcoal. Even smoked meats can produce all three of these classes of potent carcinogen.

Safe Grilling Recommendations

· Cook at temperatures below 400°F.

· Marinate meats to decrease the effective temperature.

· Use garlic, onions, turmeric, or rosemary in marinades for protective phytochemicals.

· Do not add honey or sugar to marinades because this will form other harmful amines.

· Microwave meat a minute or two before grilling.

· Grill to the side or just off the high heat.

· Turn meats frequently during cooking.

· Wrap food in aluminum foil.

Although the message here is to select and prepare meats to avoid consuming PAHs, nitrosamines, and heterocyclic amines, we know that flavonoids found in fruits and vegetables can counteract the carcinogenic effects of these agents. For example, I, as well as other investigators, have found that flavonoids are very effective in counteracting the effects of benzopyrene, one of the many PAHs associated with smoked, burned, and charred meats that have been shown to induce skin, intestinal, and lung cancer in experimental animals. And Dr. T. Sugumura and coworkers from the Japanese Cancer Center have found that green tea polyphenols are very potent inhibitors of heterocyclic amine–induced cancer in rodents. Cancer-counteracting properties of foods found in nature will be discussed in greater detail in Chapter 3.

> ### REDUCING CARCINOGENS FROM GRILLED MEATS
>
> Scientists at the Lawrence Livermore Laboratory in California found that frequently turning hamburgers and other meats helps to reduce carcinogens from the cooking process. Marinating chicken and other meats for as few as twenty minutes before barbecuing also helps reduce heterocyclic amines. A marinade consisting of a mixture of olive oil, lemon, cider vinegar, garlic, and mustard, for example, lowers cooking temperature, and the garlic contains phytochemicals that help to neutralize dangerous chemicals that may be produced.

4. Avoid Preserved Foods

Nitrosamines can also be formed when the nitrites from preserved foods combine with amine-containing foods and certain drugs in the acid environment of the stomach. Baseball wouldn't be the same without beer and hot dogs—a good example of such a combination—but the result can be very dangerous to our health. So limit those ballpark favorites. Some meats are now preserved with sodium ascorbate, a form of vitamin C, which is a healthier option. Read the labels of preserved meats and other foods very carefully. Vitamin C, as well as several other antioxidants, has been found to inhibit the formation of nitrosamine in the acid environment of the stomach. Dr. S. Mirvish at the Epply Cancer Research Institute found that vitamin C (ascorbic acid) or other antioxidants introduced at the same time as nitrites, prevented them from reacting with amines in the stomach and led to a decrease in the development of cancer.

Preservative-free turkey and other luncheon meats are available in the deli case of many health-food stores.

5. Drink and Use Clean Water

Are water standards high enough to protect us from the hundreds of dangerous chemicals present in the water supply (including chlorine, a widely accepted disinfecting agent, and its known cancer-causing by-products)? Probably not.

One practical solution for minimizing exposure to the dangers of a less than pure water supply is in-home point-of-use water filtration. NSF International (see Resource Guide), an independent testing organization sanctioned by the EPA, regularly evaluates most of the commercial filters on the market for effectiveness in removing a list of substances identified as harmful to humans, including lead, mercury, pesticides, herbicides, asbestos, turbidity, trihalomethanes (chlorine by-products), as well as bacteria including cryptosporidium and giardia lamblia. Point-of-use filters should be used at the kitchen and bathroom taps and at showerheads for protection against chlorine and other dangerous chemicals that can be absorbed through the skin. The cartridges in point-of-use filters should be changed regularly.

When purchasing a point-of-use water filter, be sure it is certified by NSF International for both aesthetic effects (Standard 42) and health effects (Standard 53).

6. Eliminate Bugs and Weeds the Natural Way

A disturbing 1998 report in *Environmental Health Perspectives* noted that some childhood cancers could be prevented by reducing exposure to pesticides. The many indoor sprays and powders used to fight roaches, ants, termites, and mice expose the whole family to toxic chemicals and free radical–producing substances. Pesticides remain active and airborne for days after use. So it's important to minimize their use.

Safe, effective botanical insecticides are becoming more widely available. One alternative is the combination of Borax and powdered sugar to eliminate ants, roaches, and silverfish. Here are some other suggestions for keeping your house pest (and pesticide) free.

- Use bait traps. Be sure to keep them out of reach of children.

- Seal entry points to your home.

- Clean and sweep up all crumbs and spills quickly.

- Store food properly.

- Use a garbage disposal for waste products if possible. Wash disposable food containers and packaging before discarding and remove garbage promptly.

- Use a dehumidifier if necessary.

A good doormat will limit the amount of outdoor pesticides your family will carry inside on their shoes. Better yet, adopt the Japanese habit of leaving shoes just inside the door. Of course, it is very important to vacuum, mop, and shampoo the rugs and carpets regularly. Environmentally friendly and safe cleaners are becoming more popular.

If they are not available at your supermarket, try the local health-food store. If an exterminator is required, find one that uses natural methods.

7. Reduce Exposure to Heavy Metals from Fish Consumption

Pregnant women and those wanting to become pregnant should avoid shark, swordfish, king mackerel, and tilefish, because they contain enough mercury to hurt a baby's developing brain. Fish that live a long time probably have the highest amounts of both mercury and PCBs. Tuna, king salmon, and swordfish are not as safe as smaller fish such as coho and Atlantic salmon, sardines, mackerel, and striped bass. When eating fish such as whole salmon, for example, make sure you trim off all the visible fat, which contains fat-soluble PCBs and heavy metals. This is also true for beef, chicken, and pork.

8. Protect Against Polluted Air in Your Home

Indoor air quality affects us daily and is often overlooked as a source of harmful chemicals. Studies going back as many as ten years have shown home air pollution to be as serious a health concern as outdoor air. The University of California at Berkeley *Wellness Letter* recently reported on a large study of rural and industrial populations, which showed that exposures to home air pollutants were up to seventy times higher than the most serious outdoor levels! Sources of indoor air pollution include primary and secondary smoke from cigarettes, cigars, and pipes; radon; cleaning products; and outgassing from chemicals in fabrics and carpets. It is important to provide adequate ventilation by opening windows and doors. Be sure to change furnace filters often. I highly recommend investing in a good room air filter as well.

9. Ensure Proper Ventilation

The problem here is the potential for carbon monoxide poisoning and many chemicals associated with combustion such as hydrocarbons and PAHs. Clean furnace flues and chimneys annually and never use gas ovens for heat. Never barbecue indoors without adequate ventilation. Never run machines with internal combustion engines, such as automobiles and lawn mowers, in enclosed spaces, and never sleep or spend long periods of time in rooms with kerosene space heaters, unless adequately ventilated. Remember, too, that a carbon monoxide detector may well save your life.

10. Select Household Products with Low Toxicity and Natural Ingredients

Wood polish, drain cleaners, and pesticides can contain toxic substances, and in some cases, they can cause genetic changes leading to cancer. As a replacement for the very toxic commercial products used for oven cleaning, try this: sprinkle the inside of your oven with water, add baking soda, leave it overnight, and scrub off.

There are many other natural cleaning alternatives, such as white vinegar and water, that can be made from products in your kitchen. A catalog of safe cleaning products is available from the American Environmental Health Foundation. (See Resource Guide for contact information.)

11. Select Nontoxic Building and Decorating Materials

Many paints, woods, and carpets contain chemicals such as formaldehyde and petroleum distillates, which are known potential health hazards. When using paint, strippers, thinners, and other such materials, adequate ventilation is a must. Regarding building materials, if wood is not available, look for unfinished pressed wood, but make sure it's stamped with the HUD (Housing and Urban Development) emissions seal. Look for carpet and padding that have the green label from the Carpet and Rug Institute's indoor air-testing program. This ensures that government standards have been met for the emissions of volatile organic compounds.

12. Keep Household Dust to a Minimum

Household dust is the greatest source of lead poisoning in children. Dust can also harbor pesticide residues, asbestos and other chemicals, and animal dander. If you live in a home with old carpets or area rugs, pay special attention to the dust buildup problem, especially if you have children. I highly recommend that you also use an air purifier.

13. Prevent or Remove Mold Spores

Humidity or a leak in the foundation or roof of a house can supply enough moisture for the creation of colonies of molds. Air-conditioning systems and dehumidifiers, because of condensed water, can also help various molds to flourish. If mold is present or the familiar odor of mildew is detectable, the source must be cleaned. Where access is limited, such as in air ducts, professional help may be necessary. Incidentally, keeping pots covered when cooking will help reduce humidity levels in the home, thereby reducing mold. Molds can contain several chemical toxins. Moldy corn and grains can produce aflatoxins, which are carcinogenic.

USE A DEHUMIDIFIER

High humidity increases the chance of mildew and mold problems. Use a dehumidifier if possible.

---

14. Rethink the Way You Store Your Clothes

Mothballs for storage can produce naphthalene fumes, a known carcinogen. As an alternative, store only clean clothes in airtight containers—without mothballs. Opt for lavender, bay leaves, or cedar instead. Dry-cleaned clothes are usually treated with perchloroethylene (perc), a toxic solvent that can effect the health of workers who use it. Even though the dry-cleaning industry has been attempting to eliminate its use, until it does so, it is important to take precautionary steps. If the garment smells of chemicals, hang it outdoors or in a well-ventilated room. Always wash permanent press garments before first wearing them.

TOXIN-FREE DRY CLEANERS

Look for dry cleaners that advertise perc-free dry cleaning.

---

15. Read the Labels on Personal-Care Products

Become a label reader. The volatile chemicals in commercial brands of nail polish remover, hairspray, and perfume include aerosol propellants, artificial colors and fragrances, and petrochemicals that are easily absorbed by the skin and hair. Adding to the concern, these chemicals evaporate, eventually, and researchers are uncertain about the health effect at the levels commonly measured in homes.

A chemical called dibutylphthalate (DBP) commonly used to make nail polish, cosmetics, and perfume has been found to cause birth defects in animals. The Environmental Working Group in Washington, D.C., wants additional research on this chemical because the Centers for Disease Control and Prevention's National Center for Environmental Health found DBP in the urine of one in every 289 adults tested.

Read the label on all personal-care products and make sure you have adequate ventilation when using nail polish removers, hairsprays, and perfumes.

16. Wash Produce Repeatedly

It is important to wash fruits and vegetables under running water, even organic produce, which can absorb chemicals from the soil or the environment. I suggest that foods be rinsed at least five times to ensure removal of chemicals such as pesticides and herbicides.

Use slightly warm water instead of cold water when rinsing foods. The solubility of most chemicals increases with temperature. If you use a product that helps to remove fat-soluble compounds from foods, rinse at least three times after with slightly warm water.

17. Avoid Air Fresheners

Contrary to popular belief, air fresheners do not remove odors. Only ventilation and frequent cleaning can do that. But air fresheners do contain paradichlorobenzene, a carcinogen, so don't use them. Scented candles might also seem like a good idea but most of them give off polyaromatic hydrocarbons, agents that generate free radicals, much like the chemicals produced by charcoal grilling. Safe scented candles are available in health-food stores. Another option is to burn pure essential oils, which are also available in health-food stores.

18. Manage Caloric Intake: Eat Less, Live Longer

In our culture of excess, it is very easy to overindulge when it comes to food. Accordingly, we must be ever conscious of the fact that huge portions of food carry dangerously unnecessary additional calories, as discussed in Chapter 1. The fact is that the amount of food we eat has a direct bearing on the body's ability to fight disease. As a nutrition researcher, I am aware of the many dramatic studies on

Children at Increased Risk with Environmental Toxins

From the developing fetus to early adulthood, the rapid cell proliferation needed for the growth, brain function, and vital systems including those for detoxification and immunity make children very vulnerable to environmental toxins. That's the reason for the strong warning for women to avoid cigarette smoking, drinking alcohol, and other unhealthy lifestyle activities during pregnancy.

Childhood cancer and birth defects are not the only problems caused by environmental toxins. According to the EPA, lead poisoning contributes to rising rates of attention deficit disorder (ADD), hyperactivity, and aggression. The effects of air pollution, another threat to children's health, are heightened in the presence of ozone. And polychlorinated biphenyls (PCBs) have recently been linked to hyperactivity and poor concentration in children. Dyslexia, autism, aggressive behavior, ADD, and other maladies currently on the rise in America's children are directly traceable to the effects of environmental toxins.

In 2000, the National Academy of Sciences reported that environmental chemicals called neurotoxins intimately interact with genes, causing nearly 25 percent of all developmental problems in children. Normal brain development requires a precise process, beginning before birth and concluding for the most part after puberty. Neurotoxins are thought to disconnect this process.

Scientists are concerned about the toxic effects of many neurotoxic compounds on children. For example, chromated copper arsenic (CCA), commonly applied to pressed wood used for playground equipment, combines three neurotoxic compounds. Studies show that CCA has an adverse effect on intelligence. (See the Resource Guide for information on chemical-free playground equipment.)

It is possible to determine your child's level of exposure to lead, mercury, pesticides, and other harmful substances, something you may want to do if you suspect your child has learning disabilities.

Specific supplements—administered according to the child's body weight—for the detoxification of potentially harmful chemicals and metals are discussed in Chapter 6.

caloric management. Although I'm subject to the same temptation to overeat as others, because I know that caloric restriction can protect against cancer, it's easier for me to make the decision to limit portion sizes. The following adjustments to our eating habits can have a positive influence on long-term health and keep us free of many degenerative diseases.

- Learn what reasonable portion sizes really are. For packaged foods, use the serving size information found on the nutrition label as a rough guideline for how much to eat. If necessary, measure out portions to prevent overeating. When you're on the go and time is short, amounts can be approximated as follows:
  - A cup of whole grains is the size of your fist.
  - One serving of raisins is around half the size of your cupped hand.
  - A tablespoon of parmesan cheese is approximately the size of your thumb.

- Develop healthier habits regarding decisions about food, such as splitting a restaurant entrée with your dining partner.

- Select foods higher in fiber, such as vegetables, fruits, beans, and whole grains, to take up most of the plate. Meats, chicken, and fish should be limited to about one-third of the total meal.

- Get rid of the habit of going for the stuffed feeling; instead learn to walk away from the table before finishing what's on your plate. Eventually your stomach will shrink and adjust to smaller portions of food, eliminating that empty feeling.

- Use smaller plates and bowls.

- Many people can't control eating behavior without help. If necessary, seek counseling with a licensed therapist to discuss the emotional component of overeating.

19. Moderation in All Things—Even Exercise

It's a fact: weekend warriors may be shortening their lives.

We exercise to look and feel better and because we know it's good for us. However, research shows that infrequent (only one or two times a week) and excessive (hard) exercise is unhealthy. One should exercise four to five days a week for at least thirty minutes a day. The use of

weights can be very beneficial for building bone density and muscle mass, but keep the weight low to moderate; using heavy weights can actually trigger the production of free radicals in the body.

LESSONS FROM FRUIT FLIES

Studies examining life span and physical activity in flies found that the group that flew a moderate amount of time lived the longest whereas the groups that flew either the longest or the shortest lived the shortest amount of time. Thus, moderate physical activity is best.

Overexercising causes free radical damage and depletes the immune system. Athletes, for example, have been shown to become very susceptible to colds and viruses after a strenuous competition. Too much exercise also produces natural chemicals, including cortisol and cytokines, which can produce many adverse side effects. Moderate daily exercise, enough to work up a sweat but not hurt muscles or abuse joints such as the knees, can provide extraordinary health benefits. Exercising sensibly and regularly has been shown to strengthen the immune system and lower the risk of breast cancer, cardiovascular disease, headaches, stress, and depression.

──────────── ⁓ ────────────
Benefits of Moderate Exercise

Regular to moderate exercise, such as walking, doing chores, and working outdoors, helps our health in many ways. Sensible exercise helps to

- · lower weight, cholesterol, and blood pressure
- · burn calories
- · improve mood
- · lower stress

──────────── ⁓ ────────────

20. Learn to Manage Stress

When faced with emergencies, the body produces special chemicals that support the immune system and boost energy to help pump blood through the system. However, if stress continues, these protective changes can cause problems. Some of the potential problems are listed here.

- The body becomes susceptible to infection because the immune system is overloaded.

- Increased adrenaline levels exhaust the digestive system. Prolonged decrease in digestive enzymes impacts the body's ability to eliminate all kinds of toxins.

- The body overproduces natural hormones and other chemicals that are a source of free radicals.

Activities such as relaxation and recreation can help to reduce stress. Spending time with people who help us to relax is also important. In addition, being able to talk about feelings to people who care helps our health. Researchers know that people who feel isolated and lonely are less able to fight disease.

Here are some suggestions for dealing with stress.

- Group or individual therapy can help us learn to express feelings and to connect with others.

- Adequate sleep provides needed rest, which in turn brings about more positive feelings.

- Moderate daily exercise helps provide deeper sleep at night and a more relaxed feeling throughout the day.

- If necessary, investigate the many natural options available for the treatment of anxiety, such as the herbs kava kava and Saint-John's-wort. SAMe (s-adenosylmethionine) is also an option for people who are depressed. Herbal supplements should be used only when needed and/or as prescribed by a licensed physician.

Although a certain amount of stress can help us to cope during an emergency, it is not a normal state of being and must be dealt with if we are to maintain our health.

In this chapter we have surveyed the main sources of destructive chemicals in our daily lives—both environmental and those made in our bodies. I have shared some suggestions we offer at AMC for keeping these toxins at bay. The more successful we are in doing this, the better the chances for our detoxification systems to operate as nature intended, provided of course that we nourish them with the right foods and supplements. We will discuss both these factors at length in the coming chapters.

CHAPTER THREE

Superfoods
That Detoxify

$\mathcal{L}$

$\mathbf{A}$t the time of my postdoctoral fellowship at the McArdle Laboratory for Cancer Research, University of Wisconsin Medical School, 1968–1971, my research was focused on investigating the process by which environmental agents cause cancer. We knew that certain combustion by-products called polycyclic aromatic hydrocarbons, which are found in cigarette smoke, charcoal-grilled and burned meats, burning fuel, forest fires, and chimney smoke, played a role in cancer formation by damaging our genetic material. We observed this in laboratory experiments we performed using a group of mice, each of which possessed a similar genetic characteristic of an increased susceptibility to cancer. Every time we exposed the mice to these compounds, they would, without exception, get cancer; if they were not exposed, they would not. But we did not understand how this happened, as polycyclic aromatic hydrocarbon molecules are inert, meaning they should not be active in the body. Eventually we discovered that when the body tries to rid itself of clearly carcinogenic compounds by attempting to change them from lipid or oil-soluble to water-soluble, it falters and malfunctions. A natural attempt to heal itself instead results in the oxygenation of these compounds into a form (epoxides) that can easily bind with our genetic material and do extensive damage. If this damage is not repaired, genetic mutations can result and lead to cancer.

We studied ways to interfere with this binding process. That was when I began to work with flavonoids, a class of simple plant compounds in fruits and vegetables, which my colleagues and I believed might have just such ability. We were absolutely amazed to discover through our research just how effective flavonoids and later other nutritionally related compounds and specific vitamins were in counteracting the effects of combustion by-products and preventing cancer.

WHAT ARE FLAVONOIDS?

Flavonoids are ubiquitous in plants. There are at least two thousand different naturally occurring flavonoids. The flavonoids consist mainly of flavonols, flavones, and their glycosides (sugar attached), proanthocyanidins, anthocyanins, and catechins. Among the most common are the flavonols quercetin and rutin, which are present in tea, coffee, grains, and a variety of fruits and vegetables. Proanthocyanidins, or condensed tannins, are polyflavonoid in nature and are widely distributed in foods such as apples, grapes, berries, plums, and grains. Anthocyanins are responsible to a major degree for the various brilliant colors of flower petals and fruits. The catechins are also widely distributed in plants but are in the highest concentrations in tea leaves. Because of their common presence in plants, flavonoids are an integral and important part of our diet.

As you might imagine, flavonoid-rich foods started to look pretty significant to us in preventing cancer by specifically supporting the processes of detoxification. I was so impressed with our findings that I began to include more flavonoid foods in our family's diet. We even started supplementing with vitamins, although at that time we really didn't understand that vitamins such as the powerful detoxifyers, C and E for instance, should be taken together because they support each other's functions. As the years went by, nutrition science evolved, giving us more information about not only what kinds of foods and supplements are important, but also in what combinations they provide the optimum health-protective benefits.

Some people have greater genetic susceptibility to the adverse effects of environmental toxins than others. For them, it is extraordinarily important to realize that their health is not up to fate: there is something that can be done to counter a predisposition to cancer and other diseases. Eating healthier foods containing flavonoids is important, but it's just one of many lifesaving tools available to all of us. This and the next chapter cover foods that pack the most detoxifying elements. My corresponding nutrient and vitamin programs will be covered in Chapters 5 and 6.

SAVE THE COOKING WATER

Powerfully protective flavonoids and other beneficial phytochemicals from cooked vegetables are released into the cooking water. It's a good idea to reuse this water for stocks and soups.

Mother Was Right!
Eat Your Fruits and Vegetables

Results of more than two hundred epidemiological studies and literally thousands of human and experimental animal studies support the scientific view of the mantra of this book: a diet based on plant foods leads to a decrease in cancer and other degenerative diseases. And since these foods generally possess different nutritional components, eating a variety of them is the key to achieving a good balance of carbohydrates, proteins, and fats, essential vitamins and minerals, and beneficial phytochemicals including flavonoids. Let's take a look at cruciferae, allium, and leguminosae, three families that have the largest backing with published scientific data based on their effectiveness in detoxification especially as related to cancer.

Of all the botanical families, none has greater scientific association with the prevention of cancer, especially breast and prostate cancer, than cruciferae or cruciferous vegetables, including broccoli, cabbage, and cauliflower. These hardy plants also provide protection against ischemic stroke, the most common type of stroke. In the ongoing Nurses' Health Study and Health Professionals' Follow-Up Study of more than 75,000 women and 38,000 men, Dr. Joshipuna and colleagues found that people who eat a diet loaded with fruits and vegetables, with cruciferous vegetables being the most beneficial, were one-third less likely to suffer stroke.

The Families of Fruits and Vegetables

Knowledge of the edible plant kingdom is the good-health equivalent of memorizing the multiplication tables, just more enjoyable. The list below shows the different families of plants and which fruits and vegetables are in each. Try to choose from a wide variety of families to get the most benefit.

ACTINIDIACEAE
  Chinese gooseberry
  kiwi

AGARICACEAE
  mushroom

ALLIUM
  asparagus
  chives
  garlic
  leeks
  onions
  scallions
  shallot

ANACARDIACEAE
  black currant
  mango

ANNONACEAE
  cherimoya
  custard apple
  paw paw
  sugar apple

BROMELIACEAE
  pineapple

CARICACEAE
  papaya

CHENOPODIACEAE
  beet greens
  beets
  spinach
  Swiss chard

COMPOSITACEAE
  artichoke
  chicory leaf
  dandelion
  endive
  lettuce (iceberg, red leaf,
    romaine)
  tarragon

CONVOLVULACEAE
  sweet potato

CRUCIFERAE (CRUCIFEROUS)
  bok choy
  broccoli
  broccoli spouts
  Brussels sprouts
  cabbage (green, red, Chinese)
  cauliflower
  collard greens
  horseradish
  kale
  kohlrabi
  mustard greens
  radishes
  rutabaga
  turnip greens
  turnips
  watercress

CUCURBITACE
cantaloupe
crenshaw
cucumber
honeydew
pumpkin
squash (summer, winter,
  zucchini)
watermelon

ERICACEAE
blueberry
cranberry
huckleberry
lingonberry

GRAMINEAE
bamboo shoots
corn
lemon grass

LABIATAE
basil
marjoram
mint
oregano
rosemary
sage
savory
thyme

LAURACEAE
avocado
cinnamon
sassafras

LEGUMINOSAE (LEGUMES)
alfalfa sprouts
black-eyed peas
broad beans
fava beans

garbanzo beans
green beans
green peas
kidney beans
lentils
lima beans
mung beans
navy beans
peanuts
pink beans
pinto beans
soybeans
yellow beans

MUSACEAE
bananas
plantains

PALMAE
coconuts
dates
palm hearts

POLYGONACEAE
rhubarb
sorrel

ROSACEAE
apple
apricot
blackberry
cherry
juneberry
loganberry
peach
pear
plum
prune
raspberry
salmonberry
strawberry

(continued)

The Families of Fruits and Vegetables *(continued)*

RUTACEAE
grapefruit
kumquat
lemon
lime
Mandarin orange
orange
tangerine

SOLANACEAE
eggplant
peppers (green, red, chili)
pimiento
potato

tomatillo
tomato

UMBELLIFERAE
carrots
celery
coriander (Chinese parsley)
dill
fennel
parsley
parsnips

VITACEAE
grapes
raisins

The odor that we commonly associate with cruciferous vegetables is actually caused by a class of nitrogen, sulfur, and glucose-containing chemicals called glucosinolates. When the plant tissues are disrupted in any way, whether by mastication, fermentation, cooking, or digestion, glucosinolates rapidly break down into isothiocyanates, particularly sulforaphanes, dithiolethione, and indole-3-carbinol. These are very important phytochemicals with tremendous anticancer properties because of their specific effect on xenobiotic Phase I and Phase II detoxification. Cruciferous vegetables also contain D-glucarate, which significantly aids Phase II detoxification.

Isothiocyanates and D-glucarate are particularly active against carcinogenic nitrosamines. Isothiocyanates and dithiolethiones have been found to inhibit various forms of cancer including lung, breast, esophageal, liver, small intestine, colon, skin, pancreatic, and renal. Indole-3-carbinol and D-glucarate offer tremendous protection against sex hormone–related breast and prostate cancers by limiting overproduction of estrogens and androgens and by detoxifying environmental agents such as dioxins, which influence these types of cancers.

A word about fermentation is warranted, as this is a very common way of preparing cruciferous vegetables. Unquestionably, fermentation triggers the release of beneficial phytochemicals. But there are many

different kinds of fermentation ranging from the simple chopping of coleslaw to more complex methods using various bacterial strains. The blend of activated phytochemicals can be quite different depending on the process. At present we don't have sufficient scientific data on all of these processes to establish guidelines for preparing and eating fermented foods. Until we do, I recommend that you eat a combination of raw, cooked, and fermented cruciferous vegetables.

WATERCRESS

Chief among the members of the cruciferous family, watercress contains various phytochemicals that work incredibly well together to increase the overall activity of the xenobiotic detoxification system. So add a little watercress to your salads or sandwiches, every day, as I do.

Garlic, onions, leeks, chives, asparagus, and scallions are members of the allium botanical family and are also commonly characterized by their strong odor. This odor results from the activity of important sulfur compounds that are known to be effective in both the antioxidant and xenobiotic detoxification systems. The purified organosulfides such as allium sulfide compounds in onion and garlic extracts are protective against cancer and cardiovascular disease. Garlic extracts are also effective in lowering cholesterol and triglycerides. In addition, garlic and onions have been found to increase glutathione, a powerful antioxidant that helps to support both the antioxidant and the xenobiotic detoxification systems. For centuries, allium plants have been cultivated in the Middle and Far East for their characteristic pungent flavor and medicinal properties.

The leguminosae family, or legumes, which includes many kinds of beans and peas, is a good source of protein, carbohydrates, fats, vitamins, minerals, fiber, and phytochemicals. Among the different types of legumes, the soybean stands out as one of the world's most widely consumed food sources. Not surprisingly, it is also one of the most studied for the health benefits it possesses. The soybean is a bright green legume closely related to peas, clover, and alfalfa. It is high in protein and protective phytochemicals. Studies have shown that soy protein helps to prevent heart disease by lowering total cholesterol. In addition to having a high protein content, soybeans also have cancer-fighting isoflavones, a phytochemical in the flavonoid class of compounds. Isoflavones are also known as plant estrogens (phytoestrogens) because of their structural similarity to estrogens and their capacity to weakly bind to estrogen receptors in the body. This ability is thought to be one of the mechanisms by which soy isoflavones prevent hormone-dependent cancers such as those of the breast and prostate. In addition, soy isoflavones appear to help prevent osteoporosis. Many scientists now believe that the observed low rates of cancer, heart disease, and osteoporosis among Asian populations, especially in Japan where their consumption is most widespread, are attributable to the protective effects of soybeans.

Soy Foods for Life

Soybeans and soy products are beneficial to both men and women because they

- protect against heart disease by lowering cholesterol

- have strong antioxidant properties

- have a natural antiestrogen effect similar to tamoxifen

- protect against cancer, especially of the breast and prostate

- prevent osteoporosis

- prevent bone loss and aid in the absorption of calcium

The Power of Pigmentation

All colorful fruits and vegetables, inside or out, contain flavonoids, carotenoids, or other beneficial phytochemicals with important antioxidant properties, many of which we already know have a positive effect on the xenobiotic detoxification function. The same phytochemicals that cause the color also inhibit inflammation; lower cholesterol; and prevent cancer, heart disease, and other illnesses. The phytochemical chlorophyllin, which is found in the pigment of green vegetables and fruits, has recently been established to have such abilities. While there is much research left to do on phytochemicals (for instance, flavonoids such as proanthocyanidins and anthocyanins are not yet fully understood), there are enough studies to show that the aggregate effect of consuming phytochemical-rich fruits and vegetables is positive in terms of supporting detoxification and preventing disease. At Tufts University, sixty fruits and vegetables were studied and tested for their antioxidant potency. In these studies, blueberries topped the list for antioxidant strength, followed by strawberries, prunes, black currants, and boysenberries. Other flavonoid-rich fruits and vegetables include blackberries, raspberries, red grapes, and alfalfa sprouts. The table on phytochemicals lists the more common fruits and vegetables and the specific phytochemicals they provide.

Phytochemicals Found in Fruits and Vegetables

CLASS	EXAMPLE	SOME SOURCES
indoles	indole-3-carbinol	broccoli and cabbage
isothiocyanates	sulforaphane phenylethylisothiocyanate	broccoli and cabbage watercress and turnips
organosulfides	allyl disulfides diallyl sulfide diallyl disulfide	onions and garlic
flavonoids	quercetin apigenin proanthocyanidins anthocyanins tannins	fruits and vegetables such as berries and beets
polyphenols (part of flavonoids family)	catechins theaflavins	green and black tea and coffee

(continued)

Phytochemicals Found in Fruits and Vegetables *(continued)*

CLASS	EXAMPLE	SOME SOURCES
phenolic compounds	caffeic acid	fruits and vegetables such as apples and tomatoes; coffee
	ferulic acid	coffee and fruits
	chlorogenic acid	soybeans and coffee
	curcumin	spices
carotenoids	β-carotene	sweet potatoes, carrots, and peaches
	α-carotene	carrots, squash
	lycopene	tomatoes and watermelon
	lutein	spinach, squash, pumpkin
chlorophyll	chlorophyllin	green vegetables such as spinach and lettuce
terpenoids	mono, di-, and tri-terpenoids (limonene and limonin)	citrus fruits including oranges spices including rosemary

There is a very simple way to increase the power of pigmentation of fruits and vegetables through daily drinks. I have created both a vegetable and a fruit drink. Two glasses of each every day will increase your intake of vegetables and fruits significantly.

———————————— ✿ ————————————

Easy Vegetable Intake

DR. SLAGA'S VEGETABLE DRINK

16 ounces commercial vegetable juice (Knudsen Very Veggie or V-8)
¼ cup diced green pepper
½ cup broccoli sprouts, alfalfa sprouts, and/or bean sprouts
¼ cup water chestnuts
¼ cup roasted soybeans, walnuts, and/or sunflower seeds
1 peeled lemon

Combine all the ingredients in a food processor or high-speed blender and blend until smooth. You can adjust the amount of vegetable juice to attain the desired consistency. Drink immediately. Four servings.

Many studies have found that the flavonoids—including polyphenols and phenolic acid from green and black tea, coffee, and red wine; carotenoids and especially lycopene in tomatoes; and lutein in peas, carrots, and squashes—enhance antioxidant detoxification. Carotenoids have also been shown to be effective in preventing breast and prostate cancer. Incidentally, it is a well-established fact that carotenoids can also improve eyesight.

Easy Fruit Intake

DR. SLAGA'S FRUIT DRINK

$1/2$ cup plain nonfat yogurt
$1/4$ cup blueberries
$1/2$ cup red seedless grapes
$1/2$ cup mixed strawberries and raspberries
$1/2$ cup peeled and diced orange and grapefruit
$1/4$ ripe, medium-size banana
$1^1/2$ cup orange juice with pulp
$1^1/2$ cup grapefruit juice with pulp

Combine all the ingredients in a high-speed blender. The amount of orange and grapefruit juice can be adjusted for desired consistency and taste. Drink immediately. Four servings.

Spice Up Your Life

Not only fruits and vegetables but also spices contain important classes of phytochemicals that make unique contributions to all aspects of our detoxification systems. One such class is the ever-important flavonoids. Another is terpenoids. Mono-, di-, and triterpenoids are found in spices such as rosemary, sage, oregano, basil, and thyme. Monoterpenoids are important in the elimination of potentially carcinogenic forms of estrogens, which are associated with breast cancer. Diterpenoids and triterpenoids have potent antioxidant, anti-inflammatory properties that aid xenobiotic as well as antioxidant detoxification processes. Animal studies have shown that diterpenoids and triterpenoids are effective inhibitors of cancer, especially skin, breast, and colon cancer.

DETOXIFYING SPICES

To help detoxify dangerous forms of estrogen associated with breast cancer and to inhibit the formation of skin and colon cancer, be sure you cook with rosemary, sage, oregano, and thyme.

Spices also contain phenolic compounds, a class of phytochemicals with powerful antioxidant properties, which some studies show to be effective inhibitors of cancer development. Peppers contain several phenolic compounds that have antioxidizing activity and enhance our xenobiotic detoxification capabilities. Chili peppers (red peppers) contain capsaicinoids, which are effective antioxidants and anti-inflammatory agents and inhibit pain. Black pepper contains phenolic compounds such as piperine and related compounds that are effective in xenobiotic detoxification and help with the absorption of many phytochemicals. Curcumins are phenolic compounds present in turmeric and mustard. Possessing strong antioxidant properties, curcumins also inhibit cell proliferation and behave as anti-inflammatory agents, helping to reduce the activity of cyclooxygenase-2 (cox-2), a key enzyme associated with a number of inflammatory diseases and cancers. In terms of cancer, curcumins have been found to be a potent inhibitor of colon, breast, and prostate cancers. Additional phytochemicals in spices include ginerol, an extremely important cancer inhibitor found in ginger; eugenol from cloves; coumarins from coriander, cumin, and cinnamon; and carnosol and rosmarinic acid from rosemary and sage. Paprika supports proper detoxification functions.

As it is difficult to think of a spice that does not contain one or more of these important phytochemicals, my rather obvious advice is to make liberal use of them in your diet. Happily, spices can make a nutritious meal more protective *and* better tasting.

Top Detoxifying Spices

black pepper	cumin	rosemary
chili pepper	curry	sage
cinnamon	ginger	turmeric
cloves	mustard seed	
coriander	paprika	

The Staff of Life

Bread has been revered throughout the ages for its life-supporting properties. Bread was for hundreds of years considered a whole, nutritious food. There was simply no other way to make it. Today, because of processing methods, that is no longer necessarily the case. So when it comes to grain, including foods such as breads, pastas, crackers, and tortillas, we have to caution people to make sure the whole grain is used. Remember, only whole grains convey meaningful health benefits. Anything else amounts to empty calories.

By definition, a whole grain has three components: the thin fiber-rich husk or outer layer called bran, the large middle mass called endosperm, and the core called the germ or embryo. Whole grains include wheat (bulgur, wheat berries, cracked wheat, couscous), rice (brown and wild rice), oats, rye, barley, buckwheat, amaranth, and even popcorn. I recommend three to four servings daily. Inadequate consumption of a variety of whole grains is a definite factor in cancer formation. Unlike refined grains—white flour, most commercial grain-based snack foods, cakes, breads, and pastries—whole grains are a rich source of nutrients plus soluble and insoluble fiber, vitamin E, folic acid, niacin (B_3), riboflavin (B_2), selenium, magnesium, and zinc. Significantly, they also contain beneficial phytochemicals such as ferulates and inositol hexaphosphate (1P6 or phytic acid). Ferulates have strong antioxidant, anti-inflammatory, and xenobiotic Phase I and Phase II detoxification-boosting properties. Phytic acid is found in the fiber of whole grains. Recent animal studies have found this phytochemical to be an effective inhibitor of skin, breast, prostate, and colon cancer due to its limiting effect on cell proliferation and apparent support of the immune system. We also know that the bran, which contains most of the insoluble fiber in whole grains (five times that of refined grains), protects against colon cancer. In general, eating sufficient whole-grain foods provides protection against many illnesses including cancers of the stomach, ovaries, breast, prostate, and pancreas.

WHOLE GRAINS ARE HEALTH PROTECTIVE

When it comes to wheat-based products, including bread, crackers, pasta, tortillas, bagels, and cereal, look for the word *whole* on the label. In terms of cereals, oatmeal, shredded wheat, and even Cheerios, Wheaties, and Nutrigrain are good choices. Although All-Bran is not made from whole grain, it is loaded with bran and therefore still considered a nutritious food.

Essential Fats for Disease Prevention and Detoxification

In today's diet-conscious culture, the phrase *essential fats* seems like a contradiction in terms. After all, how can fat be necessary when we spend so much time trying to avoid or lose it? Of the fifty or so nutrients identified as essential because our bodies can't make them and they must be obtained from nature, two just happen to be, yes, fats. As scientists have known for some time, these essential fats, together with essential vitamins, minerals, and amino acids, are critical components of our body's chemistry and therefore are necessary for life.

In recent years, there has been a lot of misleading, contradictory, and in some cases just plain wrong information about fat in our diets. Because of the confusion this created, fats have gotten a bad reputation to the point where we feel pressured to reduce or eliminate them altogether. The truth is the only low-fat or fat-free movement that makes sense for our health and appearance is one that applies to the consumption of *saturated fats* and more specifically, *trans-fats*. These fats unfortunately make up the bulk of the fat content of the standard American diet (the acronym for which is, appropriately enough, SAD). You know these fats when you see them. At room temperature they are solid, such as the saturated fat from raw or cooked meat that has cooled and from butter and lard, or the trans-fats from shortening and margarine. Most of the time they remain in a solid state even inside the body. While there seems to be some evidence that small amounts of saturated fat can be beneficial, when consumed in large amounts saturated fats and trans-fats can lead to the development of diseases such as atherosclerosis, heart disease, and cancer. With respect to trans-fats in particular, my recommendation is to play it safe. These fats, which are more commonly labeled *hydrogenated* or *partially hydrogenated* fats, are pervasive in our food culture and until we know more about them, it's best to avoid them.

So what are the good fats, these two so-called essential fats that are actually beneficial to our health? They are polyunsaturated omega-3 and omega-6 fats, or more correctly, fatty acids. You may also hear them called, respectively, alpha-linolenic acid and linolenic acid. These fats are liquid at room temperature and remain that way in the body.

There have been thousands of scientific studies documenting the beneficial effects of these essential fatty acids against heart disease, stroke, inflammatory disease, immunological disorders, cancer, and neurological degeneration. Omega-3 and omega-6 essential fatty acids are important building blocks of nerve cells and cell membranes in general; they serve as messengers such as prostaglandins, hormonelike substances that initiate key functions throughout the body. And they are important in many aspects of detoxification. Fat is quantitatively the most important structural unit in the brain and nervous system and the second most important in all other soft tissue. This structural fat is built from essential fatty acids and the derivatives the body then produces, in a manner similar to the way in which proteins are built from essential amino acids and their derivatives.

Polyunsaturated fats containing the essential fatty acids, omega-3 and omega-6, are vitally important for proper cell membrane fluidity, efficiency, and functionality. If our diets are lacking in these fats, saturated fats will replace them within cell membranes. If this substitution continues for a long time, the outcome can be rapid aging and various disease states.

It is important to consume essential fatty acids in the right proportion. To the best of our scientific knowledge, especially related to ideal cholesterol levels, two to four parts of omega-6 fatty acids to one part of omega-3 fatty acids appears to be an ideal ratio. This proportion has been shown to reduce total cholesterol and bad LDL cholesterol while raising good HDL cholesterol. Unfortunately, the typical American consumes too many omega-6 and not nearly enough omega-3 fatty acids. The reason for this is simple. With the exception of olive and canola oils, which are rich sources of the nonessential omega-9 fatty acid that has been shown to have extremely beneficial properties, most if not all commercial cooking oils—mainly sesame, corn, and safflower—tend to have high omega-6 content. This is because omega-6 oils are more stable chemically, meaning they have a longer shelf life than the omega-3 fatty acids, which typically must be refrigerated to maintain freshness. So the imperative for convenience in the modern world has created this imbalance of essential fatty acids. Many of these same commercial oils are processed and overheated to reduce color and odor and to increase shelf life even further by reducing the fatty acid's sensitivity to light. Consuming these oils only compounds the imbalance by adding omega-6 fatty acids that have been chemically altered, something science has already identified as a potential health issue. Be sure to read labels and only buy fresh, cold-pressed oils packaged in dark containers.

To correct the imbalance of omega-6 to omega-3 essential fatty acids, it is not as necessary to reduce consumption of the former as it is to boost consumption of the latter. Ideally, we should all add high-quality sources of omega-3 essential fatty acids to our diets. There are many such sources, including walnut and perilla oil, but by far the richest known plant source is the flaxseed. Flaxseed oil can be taken in liquid or capsule form. Flaxseeds and products are widely available in health-food stores. If flax oil is not available, cold-water fish including salmon, tuna, halibut, herring, bluefish, mackerel, and sardines are excellent sources of omega-3 fatty acids as well. Try to include omega-3-rich foods in your daily diet.

Remember essential omega-3 and essential omega-6 fatty acids are only found in the plant world. In healthy people, the body converts these essential fatty acids to nonessential forms. The main nonessential fatty acids converted by the body from omega-3 are DHA and EPA; the main one from omega-6 is GLA. These derivatives of the essential fatty acids are very important in preventing cardiovascular disease, inflammatory diseases, neurological degeneration, and cancer. Studies have shown that DHA is of major importance for the development and continued healthy function of the brain and nervous system. DHA and EPA aid in the prevention of cardiovascular disorders and cancer and also have a positive effect on the immune system. For those whose bodies for health reasons cannot make the conversion from the essential to the nonessential fatty acid derivatives, or who don't have access to omega-3-rich plants, these essential fatty acid derivatives are already present in range-fed meat and cold-water fish. Inuits do not have a growing season to sustain plant life but they have healthy cardiovascular systems. The reason is simple: their diet is very high in omega-3-rich salmon, whale, and seal meat.

The fats you eat affect your body's ability to get rid of toxins. First, a diet overloaded with bad fats such as hydrogenated shortening stresses the detoxification system simply because the fats remain semisolid in the body. Both Phase I and Phase II detoxification as well as antioxidant detoxification can only work efficiently with healthy membranes. Second, the healthy sources of fats that I have described—plant oils, fatty-acid-rich cold-water fish, and even monounsaturated olive oil— help to dissolve oil-soluble toxins. Without them, some toxins may remain in the body for longer periods of time or they may never be totally eliminated. Third, vital oil-soluble nutrients needed for detoxification, such as antioxidant vitamin E and lycopene, depend on these healthy fats to be efficiently absorbed by the body. They are only soluble in oil.

Not only are healthy fats necessary for general health, but they also help the processes of detoxification. You must include healthy sources of fats and oils in your daily diet.

Dr. Slaga's Top Superfoods for Detoxification

From my survey of the various botanical families of fruits, vegetables and legumes, fats and oils, grains, fish, and even meat, I hope it is apparent that the many necessary nutrients and phytochemicals needed for good detoxification are available in a wide variety of foods. Try to find a convenient way to include as many of these foods in your diet as you can. This will require a conscious effort until good eating habits develop. The recipes in Part Two of this book are designed to help you get off to a good start. I urge you to put these tasty and healthful recipes to good use.

Of course some foods are better than others in terms of their nutrient and phytochemical content. Let's call them superfoods, and, yes, I have a list of favorites, based on years of research. And I guarantee that one or two will surprise you. Let's take a look.

Broccoli Sprouts and Watercress

These are loaded with nutrients and phytochemicals that detoxify. Broccoli is great, but the sprouts are even better; they actually contain twenty times more sulforaphane. They also contain other important phytochemicals, including D-glucarate, dithiolethione, and indoles, which work synergistically in all aspects of detoxification. Broccoli sprouts are starting to show up in grocery stores.

Among the many beneficial phytochemicals in watercress, isothiocyanate has been shown to protect against esophageal, stomach, and lung cancer.

Both of these foods are easy to prepare as raw salads or garnish. Put them right at the top of your list for daily lunches and dinners.

Blueberries

Blueberries are rich in important flavonoids and phenolic compounds that are protective against many diseases because of their potent antioxidizing activities and xenobiotic detoxification capabilities. I have put together a snack mix containing a variety of berries, nuts, and seeds, which is a great way to boost your body's detoxification. Parents with young children may want to add a small amount of dark chocolate chips that aren't too heavily sweetened.

Easy Power Snack

DR. SLAGA'S HEALTHY MIX

¹/₂ cup dried blueberries
¹/₂ cup dried cranberries
¹/₂ cup raisins
¹/₂ cup dried apricots
¹/₂ cup roasted soybeans
¹/₂ cup walnuts
¹/₂ cup almonds
¹/₂ cup sunflower seeds

Mix all the ingredients. This mixture can be eaten as is, or try adding it to yogurt, salads, or cereal. Sixteen servings.

Onions and Garlic

Any healthy diet, especially one designed to support detoxification, simply must contain onions and garlic. They contain many important sulfur compounds, including organosulfides, which increase overall detoxification and protect the body from cardiovascular diseases and cancer.

Grapefruit and Oranges

These are my top choices in the citrus fruit family because of the many beneficial vitamins, minerals, D-glucarate, and flavonoids they contain. Oranges also contain many important terpenoids. I like to combine grapefruit and orange juice into one drink to get a better taste and the full benefit of these nutritious fruits. Nutrients and phytochemicals work not only individually to improve detoxification, but also synergistically. The flavonoids in grapefruit and oranges keep vitamin C in a state necessary for it to function as a powerful antioxidant. In addition, D-glucarate and flavonoids work in tandem to bring about effective xenobiotic Phase I and Phase II detoxification.

Spinach

Everyone over forty probably knows how important spinach was to the cartoon character Popeye. But back in the days of Popeye, spinach's value must have been a closely kept secret because nobody was eating it. In fact, it had a reputation for tasting awful. Today we know that spinach contains vitamins, minerals, fiber, and beneficial phytochemicals such as chlorophyll and flavonoids, all of which are intrinsic to good detoxification. And guess what, it actually tastes delicious raw, very lightly sautéed, or mixed in a variety of dishes.

Apples

In my opinion, the apple is a very special fruit. It's loaded with fiber, vitamins, minerals, and other beneficial phytochemicals (such as phenolic compounds, flavonoids, terpenoids, and D-glucarate), all of which combine to aid all aspects of detoxification. There is definitely something to the old saying "An apple a day, keeps the doctor away."

Tomatoes

In the last several years tomatoes and tomato products made their way onto my list of superfoods because they contain many vitamins and minerals, fiber, beneficial flavonoids, phenolic compounds, and some terpenoids. Tomatoes also contain tremendously protective carotenoids, including lycopene, a powerful antioxidant, which is one reason for the lower levels of cardiovascular diseases and cancer in populations with tomato-based diets.

Watermelons

Watermelons contain the important carotenoid lycopene, which, by the way, is what gives the red color to watermelon and tomatoes. Watermelon is a good source of the vitamins, minerals, phenolic compounds, and flavonoids we need to be healthy.

Carrots

Carrots have large amounts of carotenoids as well as other important phytochemicals, including flavonoids. The carotenoids in carrots, such as α-carotene and β-carotene—important for making vitamin A—as well as lutein, β-cryptoxanthine, and xanthophyll are all good antioxidants that help in disease prevention.

Whole Grains

As a class, whole grains are one of my superfoods because of their importance in preventing obesity, diabetes, heart disease, and cancer. In addition to important fiber, whole grains are rich in vitamins, minerals, flavonoids, and compounds such as ferulate and phytic acid. Ferulates are potent antioxidants and phytic acid has many beneficial properties but is especially known for its positive effect on the immune system.

Soybeans

No superfoods list would be complete without soybeans. Besides being a good source of protein and some essential fat, soybeans are a good source of isoflavones such as genistein. Eating soybeans and derivative soy products decreases the risk of heart disease and cancer and mitigates bone loss and osteoporosis because of its positive effect on the body's ability to absorb calcium. Moreover, the protein and soluble fiber in soy support kidney filtration and regulate glucose levels. This helps to protect against kidney problems and diabetes.

Salmon and Halibut

These cold-water fish are among my favorite sources of protein and two omega-3 fatty acids, EPA and DHA, which I have already mentioned are critical for good health and detoxification.

Walnuts and Almonds

These nuts definitely make my list of superfoods because of their many health benefits, especially related to heart disease and cancer. They are particularly rich in protective essential fats. They are also important sources of fiber; vitamins and minerals such as calcium, folic acid, magnesium, potassium, and vitamin E; as well as antioxidants such as quercetin and kaempferol. By the way, almonds, walnuts, and other nuts as well as peanuts—which are actually legumes—make excellent protein and fat substitutes for meat, cheese, and other high-fat foods.

Rosemary and Ginger

These are the spices that make my superfoods list. They are good sources of simple phenolic chemicals, flavonoids, and terpenoids, potent antioxidants that contribute to all aspects of detoxification. Right behind ginger and rosemary are turmeric, curry, and mustard, all of which also contain important phytochemicals such as curcumins, which have clear health benefits.

Chocolate (Really!)

Now I'm going to happily surprise you. Chocolate, especially dark semi-sweet chocolate, is definitely one of my detoxification superfoods. The botanical name for cocoa is *theafroma cacao*, which means "food of the gods." Cocoa beans and the resulting chocolate, especially dark chocolate, are rich in antioxidants—specifically, phenolic compounds and flavonoids. Chocolate also contains some healthy fat such as stearic acid, which is converted in the body to oleic acid, a monounsaturated fat that is also found in olive and canola oils. Oleic acid is considered a healthy fat in terms of heart disease prevention. Now before we get carried away with the health benefits of chocolate, remember most chocolate still contains large amounts of sugar and fat, which aren't healthy for us, so overindulging can have negative effects. In making desserts with chocolate, use semisweet dark chocolate and add less-refined sugars to the recipe. The glycemic index (a measure of the ability of a food to raise blood sugar) for this kind of chocolate is surprisingly low, which means it is very good in terms of preventing diabetes and obesity. Later in this book you will find a healthy chocolate dessert made from semisweet dark chocolate and chickpeas. It is absolutely delicious!

And Coffee Too!

I may surprise you again here. Coffee makes my list of superfoods, too. Coffee, like tea, contains several phenolic compounds and flavonoids that increase our ability to detoxify and therefore provide protection against most degenerative diseases. For example, recent epidemiological studies have shown that moderate coffee drinking can actually decrease the risk of colon cancer. We scientists at the AMC Cancer Research Center have found a way to significantly increase the healthy phytochemicals in brewed coffee by changing the typical roasting process of coffee beans. This healthy process will soon be available to coffee drinkers.

Red Wine

Believe it or not, red wine makes my list of superfoods. The same phenolic compounds and flavonoids in chocolate are also present in wine, particularly red wine. In fact, a five-ounce glass of your favorite red wine has about the same amount of phenolic acid (200 mg) as a 1½-ounce bar of dark chocolate. White wine also contains many of the same protective phytochemicals as red wine but in lesser amounts.

———————— C H A P T E R   F O U R ————————

Insights from
Traditional Diets

—————————— ⚘ ——————————

So many aspects of our ancestors' diets helped the process of detoxification. They ate more fiber, which encourages the body to eliminate cancer-initiating toxins (and may even prevent colon cancer genes from initiating cell growth, as scientists are currently investigating). Their diets were low in foods containing saturated fat, but high in health-protective sources of essential fats, such as nuts, seeds, avocados, and olive oil—all important to help the body flush out oil-soluble toxins. Our grandparents' diet contained more minerals because the soil was not as overworked and depleted as it is today. A deficiency in one such mineral, selenium, is a factor in every type of cancer. Those areas of the world, including Southern China and the Rocky Mountains in the United States, with high selenium soil content have a lower risk of cancer, and conversely those areas with low selenium soil—including Northeast China, Finland, and the Carolinas in the United States—have a higher risk. We will examine the very strong properties of selenium as they relate to the process of antioxidant detoxification in Chapter 5.

Take a moment to contemplate just how much our eating habits have changed. Today, the health benefits of whole foods have been sacrificed for foods that are convenient and save time. Fresh foods have become too much trouble for us to prepare on a daily basis—and forget about taking the time for canning or making soup stock.

Science has answered our modern needs with processed, preserved, and packaged convenience foods. Unfortunately it has done so at the expense of our health. That's why the traditional diets of our ancestors are so instructive today even if we can't fully implement them anymore. The rates of cancer and other degenerative diseases are lower in countries where people observe more traditional diets and eat in moderation. It's as simple as that.

My Grandparents' Diet

My Polish and German grandparents ate a variety of fruits, vegetables, beans, and whole grains. They ate meat in small amounts because it was expensive. As a nutrition scientist, I have seen the clear health benefits of eating this way. Cabbage rolls, for instance, one of my grandparents' favorite meals, contained rice, onions, garlic, tomatoes, some meat, and paprika. The health benefits of these ingredients are outstanding. Let's take a look.

Cabbage

Cabbage contains several sulfur compounds, indoles, and D-glucarate, which we now know are important to countering the effects of toxins. D-glucarate, in particular, rids the body of both tumor-initiating and tumor-promoting chemicals from the environment as well as potentially carcinogenic and/or cancer-promoting steroidal hormones.

Rice

Whole grains such as brown rice contain beneficial fiber, vitamins, and minerals, as well as ferulic acid, which helps to induce Phase I and Phase II detoxification; and phytic acid, also called inositol hexaphosphate (1P6), a compound with strong anticarcinogenic and immunity-enhancing properties.

Onions and Garlic

We have seen that people with diets high in onions and garlic have lower rates of many different kinds of cancer such as skin, esophageal, stomach, colon, liver, lung, and cervical. This is in part due to the fact that the plant chemicals in onions and garlic have properties that block dangerous nitrosamines, which can form in the stomach as the result of eating cured meats.

Tomatoes

The antioxidant compound lycopene, which is abundant in tomatoes, has extraordinary ability to protect against cancers of the prostate and breast.

Meat

My grandmother added a small amount of lean pork or beef to the rice. This was enough meat to provide the amino acids necessary to produce glutathione, an antioxidant central to several important enzymes required for proper detoxification function. Any more meat and the benefits would have been offset with the consumption of too much saturated fat. (Not that she necessarily knew any of that—but she knew it was economical.)

Paprika

Paprika is a potent antioxidant spice that helps to neutralize free radicals and support proper detoxification function. My grandmother used paprika to flavor vegetables, salads, and meat.

So you see, this old family recipe for cabbage rolls has foods rich in essential nutrients and protective plant compounds to help the body's detoxification system reduce the risk of cancer. My parents continued this tradition. As a child, I remember eating a lot of fruits and vegetables. We had apple, cherry, and peach trees on our property and a garden of tomatoes, cucumbers, asparagus, beans, potatoes, peas, corn, peppers, cabbage, broccoli, cauliflower, blueberries, raspberries, strawberries, and rhubarb. And we gathered wild mushrooms as well. Ritually, my mother saved the flavonoid-rich cooking liquid from vegetables as a stock for soup, and she canned fruits and vegetables for the winter. This was a pretty common way for people to live, until the advent of fast foods. Today, my folks still have a pretty good-size garden and, thankfully, a great deal of vitality despite the fact that they are now in their eighties.

> ## MORE THAN THE SUM OF ITS PARTS
>
> Scientists involved in nutrition research are aware that plant compounds behave synergistically in supporting each other's specific detoxification responsibilities. In other words, together they act more beneficially than any of them would on their own. A recent area of nutrition research at AMC Cancer Research Center is the study of the benefits of people eating many different fruits and vegetables instead of just adding one healthy food or nutrient to their diet. In addition to providing a good balance of nutrients— vitamins, minerals, phytochemicals, and essential fats—we are seeing that variety is the key to detoxification.

Lessons from Okinawa

In the Andes Mountains in South America, the Caucasus Mountains in the former Soviet Union, and the Hunza Valley in Pakistan, there are areas where people routinely live to be one hundred years old or more. Scientists have evidence that the secret to these people's longevity lies in a healthy lifestyle in which diet is obviously a factor. But nowhere on earth do we have better documentation of this than on the Japanese islands of Okinawa. According to doctors Craig Wilcox, Bradley Wilcox, and Makoto Suzuki, these people are the healthiest in the world. The doctors' conclusions are based on a twenty-five-year study of Okinawans who have lived one hundred years or more. This study revealed that Okinawans are at a much lower risk than other people, including other Japanese, for chronic degenerative diseases including heart disease, diabetes, stroke, dementia, and several types of cancer.

Okinawans eat a low-calorie, plant-based diet of about 1,000 to 1,200 calories per day. This diet is high in complex (unrefined) carbohydrates, such as those found in vegetables, fruits, and whole grains, and low in protein and sodium. They get important omega-3 fatty acids from fish, vegetables, and other plant foods, particularly soy products and freshly ground flaxseeds. They eat vegetables, soybean-based products, and fruit in abundance (ten to twenty servings per day). They stir-fry foods in canola oil, rich in omega-9 and omega-6 fats from the indigenous rapeseed plant. Canola oil is associated with a reduction in breast cancer.

Okinawans are also physically active and participate in tai chi, traditional dance, gardening, and walking, which help control stress.

The low calorie intake of the Okinawan people is truly a calorie-restricted diet compared to what most people consume daily in the United States (on average more than 2,000 calories per day). In general, the Okinawans are a lean and healthy people; they are virtually free of obesity.

The Mediterranean Diet

The Mediterranean region including Spain, Portugal, Southern France, Southern Italy, and Greece provides perhaps the best modern-day example of a traditional diet that can promote good health and prevent heart disease, cancer, diabetes, and weight gain. What's so special about it?

First of all, 40 percent of the calories in a Mediterranean diet come from fat, which on the surface sounds high. But it's really not high, considering the quality of the fats. In fact this amount of fat in the form of omega-3, omega-6, and omega-9 is actually very healthy. The Mediterraneans get an abundance of these fats from fish (sardines, tuna, and salmon), avocados, walnuts, purslane, and, of course, olive oil—a mostly omega-9 monounsaturated fat that decreases bad cholesterol (LDL, vLDL) and raises good cholesterol (HDL). They do use butter, but that's acceptable because they eat it in small portions, and it's a far healthier choice than trans-fat-laden margarine.

Vegetables, whole grains, and beans are very popular, and Mediterranean cultures are blessed with a wide variety including green beans, beets, artichokes, asparagus, greens, onions, leeks, scallions, garlic, broccoli, cabbage, cauliflower, bok choy, rutabaga, kale, turnips, tomatoes, eggplant, peppers, spinach, carrots, squash, celery, parsley, potatoes, and mushrooms. Rice, couscous, polenta, and bulgur are the most commonly eaten whole grains. Beans include chickpeas, lentils, cannelloni, and fava beans. Lean meat—beef, lamb, and chicken—is usually eaten in small portions as a condiment or for seasoning.

Aside from butter and cheese, which form a very small part of their overall dietary habits, milk products are not generally part of the Mediterranean diet. They get sufficient calcium from other sources including whole grains, beans, green leafy vegetables, seeds, and nuts. Interestingly, they have a lower incidence of osteoporosis than we do in the United States, where we consume large amounts of dairy products.

The Mediterranean diet also contains very few processed and simple carbohydrate sugars. Fresh fruit is the typical dessert. Berries, grapes, apricots, figs, prunes, lemons, oranges and orange peels, and melons are the most commonly consumed fruits. Sweets that contain sugar and/or saturated fats are consumed infrequently and in small amounts. Wine is commonly consumed with meals in small amounts.

Finally, the Mediterranean diet features herbs and spices including basil, bay leaf, rosemary, thyme, hot red and green peppers, and turmeric, which are known to help in the overall process of detoxification.

ONE HABIT OF OUR ANCESTORS THAT SHOULD *NOT* BE PERPETUATED

Traditional diets are better in many ways, except for the propensity toward smoked and cured meats. The unhealthy aspects of these processes have already been discussed. In addition, excessive use of pickled vegetables is not good. Certain areas of China that eat these types of foods have high rates of esophageal and stomach cancer. Refrigeration has significantly decreased the routine eating of these types of foods. In the United States, the increased use of refrigeration paralleled a decrease in stomach and esophageal cancer.

Range-Fed or Grain-Fed Animals

Throughout time the ethical issue of killing animals has been subordinated to our basic instinct for survival. The truth is, meat from animals provides a concentrated and practical source of essential amino acids that we all need for good health. Before the popularization of supplementation, it was considered too difficult to get these same concentrations from the plant world. Today, it is possible to get essential amino acids without resorting to meat, so now we have the ability to achieve a healthy diet without it. But the traditional diet of our ancestors did include meat whenever possible. They usually ate it in small amounts not because of health concerns but rather because it was very expensive compared to plant foods. Back then animals were free to roam the fields grazing on grass and other vegetation. As a result, the meat the people did eat was much better nutritionally than the meat we consume today, which is generally grain-fed. Meats and eggs from so-called free-range-fed, or grass-fed, animals are lower in fat and because grass-fed meat is so lean, it is also low in calories. Remember that fat has nine calories per gram while proteins and carbohydrates have only four calories. Obviously, the greater the fat content, the greater the number of calories. A six-ounce steak from a grass-fed steer has almost a hundred fewer calories than a six-ounce steak from a grain-fed steer. This is why wild game such as deer, bison, and elk are healthier red meat sources. This type of wild game, if properly cooked, will have very few cancer-causing agents. You might find it interesting that certain countries in the world eat more meat than we do in the United States but have a lower rate of heart disease and cancer. Argentines, for example, eat more than twice the amount of red meat that we do in the United States, but because they tend to eat meat from range-fed cattle, their rates of heart disease and cancer are much lower than ours. Range-fed animals provide a rich source of important vitamins such as beta-carotene and vitamin E, and essential fats such as omega-3 fatty acids. These important nutrients have been shown in many scientific studies to reduce the risk of cardiovascular disease, cancer, diabetes, and obesity, as well as other degenerative disease. Grass-fed meat is low in saturated fat but has two to six times more essential omega-3 fatty acids than its grain-fed equivalent. Meat and eggs from pastured (range-fed) poultry are good sources of omega-3 fatty acids as well. An egg from a free-range hen can contain up to twenty times more omega-3 fatty acids than an egg from a pen-raised hen. The relative abundance of omega-3 fatty acids in grass-fed animals may surprise you. But it is not all that difficult to understand once you realize that, just as salmon and other fish get their omega-3 fatty acid content from sea vegetation, these animals are feeding on vegetation similarly rich in essential omega-3 fatty acids.

Grass-fed products also offer a significant supply of another type of good fat, a potent anticarcinogen called conjugated linolenic acid (CLA), which will be discussed further in Chapter 6. When dairy cows are raised on fresh pasture alone, their milk has five times more CLA than that of cows fed a regular diet of grains. Finally, the leaner meat from range-fed animals can actually help to lower cholesterol levels. By staying with range-fed animals, you can eat meat in small portions (six ounces or less) with approval from nutritionist scientists like me.

Detoxification Food Guidelines

It should not be surprising to you that my best advice for ensuring a healthy, long life is to base your diet as our ancestors did on a foundation of many different plant foods. Eating fruits, vegetables, beans, and whole grains in abundance will unquestionably help to eliminate carcinogenic agents from the body. We have done enough population studies to prove such foods decrease the risk of all cancers. Here are some specific recommendations we make at the AMC Cancer Research Center:

Fourteen Recommendations for Eliminating Carcinogens from Your Body

1. Eat a plant-based diet containing five to nine servings of fruits and vegetables per day.

2. When it comes to calories, less is more. Calorie restriction decreases risk of cancer and keeps us from aging prematurely.

3. Eat healthy meals at regular times. Don't skip breakfast. If you get hungry between meals, eat fruits and raw vegetables and/or whole-grain snacks or nuts.

4. Drink six to nine glasses of water per day.

5. Minimize refined sugars as well as processed carbohydrates.

6. Keep fat intake to 20–30 percent of your diet and make sure the sources of fat contain omega-3 and omega-6 fats (flaxseed oil, walnuts, seeds, avocados, olives, and cold-water fish such as salmon and tuna).

7. Eat small portions (six ounces or less) of lean meat from range- or grass-fed animals.

8. Avoid overcooked and burned meats, charcoal barbecued meats, salt-cured and smoked meats, and salt-pickled foods, which contain dangerous chemicals that can trigger the process of cancer. The recipes provided later in this book illustrate many delicious and health-protective methods of preparing foods.

9. Avoid processed, polished grains but consume whole grains such as brown rice, whole wheat, oats, and barley. This will increase your intake of both soluble and insoluble fiber as well as beneficial phytochemicals.

10. Avoid consumption of excessive protein.

11. Decrease salt content of food. Season sparingly or better yet, season instead with pepper, which contains phytochemicals that help in the absorption of other phytochemicals.

12. Do not drink more than two alcoholic beverages per day if you are a male and one and a half or less if you are a female. Wines, especially red wines, contain several beneficial phytochemicals but should still be consumed in moderation.

13. Try to maintain an ideal weight and avoid obesity.

14. Exercise regularly. Do cardiovascular and weight-bearing exercise at least three times a week for at least thirty minutes per day (more if possible). This will increase your metabolic rate and allow you to use calories more efficiently, as well as decrease stress.

Problems with the U.S. Government Dietary Guidelines

This brings me to the U.S. Food Guide Pyramid developed by the Department of Agriculture. If our government is attempting to take a leadership role in directing Americans to a healthy way of eating, it is not succeeding. Obesity and type II diabetes continue to rise and we as a nation are just getting fatter. It is estimated that 61 percent of us weigh too much and 25 percent are obese. An investigation of women in the Nurses Health Study found that those who followed the USDA's pyramid were no healthier than those that didn't. And what about the multitude of cultures attempting to assimilate in our country with dietary habits based on traditions that bear little resemblance to our own? The government's pyramid fails to address the health needs of these people.

USDA DAILY FOOD GUIDE PYRAMID

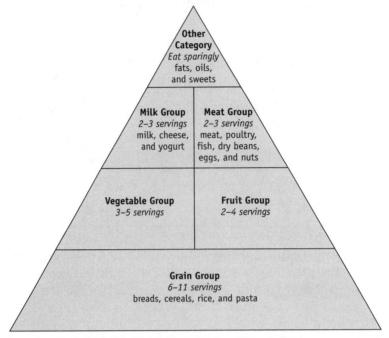

Other Category
Eat sparingly
fats, oils,
and sweets

Milk Group
2–3 servings
milk, cheese,
and yogurt

Meat Group
2–3 servings
meat, poultry,
fish, dry beans,
eggs, and nuts

Vegetable Group
3–5 servings

Fruit Group
2–4 servings

Grain Group
6–11 servings
breads, cereals, rice, and pasta

Source: Department of Agriculture U.S. Department of Health and Human Services

In my view, there are four problems with the USDA Daily Food Guide Pyramid. First, the relative weight it gives to the key food groups is out-of-date with current research. Dr. Walter Willett, a well-known nutrition researcher from the Harvard School of Public Health, also believes the government's pyramid is outdated to the point that it may actually contribute to obesity, poor health, and unnecessary early deaths. Dr. Willett discusses the changes that are needed in the food pyramid in his new book *Eat, Drink and Be Healthy*. The pyramid treats the different food groups in a far too general and oversimplified way. It fails to include exercise and a healthy mental state as significant factors, and it erroneously assumes Americans are a homogenous people.

The grain group forms the foundation of our government's food pyramid. Apparently, the old saying "Bread is the staff of life" is alive and well at the USDA. As a nutrition scientist, I do not disagree with the necessity of grain-based foods in a healthy diet. But I differ with the government's recommendation in the relative weight grains are given in the pyramid and its lack of distinction between simple and complex carbohydrates. Bread is indeed still the staff of life, but not as much as it used to be and certainly not when it is made with processed bleached white flour. Grains should only be consumed in as close to their original state as possible, meaning they should be eaten whole and unprocessed—for example, brown rice, whole wheat, oats, and barley. Even pasta, crackers, chips, and yes, bread, are acceptable but only if they are made from the whole grain. We call these complex carbohydrates. They are loaded with fiber, vitamins, minerals, and phytochemicals, all of which are protective against obesity, diabetes, heart disease, and cancer. Snack foods and bread made from bleached flour and white rice are simple carbohydrates—the not-so-good ones that have little nutritional benefit but are very good at making us a fatter nation. Since simple carbohydrates usually taste better, are more convenient, and cost less than complex carbohydrate foods, the USDA has unwittingly given us a green light to eat them by not providing a crucial distinction in its pyramid.

The relative weight the USDA has given the fruit and vegetable group should be reconsidered in light of the overwhelming number of scientific studies showing that fruits and vegetables are quite simply more important to good health than grains. Both are crucial, of course, but research has shown fruits and vegetables to be more so, providing a balance of complex carbohydrates and essential nutrients and an incredible array of beneficial phytochemicals to supercharge detoxification and other vital functions of the body. Fruits and vegetables should replace grains as the foundation of the pyramid.

Dairy is one of the protein groups in the government pyramid. But because it was developed with Caucasians in mind, it is also fundamentally flawed. African Americans, Hispanics, Asians, American Indians, and others complain that their traditional foods and ways of eating were forgotten when the Daily Food Guide Pyramid was built. For example, the majority of the ethnic populations in this country are to various degrees lactose-intolerant (they cannot consume dairy products) but the government's pyramid identifies dairy products as a major source of protein and the only good source of calcium. The fact is, the use of dairy products is typically quite low in Asian populations, where calcium is obtained instead from soybean products, seaweed, and cruciferous vegetables. These and other foods, including spinach, turnip greens and other leafy vegetables, nuts, seeds, whole grains, and beans, are just as good and in many cases better sources of calcium than dairy products.

——————————— ❧ ———————————

Supplementation with Essential Fatty Acids

Most Americans generally get too many omega-6 fatty acids and not enough omega-3 fatty acids. Following is a good formula for achieving a balance of not only omega-3 and omega-6 essential fatty acids, but omega-9 fatty acids as well. Rosemary extract, vitamin E, and ascorbyl palmitate are added to prevent rancidity and extend shelf life.

	PER DAY
black currant oil (GLA/LA/αLA)	200–400 mg
flaxseed oil (αLA/LA)	250–500 mg
perilla oil (αLA)	250–500 mg
fish oil (EPA/DHA)	250–500 mg
rosemary extract	50–100 mg
vitamin E	50–200 IU (International Units)
ascorbyl palmitate	50–100 mg

Abbreviations: GLA (omega-6 derivative); αLA (essential omega-3); LA (essential omega-6); EPA (omega-3 derivative); DHA (omega-3 derivative).

At the moment there is no single source containing all of these beneficial oils. But that will soon change. Check with the AMC Cancer Research Center periodically for new developments in this area. Until then it is necessary to get these oils separately. Just go to your favorite health-food store and ask for recommendations.

——————————— ❧ ———————————

The reason our fat nation keeps getting fatter despite the lowest placement of fats and oils on the pyramid is that the pyramid fails to take into account the difference between good fats and bad ones. This is a major oversight. Before we even get to the fats and oils category at the very top of the pyramid, Americans, thanks to the generality of the government guidelines, will have consumed far too much saturated fat in the form of dairy and meat, as well as hydrogenated fats from most convenience foods; but they will not have eaten enough of the beneficial unsaturated fat found in fish (especially cold-water fish), whole grains, nuts, and seeds. The government's advice that fats be consumed sparingly is undermined by our heavy reliance on saturated fat–laden meat, dairy, and convenience foods

DR. SLAGA'S FOOD PYRAMID

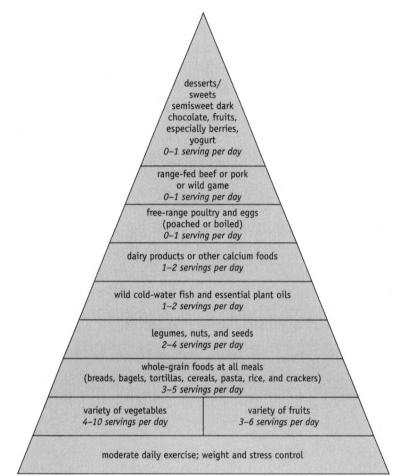

desserts/
sweets
semisweet dark
chocolate, fruits,
especially berries,
yogurt
0–1 serving per day

range-fed beef or pork
or wild game
0–1 serving per day

free-range poultry and eggs
(poached or boiled)
0–1 serving per day

dairy products or other calcium foods
1–2 servings per day

wild cold-water fish and essential plant oils
1–2 servings per day

legumes, nuts, and seeds
2–4 servings per day

whole-grain foods at all meals
(breads, bagels, tortillas, cereals, pasta, rice, and crackers)
3–5 servings per day

variety of vegetables
4–10 servings per day

variety of fruits
3–6 servings per day

moderate daily exercise; weight and stress control

and it *does not* take into account that essential fatty acids are absolutely needed for health. Omega-3 and omega-6 fats from these sources are vital for proper body function, including detoxification and, when consumed in reasonable amounts, *they will not make you fat.* In fact, omega-3 fats can actually speed up metabolism and aid in weight loss. Absolutely, good fats and oils should be a regular, prominent part of our diet. And by working our way up the pyramid we can get these fats from vegetables, whole grains, seeds, nuts, legumes, and cold-water fish. Unfortunately, the government's pyramid, to put it kindly, has done nothing to enlighten us on this fact. Consequently, we are a nation deficient in the good fats, particularly omega-3 fats. Until this changes, omega-3 and omega-6 fats should have their own category, with the recommendation to supplement, if necessary, to ensure the proper nutritional balance.

The other protein group in the food pyramid includes meat. While meat is a good source of protein and essential amino acids, we as a society eat far too much of it—and we eat the wrong kind. As discussed earlier in this chapter, range-fed animals and eggs from range-fed chickens are lower in saturated fat and cholesterol, and higher in vitamins, omega-3 fatty acids, and CLA than their grain-fed counterparts (the kind most of us eat). Again, the government's food pyramid misses the opportunity to guide us in this area, leading us instead to believe that meat, any kind of meat, is a necessary dietary component. So the meat lovers in us make the most of it.

Diet, Exercise, and Stress Reduction

I realize that some may think it would be inappropriate to include exercise and good mental health on a food pyramid. But we cannot deny the linkage and synergistic effect these elements have on good health when combined with proper diet. My pyramid finds a place for moderate exercise and stress reduction and it would form the real foundation of a good dietary plan. With the changes I am recommending, doesn't the new pyramid begin to take on a look remarkably similar to the traditional ways our ancestors ate and lived? There is no coincidence here. The truth is there has been and always will be one and only one proper way for humans to eat.

Young people and future generations yet unborn have a unique opportunity to actually live even healthier and longer lives than our ancestors, provided they are wise enough to return to the traditional ways of eating. This is because of a couple of very important health factors that our grandparents didn't have. One is access to much better medical care. Advances in medicine and early diagnosis of diseases allow us to have a better chance of correcting genetically oriented degenerative problems at an early stage. Another factor is greater access to many different types of fresh fruits and vegetables, which allows us to eat a healthy diet throughout the year, not just seasonally. And one final factor: the emergence of nutritional supplements, which ensures that we can have all the nutrients we need to help prevent cancer and other degenerative diseases. Those of us who learn from the past, take advantage of modern advances in protecting our health, and practice the recommendations from the AMC Cancer Research Center will be much more likely to lead healthier, longer, and more active lives than our ancestors.

CHAPTER FIVE

The Need for Basic Supplementation

$\mathcal{L}$

For basic health and detoxification, the human body needs proteins, carbohydrates, fats, and micronutrients consisting of vitamins, minerals, and other beneficial compounds. In an ideal world food alone would provide the full spectrum of these nutrients. In reality, however, the demands of modern life work against that. As those of you who have tried and perhaps succeeded in getting that full spectrum solely from food sources have no doubt discovered it is a consuming daily routine around which pretty much everything else must be arranged. Even so, it may not be enough for some people. Unusual physical or mental activity, stress, medication, and environmental pollution can each create a greater demand for nutrients. The truth is that most of us have many other things to do with our time. Adding to the difficulty is the fact that concentrations of nutrients vary with food growth patterns, processing, preparation and cooking methods, variations in dietary habits, and bad eating habits. Whether you are among those who make a conscious effort to eat nutritiously or those who think an order of fries constitutes a daily quota of vegetables, the central question is not whether you have a nutritional deficiency, but to what degree And that begs a second question that nutrition scientists are still struggling with: How do we know whether we are getting the right amounts of the essential nutrients from our diet to ensure good health? Most experts are in agreement on the specific amounts of these nutrients that are needed to prevent conditions of deficiency. That is what the government's recommended daily allowance (RDA) deals with. But there is disagreement not only about the amounts necessary for optimal health and energy, but also about how best to obtain them. This chapter provides a very easy-to-understand, implementable program of fundamental nutrient supplementation with a nutrition scientist's focus. I will go over what may seem fairly basic: vitamins and minerals. We all know we need them, but even nutrition experts disagree on how much we need. To make the case for my recommendations, I'll cover what each one does.

Vitamin and Mineral Deficiencies

Nutritional deficiencies arise from food and lifestyle choices but also from other factors such as:

- poverty

- psychiatric disturbance

- individual idiosyncrasies

- religious beliefs

- food fads

- excessive alcohol consumption

- poor appetite

- dieting to combat obesity

- restricted diets prescribed by physicians for the management of specific diseases

- a variety of conditions, including diseases of the liver and biliary tract, prolonged diarrhea from any cause, hyperthyroidism, pernicious anemia, and various disorders of the digestive system

- treatment with antimicrobials

- increased tissue requirements such as during periods of growth, hard physical work, exercise, and during pregnancy, lactation, and menstruation

- diseases associated with an increased metabolism, such as hyperthyroidism, and conditions accompanied by fever or tissue wasting as well as periods of stress and following injury

The following choices or conditions bring their own nutritional demands.

- Smoking causes a need for greater amounts of vitamin C.

- People who consume a lot of wine need extra B-complex vitamins.

- People who take certain prescription drugs, such as those for high blood pressure, need to ensure that they are obtaining adequate levels of potassium and folic acid.

- Aging can decrease the body's ability to absorb vitamins B-complex, C, and D and calcium.

Constructing the Optimum Nutritional Supplement Formulation

Since deficiency of a single vitamin, mineral, or other essential micronutrient is rarely encountered clinically, it is customary practice in cases of suspected deficiency, as well as in preventative treatment, to use a multiple-nutrient approach. Such formulations should provide the highest number of the essential micronutrients needed by healthy individuals.

These formulations should include electrolytes and trace elements. The optimum formulation should also include other antioxidants and/or free radical scavengers, which have been shown to enhance the immune system; prevent certain cancers, cardiovascular disorders, and inflammatory diseases; and slow aging. And they should include important compounds such as myo-inositol, choline, methionine, glutamine, taurine, lycine, L-carnitine, and trimethylglycine, all of which work synergistically with other antioxidants and help with methylation, liver function, cell membrane integrity, and energy. Most importantly, the constituents of a good formulation must be stable and taken in amounts and forms that can be properly absorbed and utilized by the body. Here is a rundown of what each group does for you.

The Oil-Soluble Vitamins

Vitamin A

Vitamin A is integral to many biochemical and physiological processes in the body. It is required in cell differentiation, especially related to epithelial tissue such as skin; mucous membranes; and linings of the respiratory, the gastrointestinal, and urogenital systems. It is important for good vision, immunity, and healthy skin and hair as well as cancer prevention. Vitamin A is necessary for proper reproduction, bone growth, and tooth development. Deficiencies have been associated with a higher incidence of certain cancers. Vitamin A works synergistically with several carotenoids; other vitamins such as vitamins C, D, and E; minerals; and other antioxidants to lower cancer rates and to increase longevity.

Vitamin A can be obtained as preformed or pro-vitamin A. Preformed vitamins are found in certain meats and animal products, and although beneficial up to a point, they can have toxic side effects when taken in large amounts over a long period of time, especially in adults or during pregnancy. Pro-vitamin A is formed in our bodies from the conversion of certain carotenoids, known as precursor compounds. These carotenoids are found in many fruits and vegetables and have little or no toxicity. Beta-carotene is the major carotenoid converted into active retinol-type vitamin A for use in the body. Other carotenoids such as alpha-carotene, gamma-carotene, beta-zeacarotene, crytoxanthin, and beta-apo-carotenals can be converted to vitamin A to various degrees. But not all carotenoids can be converted into vitamin A. Examples of carotenoids that are *not* converted to vitamin A include lycopene, lutein, canthaxanthin, zeaxanthin, and capsanthin. Beta-carotene is one of the major precursors to vitamin A, and there are many scientific studies detailing its beneficial effects. Beta-carotene, which has been shown to prevent certain types of cancers, has powerful antioxidant properties and works best in combination with vitamins C and E, minerals such as selenium, and certain phenolic antioxidants to prevent cancer and to increase longevity.

Vitamin E

Vitamin E is a fat-soluble essential micronutrient that functions as an antioxidant. It protects lipid membranes in the body from oxidizing.

From studies using experimental animals and humans there are hundreds of sound scientific publications on the benefits of vitamin E. Many have shown that vitamin E works synergistically with other vitamins and minerals such as vitamin C and selenium, as well as antioxidant flavonoids and coenzyme Q_{10}, to protect against cancer, heart disease, and stroke. Coenzyme Q_{10} (CoQ_{10}), a fat-soluble compound, helps to keep vitamin E in a reduced and active state, especially in lipid membranes. Vitamin E supports immune system function and aids in the repair of tissue damaged by free radicals. It also protects the body's store of vitamin A, prevents breakdown of red blood cells, strengthens capillary walls as well as blood flow to heart and brain, lowers blood cholesterol and triglycerides, and helps to regulate protein and calcium metabolism.

VITAMIN E AS A PRESERVATIVE

Vitamin E is commonly added to high-quality vegetable oils to prevent them from becoming rancid.

Natural vitamin E from vegetable oils, nuts, whole grains, and seeds actually consists of eight different forms: d-alpha-, d-beta-, d-gamma-, and d-delta-tocopherol and d-alpha-, d-beta-, d-gamma-, and d-delta-tocotrienol. Cooking and processing robs foods of much of their vitamin E because it is easily destroyed by heat, light, and air. Although d-alpha-tocopherol is the most commonly occurring form of vitamin E in nature, the other vitamin E forms are now being found to have comparable, and in some cases even better, specific biological activities. For example, the activity of d-gamma-tocopherol has been found to be superior to d-alpha-tocopherol in destroying one of the very dangerous free radicals that leads to neurological degeneration. In another example, d-gamma-tocotrienol has been found to be about thirty times more active than d-alpha-tocopherol in lowering cholesterol. These and other scientific studies strongly suggest that mixing the various vitamin E tocopherols and tocotrienols would be better than taking d-alpha-tocopherol alone.

NOT ALL VITAMIN E IS THE SAME

DL-alpha-tocopherol is the synthetic form of vitamin E. It is generally less active than the natural form.

Because vitamin E is inherently unstable, it must be packaged in airtight soft gelatin capsules or esterified with acetate or succinate, which provides good stability and absorption but blocks antioxidizing activity. However, antioxidant properties can be restored once they've been absorbed into the body.

Vitamin D

Vitamin D, or more correctly Vitamin D_3, is actually a hormone needed for both the absorption and utilization of calcium and phosphorus. The primary role of vitamin D_3 is the mineralization of bones and teeth and the regulation of blood calcium levels. It is also critical for the growth and differentiation of several tissues. Further, it has been shown to reduce the rate of certain cancers. It aids in nervous system and heart function and contributes along with calcium to the prevention of rickets. Vitamin D_3 should be taken together with calcium, magnesium, manganese, phosphorus, boron, vitamin C, and the B vitamins to ensure healthy bones and connective tissue.

Vitamin K

The three forms of vitamin K are vitamin K_1 or phytonadione from plants; vitamin K_2 or menaquinones from bacteria in our intestines; and a synthetic called vitamin K_3 or menadione. Unlike the other fat-soluble vitamins—A, D, and E—vitamin K is not stored in the body. Vitamin K is a necessary factor in the formation of prothrombinogen and other blood-clotting mechanisms; the body can't form blood clots without vitamin K. Along with vitamin D_3, vitamin C, and estrogens, vitamin K is important in regulating calcium. Vitamin K has also been found to be a powerful antioxidant, which can counteract free radicals and key cytokines involved in inflammation. Deficiencies of vitamin K can lead to excessive bleeding and osteoporosis. Recently, it was approved for the treatment of osteoporosis in Japan.

The Water-Soluble Vitamins

B-Complex Vitamins

The B-complex vitamins consist of B_1 (thiamin), B_2 (riboflavin), B_3 (niacin and niacinamide), B_5 (pantothenic acid), B_6 (pyridoxine), B_{12} (cyanocobalamin), folic acid, and biotin. Choline and myo-inositol are micronutrients that are usually included with the B-complex vitamins because of their connected biological functions. Each B-complex vitamin has its own unique biological role, but in terms of efficacy, they work best in combination. They are very important in many biological processes, the most significant of which are energy production during the metabolism of carbohydrates, proteins, and fats and keeping our immune, skeletal, and nervous systems healthy. **Vitamin B_1** (thiamin) plays an essential role in the metabolism of carbohydrates into energy and helps to promote normal appetite and digestion. It is also effective in reducing fatigue, reducing buildup of fat deposits in arteries, converting fatty acids into steroids, and helping to maintain healthy nervous and cardiovascular systems.

Vitamin B$_2$ (riboflavin) is required for the repair and growth of tissues as well as synthesis of our DNA. For instance it is found in the retina of the eye and is essential for sight. Vitamin B$_2$ assists in metabolizing nutrients such as proteins, fats, and carbohydrates and therefore is critical in the formation of energy for cells; is a cofactor in glutathione reductase, which keeps glutathione in the state that is necessary for its antioxidizing activity; assists in forming red blood cells; helps to correct iron-deficient anemia; and has a significant role in antibody production.

Niacin, niacinamide, and nicotinic acid are considered three forms that have **vitamin B$_3$** activity. Vitamin B$_3$ is involved in the regulation of blood sugar, antioxidant activity, and detoxification reactions and is important for the production of energy. It is an essential constituent of coenzymes I and II that occur in a wide variety of enzyme processes involved in the metabolism of carbohydrates. Niacinamide is necessary for DNA formation and important for the integrity of the central nervous system. It also aids normal tissue function, particularly the skin and gastrointestinal tract. Niacin has also been shown to reduce cholesterol levels. However, high doses of niacin (greater than 500 mg per day for most humans but much less for some) leads to flushing of the skin, especially face and hands (redness, burning, and stinging).

Vitamin B$_5$ (pantothenic acid) is involved with the metabolism of proteins, fats, and carbohydrates in the form of coenzyme A. It is also involved in the synthesis of sterols, hormones, porphyrins, and the neurotransmitter acetylcholine. Vitamin B$_5$ helps to keep the skin healthy, prevents wrinkles, and stimulates the adrenal glands. It also aids in resisting infection and healing wounds as well as blood formation and stimulation of antibody production.

RDA IS NOT ENOUGH

A superior multivitamin and mineral formulation should contain more than the RDA. For example, amounts higher than the RDA for the B-complex vitamins—in the presence of coenzyme Q$_{10}$ and carnitine—are necessary to provide enough energy for people living in a fast-paced and stressful society.

Pyridoxine, pyridoxal, and pyridoxamine are the vitamins collectively known as **vitamin B$_6$**. Vitamin B$_6$ is important in the metabolism of proteins and amino acids, helps regulate blood glucose levels, is necessary for the manufacture of hemoglobin, is important in normalizing nervous system function, and plays a key role in enabling the brain to transmit nerve impulses. Vitamin B$_6$ promotes healthy skin, teeth, gums, and blood vessels. It also helps the body in the utilization of carbohydrates and essential fatty acids for energy, promotes the production of antibodies, and provides support for the overall healthy function of the immune system. Vitamin B$_6$ is one of the most critical of all the vitamins; it participates as a coenzyme in more than sixty enzymatic reactions.

Vitamin B$_{12}$ (cyanocobalamin) is a very important vitamin that contains the trace mineral cobalt. Known as vitamin B$_{12}$, it works together with folic acid in reactions that are critical to the process of cell division and in making DNA and RNA. It is critical for bone growth, the integrity of the central nervous system, and normal blood formation. Vitamin B$_{12}$ deficiencies, especially as a result of poor absorption, are related to certain anemias, especially pernicious anemia. Vitamin B$_{12}$ promotes utilization of proteins, fats, and carbohydrates.

In addition to its significance in cell division and the making of DNA and RNA, as with other B vitamins, **folic acid** is important in red blood cell maturation and other metabolic processes. It is essential for the functions of vitamins A, D, E, and K and it aids in the digestion of proteins. Folic acid is necessary for normal neural tube formation during development and it is especially needed during pregnancy and childhood development. Folic acid, together with vitamins B$_{12}$ and B$_6$, is important in the process of methylation.

Biotin is a water-soluble vitamin essential for the metabolism of carbohydrates. It is a coenzyme in the synthesis of fatty acids and amino acids and it stimulates the production of proteins. Biotin has been found to enhance insulin sensitivity and increase glucose utilization in the liver.

Choline is not a vitamin, but it is related in function to the vitamin B-complex. Proper fat metabolism in the liver depends on it. A deficiency can lead to liver cancer. Choline is essential for making acetylcholine and important components of cell membranes such as lecithin (phosphatidylcholine) and an important molecule called sphingomyelin. Choline is also needed as a methyl donor in some methylation reactions, especially in the liver. Although choline can be made in the body, it is nevertheless considered to be an essential micronutrient.

Choline and **myo-inositol**, the other B-complex-related nonvitamin, are important components of cell membranes and help in the absorption and digestion of fats including the export of fats from the liver. Supplementing with choline and myo-inositol helps to prevent liver disorders, diabetes, and depression.

Vitamin C

Vitamin C is a very potent antioxidant. It prevents nitrosamine formation in the stomach; prevents the activation of PAHs to cancer-causing agents; and decreases radiation-induced toxicity, mutations, and cancer. Vitamin C works synergistically with several other vitamins and minerals as well as other antioxidants to lower cancer and cardiovascular disorder rates and to increase the protective effect of the immune system. It is critical for producing and maintaining collagen, healing wounds, aiding tooth and bone formation, and producing hormones that regulate basal metabolic rate and body temperature. Vitamin C also aids in the metabolism of amino acids and calcium. It promotes stamina and contributes to the reduction of infection, colds, fatigue, stress, and allergies. Dr. Linus Pauling, a two-time Nobel Laureate, spent years studying vitamin C's beneficial effects.

Vitamin C's effectiveness is enhanced when combined with certain other nutrients. In citrus fruits, vitamin C is kept in a reduced (antioxidant) state by various flavonoids. Without them, vitamin C would be unable to do its job of neutralizing free radicals. Once vitamin C finds its way to our cells, ascorbic acid reductase helps to keep it in a reduced state. Lipoic acid and dihydrolipoate help vitamin C (and vitamin E) to destroy many different types of free radicals. Vitamin C helps to keep vitamin E in a reduced and active (antioxidant) state so it can destroy free radicals in cellular membranes as well.

Minerals

Minerals are basic elements that come from the soil and cannot be made by plants or other living systems. Several minerals are essential to body function. They are calcium, phosphorus, magnesium, sulfur, zinc, iron, and iodine. We also need small amounts of important trace minerals. Much is known about copper, chromium, fluorine, manganese, molybdenum, selenium, and vanadium, but there is very little scientific data on other trace minerals such as arsenic, cadmium, cobalt, nickel, silicone, and tin. Not surprisingly, we get most of these minerals from plants that depend on the soil and animals that depend on the plants for survival. You can imagine that the mineral content of plants varies a lot from region to region because of the differences in the mineral content of the soil. Selenium is a good example of this. Studies show that higher amounts of selenium in the soil relate to a low cancer incidence whereas lower amounts relate to higher incidence. Our bodies need minerals for proper composition of bones, teeth, connective tissue, and blood as well as for maintenance of normal cell function.

Caution About Iron and Copper

Iron is an essential mineral needed for healthy blood and is also critical in blood formation during menstruation. Copper, another essential trace mineral, is also needed for the formation of red blood cells and the utilization of iron. Copper functions in energy formation, connective tissue metabolism, and the development of the nervous system as well. As stated before, copper is very important in detoxification because of its role in certain SODs. Iron and copper deficiencies have been linked to pernicious anemia. Copper also has a role in the prevention and treatment of cardiovascular disease and arthritis. It should be pointed out, however, that excess copper and iron can cause the formation of a very potent free radical. That is why these minerals should not be added to supplements containing antioxidants. Iron and copper are generally bound to proteins within the body, which prevent antioxidants and hydrogen peroxide from becoming free radicals. But excessive free or unbound forms of iron and copper can lead to free radical damage. Special cases, such as anemia, require iron and copper supplements but never along with antioxidant-rich supplements. Rather they should be taken several hours apart.

Selenium

Selenium works synergistically with several vitamins, particularly vitamin E, as well as minerals and antioxidant compounds to lower cancer rates and to increase longevity. It is an essential component of glutathione peroxidase, a very important enzyme that helps to prevent lipid peroxidation of cellular membranes. As an antioxidant it helps to protect cells from free radical damage and toxic effects of certain chemicals. In addition, it protects against mercury and insecticide poisoning. Deficiencies are linked with increased risk of many cancers including breast, ovary, colon, prostate, lung, bladder, and skin, as well as stroke, angina, and heart attack. Selenium helps to maintain normal immune function and plays a role in the biosynthesis of coenzyme Q_{10}. In a recent clinical trial based at the University of Arizona Cancer Center, a daily dose of 200 micrograms of yeast-based selenium was found to decrease the overall occurrence of cancer by 42 percent, with lung, prostate, and colon cancers showing the largest decrease.

Calcium

Calcium is not only vital for good bone and teeth formation and maintenance, but it is also involved in muscle contraction, the transmission of nerve impulses, blood clotting, the structure and function of cell membranes, and B_{12} absorption. And it is very important in the activity of many enzymes. Calcium appears to protect against certain types of cancer such as colorectal, and it helps to regulate the passage of nutrients in and out of cells, blood pressure, and heartbeat. Dietary deficiencies of calcium, which are all too common, have been associated with accelerated bone loss resulting in osteoporosis or porous or fragile bones, oral health problems, and hypertension. More than 99 percent of the calcium stored in the human body is contained in the bones.

Magnesium

Magnesium is also vital in bone formation and maintenance. It is an essential mineral for many biological processes including glucose metabolism, protein and nucleic acid synthesis (RNA and DNA), electrical balance of cells, and the transmission of nerve impulses. Many enzymatic reactions depend on magnesium, which is also an integral element in the structural integrity, function, and contractions of the heart and all other muscles. Magnesium helps with the utilization of vitamins B, C, and E; promotes the absorption and metabolism of other minerals; and helps to reduce blood cholesterol and regulate body temperature. Deficiencies of magnesium have been linked to cardiovascular disorders.

Phosphorus

Phosphorus is a component of RNA and DNA. It is very important in all bodily functions, including bone formation and maintenance. It is second only to calcium as the most abundant mineral in the body. Phosphorus is involved in a variety of processes that store and produce energy needed in muscle contraction, transfer of nerve impulses, hormone secretion, and membrane structure as phospholipids. It is needed in the utilization of fats, proteins, and carbohydrates and aids in the function of B-complex vitamins. The absorption, storage, and excretion of phosphorus is dependent on vitamin D_3 and parathyroid hormone, which is also critical for calcium's and magnesium's roles in bone formation and maintenance.

Manganese

Another important mineral in bone development and maintenance, manganese also supports insulin production and critical enzyme systems including mitochondrial superoxide dismutase (SOD), which is very important in the detoxification of free radicals. It helps to regulate blood sugar and is required for the synthesis of a component of cartilage called mucopolysaccharides. Manganese also activates enzymes to utilize vitamin C, biotin, and thiamin; is a catalyst in the synthesis of fatty acids and cholesterol; and aids in the metabolism of proteins, fats, and carbohydrates. Deficiencies have been linked to both epilepsy and diabetes.

Boron

Boron is essential to plant growth. It supports bone health through its important role in the metabolism of calcium, phosphorus, magnesium, and cholecalciferol (vitamin D_3) and together with these essential nutrients and manganese, is helpful in the prevention and treatment of osteoporosis. It appears, also, to increase the activity of estrogens on bone development and maintenance and to be useful in the prevention and treatment of arthritis.

Zinc

Perhaps more than any other mineral, zinc is essential to good health. Zinc is required in the function of more than two hundred important enzymes, including those key to antioxidizing reactions and those involved in the production of DNA and RNA. It also allows proteins to interact with DNA.

Zinc plays a significant role in the structure and function of cell membranes. It is critical for cell replication and tissue regeneration, healing wounds, sexual maturity, and normal growth. Adequate zinc levels are necessary for proper immune and skin system functions, vision, taste, and smell. Zinc, in the form of zinc D-glucarate, has been found to have both antiviral and antibacterial activity. It is also important to healthy sex hormone and prostate function. Zinc prevents the absorption of toxic lead and cadmium in the intestine, and it helps the liver avoid damage from poisoning due to dangerous chemicals. It aids in the absorption of B-complex vitamins and in the mobilization of vitamin A from storage in the liver to areas of the body where it is needed, such as the eyes and skin. Together with chromium and vanadium, zinc is needed for proper cellular glucose utilization and for insulin function.

Chromium

Chromium, a cofactor for insulin, is essential in the utilization of glucose as well as other metabolic processes involving carbohydrates. Chromium helps bind insulin to cells, which, in turn, allows glucose to be taken up by cells. Chromium decreases the insulin requirement of diabetics. Low levels of chromium have been linked to diabetes, hypoglycemia (low glucose levels), and heart disease. Chromium has also been found to lower cholesterol.

Trace Minerals

The essential trace mineral **vanadium** helps to regulate proper glucose levels, is involved in fat metabolism, and serves as a catalyst or cofactor for several important enzymes.

Another essential trace mineral is **molybdenum**. It supports iron metabolism and several aspects of detoxification, including the formation of the antioxidant uric acid as well as the detoxification of alcohol and sulfites. It is essential to the chelation process of iron and copper.

Iodine is critical to proper thyroid function, which regulates the basal metabolic rate. It is also an important component of the thyroid hormone, which helps to regulate growth and development. Iodine prevents some forms of goiter. It also helps to burn fat, convert beta-carotene into vitamin A, and aid in the absorption of carbohydrates from the small intestine.

Potassium is a major intracellular electrolyte, or charged molecule. It aids in the transmission of nerve impulses, the release of insulin, and the proper functioning of digestive enzymes. Potassium works with sodium to maintain the balance of fluids in the body and within cells. It stimulates the kidneys to eliminate poisons and body waste and it helps in the supply of oxygen to the brain.

> ### ANTIOXIDANT NUTRIENTS WORK TOGETHER
>
> Vitamins C and E and minerals selenium, zinc, copper, and manganese as well as vitamin A and carotenoids constitute the important antioxidant group of essential nutrients. Antioxidants work with each other or with other nutrients to produce enhanced health benefits. These important tandem reactions help to protect us from free radical damage.

Amino Acids and Related Compounds

Methionine

Methionine is an essential amino acid, with antioxidant properties. It acts in combination with other antioxidants via chelation or binding of heavy metals, whereby lipid oxidation is prevented and metal toxicity reduced. Methyl-donating activity of methionine is vital for numerous biological pathways, including the synthesis of compounds used for detoxification and methyl transferases. Methionine also aids in maintaining proper nitrogen balance in the body.

Taurine

Taurine is another amino acid considered vital in enhancing cellular antioxidizing activity. It acts in concert with several antioxidants to provide increased protection against cancer and certain cardiovascular disorders. Taurine is used by the liver for conjugation with bile acids, and it has been shown to strengthen and stabilize cellular membranes.

Glutamine

Glutamine is yet another amino acid that supports antioxidizing reactions in cells. It also serves as an amino acid donor in many reactions and can be converted to other amino acids as well. Glutamine is critical in the formation of RNA and DNA, both of which are necessary for normal cell function and replication. It is the most prevalent amino acid in the bloodstream. It is also one of the three amino acids involved in the formation of glutathione, a critical cellular antioxidant, which in turn is composed of three important amino acids: glutamine, cysteine, and glycine.

Lycine

Lycine is an essential amino acid that helps in the prevention of athero-genic (heart disease) risk factors apolipoprotein A and B. In addition, lycine appears to be important in preventing and treating herpes and possibly other viruses. In combination with another amino acid, arginne, lycine appears to be important in maintaining muscle mass.

L-Carnitine

L-carnitine—or its biologically active form, acetyl-L-carnitine—is a very important amino acid involved in the transport of fatty acids into cell mitochondria for the purpose of producing energy. L-carnitine works very closely with coenzyme Q_{10} to enhance its antioxidizing activity and critical energy role in cells. It also improves memory and helps to protect brain cells against aging-related degeneration. It also helps to maintain the immune system and, with coenzyme Q_{10}, helps to reduce the formation of the aging pigment called lipofuscin. The most important aspects of acetyl-L-carnitine, along with coenzyme Q_{10}, are the production of energy by mitochondria and free radical detoxification.

Adding It All Up:
Dr. Slaga's Optimum Formulation

Here is my preferred daily micronutrient supplement formulation. It is intended for those who are fifteen and older. If you have any kind of medical condition, discuss with your doctor whether this regimen is appropriate for you:

- Vitamin A (5,000 International Units or IU) with beta-carotene (10,000 IU)

- B-complex vitamins:
    - B_1 or thiamin (3–15 mg)
    - B_2 or riboflavin (3.6–13.5 mg)
    - B_3 or niacin (40–60 mg)
    - B_5 or pantothenic acid (20–40 mg)
    - B_6 or pyridoxine (4–20 mg)
    - B_{12} or cyanocobalamin (20–60 micrograms or mcg)
    - biotin (300 mcg)
    - folic acid (400 mcg)

(The B_1 through B_{12} levels range from two to ten times RDA levels—more active people should take the higher dosage; biotin and folic acid are given at RDA levels, which should not be exceeded.)

- Choline (200–500 mg) as bitartrate with myo-inositol (200–500 mg) (Can be considered part of B-complex vitamins.)

- Vitamin C (250–500 mg) with citrus flavonoids (200 mg)

- Vitamin E mixture (400 IU) with selenium (200 mcg) as either yeast selenium or selenomethionine and with coenzyme Q_{10} (10 mg)

- Vitamin D_3 (400 IU) with calcium (500–1,000 mg) as glucarate, citrate, aspartate, or gluconate; magnesium (250–500 mg) as aspartate or gluconate; manganese (25 mg) as aspartate; phosphorus (250–500 mg) as di-calcium phosphate and boron (1–2 mg) as aspartate

- Vitamin K (25–50 mcg as phytonadione) (I recommend less than the RDA level because it is also produced by intestinal bacteria.)

- Amino acids and related compounds:
  - methionine (200–500 mg)
  - taurine (200–500 mg)
  - L-lycine (200–500 mg)
  - L-carnitine or acetyl-L-carnitine (200–500 mg)
  - glutamine (200–500 mg)
  - trimethylglycine (200–500 mg)

- Other mineral groups:
  - zinc (30 mg) as aspartate
  - chromium (30 mcg) as aspartate or picolinate
  - vanadium (10 mcg) as aspartate
  - iodine (150 mcg) as kelp
  - molybdenum (30 mcg) as aspartate
  - potassium (100 mg) as aspartate or sorbate

- *No* iron or copper

Generally speaking, this formulation is geared to people of average size and activity. Larger or more highly active people will need the upper range of dosages given as will pregnant and nursing women, except that pregnant women should avoid high dosages of vitamin A and selenium, which could possibly cause problems early in the pregnancy.

Children today especially need a nutritional supplement to support their rapid development since many of the foods they eat are nutritionally deficient. I recommend that children from one to four years of age should take this formulation with only 25 to 35 percent of the adult range; 35 to 60 percent of the adult range for children from five to nine; and 60 to 90 percent of the adult range for children ten through fourteen. As with adults, larger kids should take dosages in the higher range.

Whether for children or adults, it is very important not to give the maximum dose of a vitamin or mineral when first starting a vitamin-and-mineral regimen. Our bodies have to adapt to supplements. Start out with approximately one-fourth to one-third of the daily amount for a week or two, gradually increasing the dosage to the full amount after three or four weeks. For our cells to function at their best, these nutrients should be taken in small amounts, continually throughout the day. My suggestion is to divide the daily dosages into three parts and take them throughout the day—always with food or at mealtime to ensure maximum efficacy.

Limits of Megadosing

When it comes to taking vitamins, minerals, and related compounds, do not fall into the trap of thinking that more of a good thing is better. Megadosing is a waste of money. Don't do it. Our bodies can only absorb and utilize so much of any compound at any given time. In the best-case scenario, whatever isn't absorbed is excreted. In the worst case, high dosages, most notably vitamin A, can lead to toxic and unhealthy conditions. This is also true for several minerals, including iron, copper, and selenium. The best way to avoid overdosing is to take a spectrum of essential vitamins and minerals and scientifically demonstrated supporting nutrients and micronutrients. This way you eliminate the temptation to overdo a good thing.

One final point before we move on to the important detoxification supplements. My optimum formulation, you may be disappointed to learn, is not yet available in one convenient package, but it will be soon. Check with the AMC Cancer Research Center for news of this important breakthrough. Until it is, you will have to do some label reading to match up all of the groups I am recommending. The best approach is to select a very good multivitamin and mineral formulation—there are several of them—and then add the other nutrients individually until you achieve the formulation.

CHAPTER SIX

Beyond Basics: Breakthrough Supplements for Detoxification

P eople have practiced detoxification throughout the ages. In India, they fasted to cleanse the body and purify the spirit. In the rainforest, natives boiled herbs into detoxifying teas. Scandinavians had the sauna to encourage the release of impurities. In every culture throughout the world, since the beginning of ancient medicine, healers used a variety of methods to cleanse toxins from the body. What our ancestors did to encourage detoxification was based on intuition, experimentation, and observation. Today, hard science gives us our understanding of detoxification and the ways we can truly achieve it. While no doubt some of the traditional ways may have validity, this chapter is about the natural compounds that research shows to offer reliable results. And we have the technological advances to be able to isolate them into convenient supplements, something our ancestors could only dream about and probably did.

Many supplements are available to promote health and longevity and prevent disease through the processes of detoxification. My focus here will be on compounds for supplementation that are supported by scientific research and have been found to have no known side effects or toxicity. I'll break them down into three categories:

1. those that enhance xenobiotic Phase I and Phase II detoxification and in most cases, also have antioxidizing activity

2. the powerful antioxidants

3. the important compounds that enhance methylation

All of the supplements covered here have been found to help prevent cancer, cardiovascular diseases, neurological degeneration, inflammatory diseases, and diabetes. In addition, these important breakthrough compounds have been found to enhance the body's immune system.

Supplements for Phase I and Phase II Detoxification

COMPOUNDS	CLASS	AMOUNT PER DAY
silymarin	flavonoid	100–250 mg
green tea catechin polyphenols (80%)	flavonoid	100–250 mg
ellagic acid	flavonoid	20–50 mg
apigenin	flavonoid	20–50 mg
isothiocyanates and dithiolethiones	sulfur compound	200–500 mg
allyl sulfides	organosulfide	200–500 mg
carnosol and ursolic acid	terpenoid	50–100 mg
curcumin	curcuminoids	200–500 mg
chlorophyllin	chlorophyll	200–500 mg
D-glucarate	glucarate	400–600 mg

QUERCETIN AND RUTIN

Since quercetin and rutin are the most common flavonoids with health benefits (for xenobiotic detoxification) and are generally consumed in reasonable amounts, they need not be taken as a supplement.

Supplements for Phase I and Phase II Detoxification

Silymarin

Silymarin is a group of flavonoids or flavonolignans from the seeds of milk thistle, a plant related to artichokes and daisies. An extract of milk thistle seeds contains 80 percent silymarin with silibinin, silidiamin, and silicristin being the active ingredients. Of these, silibinin is the most active and the one considered responsible for the health benefits attributed to silymarin, especially when it comes to liver protection and enhancing the detoxification of many dangerous toxins such as those from snakebites and mushroom poisoning. Extract of milk thistle has been used medicinally for almost two thousand years.

Hundreds of scientific research studies have confirmed the remarkable ability of silymarin to protect the liver from all kinds of toxic and carcinogenic agents.

SILYMARIN PROTECTS THE LIVER

Hepatitis B and C viral infections have been shown to be responsive to silymarin. This flavonoid has been used in Germany for several decades to treat both viral and alcoholic hepatitis and cirrhosis.

Dr. K. Flofa at the Oregon Health Sciences University found that silymarin not only protects the liver cells against toxic damage but also helps to stimulate the liver to regenerate. In a double-blind controlled study, silymarin was found to significantly reduce the mortality of patients with liver cirrhosis. In another double-blind controlled study, silymarin was shown to decrease serum enzymes SGPT (serum glutamic pyruvate transaminase) and SGOT (serum glutamic oxalacetic transaminase), which are associated with liver damage.

Many recent studies have shown that silymarin prevents cancers of the liver, skin, stomach, colon, lung, breast, and prostate. With regard to skin cancer, Dr. Mukhtar and his associates at Case Western University found that silymarin provides very effective protection against both ultraviolet light and chemical carcinogenesis.

Silymarin protects against the development of cancer by increasing the detoxification activity of Phase II enzymes including glutathione-S-transferase (GST) and quinone reductase and conversely by inhibiting both Phase I enzymes and β-glucuronidase. Silymarin is also a potent antioxidant, which counteracts many different types of free radicals. It increases the activity of the antioxidant enzymes such as SOD and glutathione peroxidase as well as levels of glutathione, all of which are critical to many detoxification reactions.

In culture tests on human cancer cells performed by Dr. Agarwal and coworkers, silymarin has been shown to be an effective inhibitor of the growth of prostate, breast, and cervical carcinoma cells through its ability to modulate important signal transduction pathways in cells. Silymarin is protective against heart disease, because of its inhibiting effect on the synthesis of cholesterol and its ability to prevent the oxidation of vLDL and LDL cholesterol. It helps with diabetes by enhancing insulin activity and preventing high levels of blood glucose, which can damage proteins and give rise to free radicals (glycation). Silymarin is also protective against inflammation and is an effective chelator of iron.

Among detoxification supplements, silymarin is one of the stars in preventing toxic overload to our bodies; in warding off disease; and in counteracting bacteria, viruses, and inflammation.

Green Tea Polyphenols

The beneficial health effects of tea have been demonstrated in numerous studies of both animals and humans. Green tea is without question the most highly regarded of the many tea varieties because of its health-giving effects. It contains polyphenols called catechins. Fresh, dried green tea leaves contain 30 to 40 percent catechins and 3 to 6 percent caffeine. In another variety, black tea, the leaves are crushed to allow the enzyme polyphenol oxidase to oxidize the catechins resulting in the formation of theaflavins and catechins polymers called thearubigens. In black tea, catechins represent about 3 to 10 percent and theaflavins, which give black tea its color and taste, represent about 2 to 6 percent.

Numerous studies have shown that green tea polyphenols have a powerful protective effect on mutagens and carcinogens. In terms of cancer prevention, green tea polyphenols, especially a catechin called epigallocatechin gallate (EGCG), have been found to inhibit cancers of the skin, lung, esophagus, stomach, liver, small intestine, pancreas, colon, bladder, and prostate. In a study related to skin cancer prevention, Dr. Mukhtar and coworkers at Case Western University showed that green tea polyphenols, especially EGCG, are very effective against the initiation, promotion, and progression stages of carcinogenesis induced by chemical carcinogens and/or ultraviolet light. In these studies, green tea polyphenols have a strong effect on both Phase I and Phase

II detoxification, destroying many types of free radicals, inflammation, cancer cell growth, and tumor blood vessel growth. In one study, the green tea polyphenol EGCG increased GST about thirty times, which is quite a remarkable increase for this Phase II detoxification enzyme.

Epidemiological studies have also shown that green tea–consuming countries such as China and Japan have a lower risk of breast, prostate, colon, skin, pancreas, and stomach cancers. Even more impressive is the fact that although the Japanese have the highest per capita number of smokers in the industrialized world, they also have the lowest rate of lung cancer. Green tea consumption is considered to be at least partially responsible for this. Epidemiological studies in the Western world have shown a relationship between tea and coffee consumption and lower risk of breast and colon cancers.

Many studies of experimental animals and humans have also shown a protective effect of green tea polyphenols against cardiovascular disorders and diabetes. The green tea polyphenols are effective in inhibiting the oxidation of LDL and vLDL, which are known to be involved in the development of atherosclerosis. The cholesterol-lowering ability of green tea polyphenols is also related to the protection against cardiovascular disorders. In terms of diabetes, green tea polyphenols have been found to lower blood sugar and thus insulin levels and glycation (the binding of sugars to proteins).

Ellagic Acid

Ellagic acid, found in a variety of fruits, nuts, and vegetables—including blackberries, raspberries, strawberries, cranberries, walnuts, and pecans—is a relatively stable flavonoid or polyphenol that is very helpful in overall detoxification.

Ellagic acid acts as a detoxifying agent in protecting against many different kinds of cancer and other diseases. It works by binding to reactive carcinogens, either produced by our cells or from external sources, and inactivating them before they can infiltrate DNA and cause mutations. Because of this effect, ellagic acid is a potent antimutagen and anticarcinogen. In addition, ellagic acid increases the activity of Phase II detoxification enzymes including GST and quinone reductase, and it has known antioxidizing properties.

Dr. Conney and associates at Rutgers University and the National Cancer Institute and Dr. Mukhtar and associates at Case Western University found ellagic acid to be a potent inhibitor of skin cancer caused by some of the strongest reactive intermediates of carcinogenic polycyclic aromatic hydrocarbons (PAHs) that we know about.

Dr. Stoner and coworkers at Ohio State University Cancer Center also found that ellagic acid prevented the induction of both lung and esophageal cancer induced by other classes of carcinogens. Ellagic acid has also been found to be effective in counteracting liver cancer brought on by a cancer-causing aromatic amine agent.

In clinical studies conducted on women with a genetic risk of cervical cancer at the Medical University of South Carolina, ellagic acid was shown to decrease cancer risk. In cervical cancer cell studies in culture, ellagic acid induced cell death (apoptosis), which may be the way ellagic acid kills cancer cells. Similar results were found using prostate, breast, pancreas, esophageal, skin, and colon cancer cells.

In other studies, ellagic acid promoted wound healing and reduced liver fibrosis. It provided protection against chromosome damage, DNA damage, and lipid peroxidation induced by radiation. These protective effects may be related to its antioxidizing activity.

Apigenin

Apigenin is a flavonoid found in parsley, artichokes, basil, celery, apples, onions, and other plants. It appears to counteract the induction of tumors by its effect on Phase I and Phase II detoxification, by increasing glutathione levels and by its antioxidizing activity. In the past several years, there have been many published reports on the protective effects of apigenin on the induction of cancer, especially skin cancer. Doctors Pelling and Birt, while conducting research at the Eppley Cancer Research Center, found that apigenin was a potent inhibitor of ultraviolet light–induced skin cancer.

APIGENIN ZEROS IN ON CANCER

Unpublished studies have shown apigenin to be protective against cancers induced by chemical carcinogens.

In a study that compared twenty-one different flavonoids, apigenin was shown to be the most effective inhibitor of the growth of human breast cancer cells. Like tamoxifen, apigenin binds to the estrogen receptors and thus prevents the overstimulation of breast cancer cells by estrogens. In addition, apigenin was also shown to inhibit the growth of human leukemia cells, thyroid cancer cells, and colorectal cancer cells. Its effects of stimulating differentiation of cancer cells and inhibiting the epidermal growth factor signal transduction pathway may be related to its ability to inhibit the growth of cancer cells. In addition, apigenin was found to be a strong inhibitor of tyrosine kinases, which are key enzymes in the growth of cancer cells. Furthermore, apigenin, like several other flavonoids, is a potent inhibitor of the growth of blood vessels (angiogenesis), which cancer cells need in order to grow and invade surrounding areas of the body.

Apigenin was also found to inhibit inflammation. This appears to be related to both its antioxidizing effect and its ability to inhibit an enzyme called cox-2 (cyclooxygenase-2), which is critical not only in inflammation but also for many cancer cells to grow.

Protective Sulfur Compounds

The sulfur compounds in cruciferous vegetables are known for their positive effect on overall detoxification. Among these, glucosinolates are very significant in terms of their effects on Phase I and Phase II xenobiotic detoxification. Scientists have isolated more than one hundred types of glucosinolates that can be further broken down into isothiocyanates, dithiolethiones, nitriles, and thiocyanates.

Dr. Steve Hecht at the University of Minnesota Cancer Center has been studying the naturally occurring aromatic isothiocyanates such as benzyl isothiocyanates and phenylethyl isothiocyanates as potent inhibitors of the induction of cancer by many cancer-causing agents, especially nitrosamines, heterocyclic amines, and PAHs. This appears to be related to their effect on both Phase I and Phase II detoxification, especially their inhibiting effect on some Phase I enzymes and a stimulation of Phase II enzymes such as GST and quinone reductase. Including sulforaphane, these isothiocyanates have been found to inhibit lung, breast, esophageal, liver, bladder, small intestine, and colon cancer.

Dithiolethiones are another important class of glucosinolates that support Phase I and Phase II detoxification. Dr. Kensler at Johns Hopkins University has been studying dithiolethiones in relationship to cancers of the lung, stomach, colon, liver, breast, skin, urinary tract or bladder, and trachea. In an ongoing study in the Qidong region of China, where liver cancer and aflatoxin exposure rates are high, Dr. Kensler and coworkers have found that supplementation with oltipraz, a specific dithiolethione, showed a significant reduction in biomarkers related to liver cancer.

These and other sulfur compounds can be taken as supplements in their pure form, such as sulforaphane, aromatic isothiocyanates, and specific dithiolethiones or in the form of a cruciferous extract containing these sulfur compounds, which is less expensive.

Allyl Sulfides from Garlic

Of the allium vegetables, garlic appears to provide the greatest protection against cancer, so it makes sense to look at extracting it as a supplement. Intact garlic cloves contain alliim, a colorless and odorless compound. When garlic is disrupted or crushed, an enzyme converts alliim to allicin, which gives garlic its characteristic odor but which is unstable and is spontaneously converted to more stable detoxification-supportive allyl sulfides.

Of these, allyl disulfide, diallyl sulfide, and diallyl disulfide compounds have proved to inhibit the induction of skin, esophageal, stomach, lung, colon, and cervical cancer by a wide variety of chemical carcinogens. Allyl sulfides have an inhibitory effect on the metabolism of carcinogenic nitrosamines, they significantly enhance Phase II detoxification especially related to GST, and several of them display direct antioxidizing activity. Both glutathione peroxidase and glutathione reductase levels as well as glutathione levels are increased by allyl sulfides, which also leads to greater antioxidant activity.

Dr. Michael Wargowich and coworkers at the South Carolina Cancer Center have done extensive research on the protective effect of garlic allyl sulfides on esophageal and colon cancer in the presence of chemical carcinogens, and found that their inhibiting effect was almost 100 percent. Elsewhere, human studies have found garlic sulfur compounds to have an effect on decreasing biomarkers related to colon and esophageal cancer.

Possibly due to its antioxidant properties, garlic sulfur compounds have been shown to have a protective effect on cardiovascular disorders, especially those related to narrowing of arteries (atherosclerosis), and some studies have even found that allyl sulfides are effective in lowering bad cholesterol (LDL and vLDL) while increasing good cholesterol (HDL).

It has long been known that garlic is an effective antibacterial and antifungal. Recent studies have shown this to be due to the antioxidant activity of the allyl sulfides.

Extract of Rosemary

The major constituents of rosemary leaves are the terpenoids: carnosol, carnosic, and ursolic acid. Due primarily to the antioxidant properties of carnosol and carnosic acid, extract of rosemary leaves has been used to prevent the oxidation of both animal fats and vegetable oils. Carnosol and ursolic acid are potent both as anti-inflammatory agents and stimulators of Phase II detoxification, especially related to increasing GST and glucuronidation. Doctors Fiander and Schneider of the National Research Council of Canada found that when compared with twenty different natural and synthetic compounds carnosol was the most effective in enhancing GST. Carnosol and ursolic acid are also very effective in preventing lipid peroxidation and DNA damage caused by radiation, chemical carcinogens, and tumor promoters.

Because of the many positive effects on all aspects of detoxification, rosemary leaf extract containing carnosol and ursolic acid is a potent antimutagenic and anticarcinogen. Recent studies by Dr. Conney and coworkers at Rutgers University have shown that a rosemary extract inhibits stomach, lung, colon, breast, and skin cancers induced by a wide variety of cancer-causing agents. When it comes to supplementing, it's probably better to take the extract than the isolated pure forms of carnosol and ursolic acid. As a prophylactic against skin cancer induction by PAHs, for example, rosemary extract has been shown to have a stronger inhibitory effect than carnosol or ursolic acid alone. This suggests that a combination of these compounds or a combination plus other constituents in rosemary are responsible for its inhibitory effect on cancer.

Curcumin

Curcumin (diferuloylmethane) is a curcuminoid and a phenolic compound related to ferulates, important phytochemicals in detoxification. Curcumin gives the yellow pigment to mustard and turmeric, a commonly used spice especially in Indian foods and curries, which comes from the root of a plant related to ginger. Traditionally, turmeric was used to support liver function especially related to increasing liver detoxification and preventing jaundice. It was also used to help digestive problems such as acidity and gastritis and to treat arthritis.

Curcumin has been found to be a potent antioxidant, anti-inflammatory agent, and inducer of Phase I and Phase II detoxification. Curcumin has been found to have considerable anti-inflammatory activity due to its ability to inhibit critical enzymes related to inflammation, such as cox-2 and nitric oxide synthase. You may recall from a discussion earlier in this book that cox-2 is a critical enzyme not only in inflammation but also in many types of cancer. When in high amounts, nitric oxide is also involved in inflammation and cancer. Recent investigations by Dr. Conney and associates from Rutgers University have demonstrated that curcumin possesses strong anticarcinogenic effects in several tissues such as skin, stomach, small intestine, breast, and colon. This inhibition of the induction of cancer by many different cancer-causing agents appears to be related to curcumin's ability to inhibit certain Phase I detoxification enzymes and enhance several Phase II reactions such as GST, quinone reductase, and glucuronidation. In addition to the above, the inhibitory effect of curcumin on cox-2 and nitric oxide and its stimulatory effect on DNA repair of carcinogen damage appears to be related to its antimutagenic effects. Curcumin has also been found to possess antibacterial and antifungal properties.

Chlorophyllin

Because of the abundance of chlorophyll in our food supply, it has been getting a lot of attention for its potential in preventing cancer. Chlorophyll, the water-insoluble green pigment in plants, and chlorophyllin, its water-soluble derivative, have been shown to possess strong antimutagen activity against a wide range of human carcinogens. Chlorophyllin has been used as a food color and over-the-counter medicine for many years without any known toxic effects.

In several experimental models, chlorophyllin has been shown to inhibit the induction of liver, skin, esophageal, and stomach cancer. It counteracts the tendency of certain chemical carcinogens such as aflatoxin to bind to our DNA, thereby preventing mutations that lead to cancer. Aflatoxin, a mycotoxin from moldy grains such as corn, is a very potent human carcinogen that causes liver cancer. Chlorophyllin prevents aflatoxin from binding to liver DNA. It appears that chlorophyllin is able to prevent this genetic damage by attaching itself directly to the carcinogen, by supporting Phase I and Phase II detoxification of the carcinogen, and by detoxifying free radicals generated by the carcinogen.

Referring again to the Qidong (China) study, chlorophyllin supplementation showed a 55 percent reduction in aflatoxin binding to DNA after three months of use. Based on this data, this could translate to a 90 percent reduction in the incidence of liver cancer. According to Dr. Groopman and coworkers at the Johns Hopkins University, the chlorophyllin intervention studies in China show promise because they are effective, inexpensive, and not associated with any adverse effects.

D-Glucarate

D-glucarate is a nontoxic natural substance found in both fruits and vegetables, which is a critical factor in Phase II detoxification. It significantly enhances glucuronidation, a major detoxification process, and inhibits the detoxification-reversing enzyme β-glucuronidase.

Many experimental animal studies have shown D-glucarate to inhibit the induction of lung, liver, breast, colon, bladder, and prostate cancer because of its role in enhancing Phase II detoxification. D-glucarate has also been found to inhibit human cancer cell growth especially related to breast and prostate cancer.

D-glucarate also acts as an effective cholesterol-lowering agent by enhancing detoxification and inhibiting the synthesis of cholesterol. D-glucarate lowers total cholesterol, LDL and vLDL cholesterol, and triglycerides but has no effect on HDL cholesterol.

Supplements for Antioxidant Detoxification

Among the vitamins, minerals, and phytochemicals needed to protect us from free radical damage are some exceptional compounds with antioxidizing activity that work synergistically with many other antioxidants as well as with the breakthrough supplements related to Phase I and Phase II detoxification.

Supplements for Antioxidant Detoxification		
COMPOUNDS	CLASS	AMOUNT PER DAY
alpha lipoic acid/ dihydrolipoic acid	cellular antioxidant	50–150 mg
coenzyme Q_{10} + acetyl-L-carnitine	cellular antioxidant	50–150 mg of each
proanthocyanidins/ anthocyanins (grape seed and skin extract)	flavonoids	200–500 mg
lycopene + lutein	carotenoids	10–50 mg of each
N-acetylcysteine (NAC)	amino acid derivative	200–500 mg

Alpha Lipoic Acid/Dihydrolipoic Acid

Alpha lipoic acid (and its reduced form dihydrolipoic acid) is a powerful cellular antioxidant. It has a unique ability to deal effectively with free radicals in both a water and a lipid environment. Made up of sulfur-containing compounds that convert back and forth depending on cellular conditions, alpha lipoic acid destroys hydroxy radicals, singlet oxygen, and hypochorous acid; and dihydrolipoic acid destroys peroxyl, superoxide, and hydroxyl radicals. With dihydrolipoic acid taking the lead, they work together in recycling many important antioxidants, including vitamins E and C, glutathione, and coenzyme Q_{10}, back to a reduced state. This antioxidant system has the ability to increase cellular glutathione levels significantly, something very important in both xenobiotic and antioxidant detoxification, and to bind or chelate heavy metals such as mercury, arsenic, cadmium, and excess iron and copper. Dr. Lester Packer and coworkers at the University of California at Berkeley have done extensive studies on the antioxidant properties of alpha lipoic acid and dihydrolipoic acid.

Experimental and clinical studies have also shown alpha lipoic acid to be effective against certain cardiovascular disorders, chronic liver disease, neurological degeneration, AIDS, heavy metal poisoning, radiation damage, cancer, diabetes, and aging. This appears to be related to both its antioxidant properties and its role in the uptake and breakdown of sugars for energy. These effects of alpha lipoic acid have led to its use in the prevention and treatment of diabetes. A recent placebo-controlled human study showed that alpha lipoic acid increases insulin sensitivity, resulting in increased glucose uptake into cells in Type II (adult-onset or insulin-dependent) diabetes.

The production of alpha lipoic acid and dihydrolipoic acid in our bodies decreases with age and levels are low in many disease states. Since only small amounts are available in our diet, supplementation is very important.

Coenzyme Q_{10} and Acetyl-L-Carnitine

Coenzyme Q_{10} (CoQ_{10}) is a lipid-soluble, natural chemical antioxidant produced by our cells. As is true of all antioxidants, to be effective it must be in a reduced state. CoQ_{10} plays a critical role in breaking free radical chains, especially in cellular membranes; it protects against lipid peroxidation and lowers LDL cholesterol. CoQ_{10} also reduces other antioxidants, especially vitamin E, providing indirect protection to cell membranes from free radical damage.

Along with alpha lipoic acid and acetyl-L-carnitine, the active form of carnitine, which is derived from the essential amino acid lysine, CoQ_{10} prevents decay or aging of the mitochondrial membrane or mitochondria, the energy powerhouses of our cells.

CoQ_{10} together with acetyl-L-carnitine (important in fatty acid metabolism) and alpha lipoic acid supply the biochemical spark that creates the energy in our mitochondria for all cellular functions, including detoxification. These essential components for all cellular energy metabolisms give us the extra energy to perform better and to fight off degenerative diseases and, especially, aging. They improve vitality, heart and circulatory function, immune function, and brain function. The father of CoQ_{10} research, Dr. Folkers at the University of Texas, found in heart attack patients with very low levels of CoQ_{10} that supplementation decreased further heart attacks and improved heart and circulatory function. CoQ_{10} also has been shown to help prevent chronic fatigue syndrome. This triad helps to prevent not only heart disease, but also cancer, diabetes, gum disease, immune dysfunction, chronic lung disease, and neurological degeneration. It also helps slow down the aging process.

Although our bodies produce both CoQ_{10} and acetyl-L-carnitine, supplementation of these compounds offers great additional benefits—and there are no side effects or toxicity even at high doses.

Proanthocyanidins and Anthocyanins

Proanthocyanidins and anthocyanins, which are found in many different types of plants and trees, are very potent flavonoid antioxidants that provide protection from a variety of free radicals. Proanthocyanidins are also called condensed tannins, oligomeric proanthocyanidins (OPCs), or Pycnogenol, a trade name for OPCs. Anthocyanins are complex flavonoids that give fruits, vegetables, and flowers their colors.

Proanthocyanidins and anthocyanins are superb antioxidants. They destroy many different types of free radicals and potentiate other antioxidants. When using different assays to measure antioxidant potency, especially the ORAC (oxygen radical absorbance capacity), proanthocyanidins and anthocyanins and their sources, most notably grape seed and skin extracts, blueberry and bilberry extracts, and pine bark extracts, are always at the top of the list. Proanthocyanidins have about fifty times more antioxidant capability than vitamin E and twenty times more than vitamin C. In addition, these powerful flavonoids help to recycle vitamins C and E back to a reduced state, which allows the vitamins to do their jobs more effectively. Proanthocyanidins and anthocyanins are very effective at increasing the levels of glutathione in cells, especially liver cells, which helps in all aspects of detoxification.

Because of their exceptional ability to help regulate nitric oxide and protect against free radicals such as hydroxyl radical, superoxide radical, and peroxynitrite radical, proanthocyanidins and anthocyanins protect against cancer, cardiovascular disorders, inflammatory diseases, allergies, diabetes, skin aging, vision disorders, neurological degeneration, and general aging. These flavonoids not only prevent many diseases but in some cases can actually restore health. Due to their antioxidant properties the proanthocyanidins and anthocyanins can

- prevent lipid peroxidation
- work synergistically with other antioxidants
- increase glutathione levels
- increase Phase II detoxification
- lower LDL cholesterol and prevent its oxidation
- inhibit cox-2 enzyme
- inhibit histamine formation and thus decrease allergies
- prevent and remove lipofuscin formation in brain, heart, and skin (aging spots)
- decrease senile dementia, Alzheimer's disease, Parkinson's disease, and multiple sclerosis (MS)
- increase brain function such as memory, learning, and coordination
- prevent skin aging and wrinkles by protecting collagen and elastin from breakdown
- prevent hardening of arteries and improve blood flow
- decrease blood sugar and prevent glycation
- help promote healing
- protect against viruses and bacteria

- chelate heavy metals

- enhance immune function

- protect against radiation damage

- prevent cataracts and macular degeneration

- prevent cancer cell growth

Overall, the proanthocyanidins and anthocyanins from grape seed and skin extracts or blueberry and bilberry extracts are remarkable vitamin-like phytochemicals that prevent diseases as well as decrease aging. Since grape seed and skin extracts are the least expensive and best way to obtain these remarkable protective flavonoids, I highly recommend supplementing your diet with them.

PYCNOGENOL

If you find Pycnogenol too expensive, there are alternative grape seed and skin extract supplements containing proanthocyanidins, anthocyanins, flavonoids, and small amounts of resveratrol, another antioxidant, on the market. In many studies these more generic formulas were shown to be as good or better.

Lycopene and Lutein

Lycopene and lutein are two very important fat-soluble carotenoids that possess exceptionally strong antioxidant activity when compared to other carotenoids such as beta-carotene. Unlike alpha-carotene and beta-carotene, lycopene and lutein are not converted into vitamin A. Tomatoes and tomato products, watermelon, red grapefruit, guava, and dried apricots contain large amounts of lycopene, which is responsible for their pink to red color. Recently, lycopene was found to be very abundant (eighteen times richer than in tomatoes) in a red berry called autumn olives, which are similar to cranberries in taste and size. Spinach, kale, and other greens contain high levels of lutein. Like vitamin E, lycopene and lutein destroy reactive oxygen species from sunlight, break free radical chain reactions, and prevent oxidative damage. Lycopene and lutein account for a significant amount of the activity of carotenoids to work synergistically to prevent free radical damage and thus inhibit cancer, cardiovascular disorders, eye disease, and neurological degeneration as well as enhance the immune function.

THE SCARCITY OF CAROTENOIDS IN FOOD

Of the six hundred or so known carotenoids, we only get about forty from food, and only a small number of these are found in appreciable quantities in human blood and tissues. The major ones are lycopene and lutein, alpha-carotene, beta-carotene, zeaxanthin, and crytoxanthin.

Several epidemiological studies have found that foods containing carotenoids such as lycopene and lutein lead to a decreased risk of cancer. The health benefits of the Mediterranean diet may be partly related to not only olive oil but also tomato products containing lycopene.

Most experimental studies have found that both lycopene and lutein have anticancer effects, especially if taken together. The anticancer effects of lycopene and lutein are the greatest for prostate, lung, and stomach cancers but only suggestive for breast, colon, pancreatic, esophageal, and oral cavity cancers according to Dr. Giovannucci at Harvard Medical School.

Lycopene is concentrated in certain tissues such as the prostate. In fact, lycopene has been found to decrease the size of existing prostate tumors, slow their spread, and lower PSA (prostate specific antigen). Lutein is concentrated mainly in the macula of the eye. Carotenoids, especially lutein, offer significant benefits to vision as well as prevent cataracts and macular degeneration.

In other studies, lycopene was found to decrease LDL cholesterol oxidation. The combination of both lycopene and lutein was more effective in preventing LDL oxidation than lycopene alone. It should be pointed out that carotenoids such as lycopene and lutein are better absorbed when taken along with some fat. The combination of tomato products and olive oil for example, as in a Mediterranean diet, would allow better absorption of lycopene.

N-Acetylcysteine (NAC)

N-acetylcysteine (NAC) is a very stable version of the sulfur amino acid L-cysteine. As a potent antioxidant, antitoxin, anticarcinogen, and antimutagen, it plays an important role in increasing cellular levels of glutathione, and in fact it is one of the three amino acids that make up this cellular detoxification compound. As there is a decreased level of glutathione in HIV infection and other human immunodeficiency viral infections, NAC also plays a very important role in increasing the level of glutathione in these immune disorders, which in turn stimulates the immune system.

NAC provides protection against many different types of free radicals as well as a broad range of toxic and carcinogenic agents found in cigarette smoke, automobile exhaust, toxic pesticides and herbicides, charcoaled and smoked meats, overdoses of drugs such as acetaminophen (Tylenol), anticancer drugs, and radiation. In terms of its antimutagenic and anticarcinogenic effects, NAC inhibits the induction of cancer in the skin, liver, breast, lung, bladder, colon, and oral cavity. It inhibits not only the tumor initiation and promotion stages, but also the tumor progressional stage of carcinogenesis. Because of the many protective effects of NAC and the fact that it is nontoxic, it has become a popular subject in clinical trials for cancer prevention studies in the United States and Europe. Preliminary results are pointing to NAC's effectiveness.

Supplements for Enhancing Methylation

Most methylation reactions in the body require s-adenosylmethionine (SAMe) and trimethylglycine (TMG), or betaine, as it is sometimes called. When TMG donates a methyl group in the methylation process to homocysteine, for example, homocysteine is converted to methionine and then SAMe, provided enough B_{12} and folic acid are present. Similarly to convert homocysteine to the very important glutathione, there must be a sufficient concentration of B_6.

Under healthy conditions, our bodies can produce enough of both TMG and SAMe. However, in many disease states—and as we grow older—production declines. To ensure that sufficient amounts are present in your body, I recommend that you take supplemental SAMe and TMG.

Supplements for Methylation Enhancement	
COMPOUND	AMOUNT PER DAY
SAMe (s-adenosylmethionine)	50–200 mg
TMG (trimethylglycine)	200–500 mg

Compounds for Preventing Breast and Prostate Cancer

There are additional specific substances besides the previously described supplements that help prevent breast and prostate cancer because of their ability to regulate the sex hormones. These substances can be taken by all adult men and women who want to decrease their risk of hormone-related cancers.

Conjugated linolenic acid (CLA), isoflavones, indole-3-carbinol, and calcium D-glucarate are very helpful in supplying additional protection against breast cancer.

These compounds help to prevent excess breast cell proliferation and prevent excess amounts of estrogens and metabolites, which can lead to breast cancer. Dr. Henry Thompson at the AMC Cancer Research Center has shown CLA to be a potent inhibitor of morphological and biochemical markers related to breast cancer. In addition, Dr. IP and coworkers at the Roswell Park Memorial Cancer Center found that CLA inhibited the induction of breast cancer. In these studies, CLA appears to inhibit breast cell proliferation and angiogenesis after the carcinogen was given. Isoflavones mimic weak estrogen and interact with estrogen receptors such as tamoxifen, helping to prevent overstimulation of breast tissue. Indole-3-carbinol causes the major estrogen, estradiol, to convert into harmless metabolites including 2-hydroxy—as opposed to 4-hydroxy and 16-hydroxy, which have been related to breast cancer in some studies. Calcium D-glucarate helps to detoxify excess estrogens and cholesterol, a precursor of estradiol. Overall, these compounds lead to an effective regulation of estrogens that prevents them from contributing to the formation of breast cancer. In conjunction with a healthy diet, exercise, stress control, and proper supplementation for basic health and to support detoxification, these compounds round out an effective and rational approach to breast cancer prevention.

Supplements for Breast Cancer Prevention

COMPOUNDS	THREE TIMES/DAY
CLA (70%)	250–500 mg
soybean isoflavones	100–300 mg
indole-3-carbinol	100–300 mg
calcium D-glucarate	200–500 mg

Supplements for Prostate Cancer Prevention	
COMPOUNDS	THREE TIMES/DAY
CLA (70%)	250–500 mg
saw palmetto extract	200–600 mg
soybean isoflavones	100–300 mg
zinc D-glucarate	200–600 mg

CLA, saw palmetto extract, isoflavones, and zinc D-glucarate are very helpful in supplying additional protection against prostate cancer.

The strategy for prostate cancer prevention is similar to that for breast cancer. Here, both androgens and estrogens must be regulated to prevent excess prostate cell proliferation. A significant number of prostate cancers appear to be related to the overproduction of androgens, especially dihydrotestosterone (DHT). Key to keeping both androgens and estrogens in check is to maintain healthy cholesterol levels. This is because cholesterol gives rise to testosterone, the major androgen, which in turn converts to estradiol.

CLA prevents prostate cancer by inhibiting cell proliferation and angiogenesis. Saw palmetto extract inhibits the formation of DHT, inhibits cox-2 enzyme, and prevents benign prostate hypertrophy (BPH). Soybean isoflavones have many beneficial effects on inhibiting the induction of prostate cancer, including the ability to regulate androgens and estrogens. Zinc D-glucarate helps to detoxify cholesterol, androgens, and estrogens. These compounds in combination with a good diet, proper exercise, healthy mental state, and my protocol for supplementation (with a particular emphasis on selenium, vitamin E—especially gamma tocopherol—and vitamin D_3) is a very rational and effective strategy for preventing prostate cancer.

CHOLESTEROL IS A PRECURSOR
TO ALL THE STEROID HORMONES

Cholesterol
↓
↓
↓
Testosterone → DHT
↓
Estradiol

CHAPTER SEVEN

Key Supplements for Chronic Disease Prevention

❧

This chapter is for those who are interested in looking beyond supplements for cancer-related detoxification to supplements that deal specifically with other chronic diseases. It includes lists of the most important supplements for prevention of cardiovascular disorders, especially those related to cholesterol management; inflammatory diseases; immune disorders; bacterial and viral infection; obesity and diabetes; neurological degeneration; and aging. The supplements will reduce your risk of these chronic diseases whether you are in a high-risk category or not. As always, when embarking on a program of supplementation, first inform your physician. (If your doctor isn't interested in nutrition, find one who is. You'll be better off.)

Preventing Cardiovascular Disorders

Maintaining healthy levels of cholesterol, homocysteine, fibrinogen (needed for blood clotting), and blood pressure and preventing c-reactive proteins (a marker of heart disease) are very important in the prevention of hardening and narrowing of arteries (atherosclerosis), heart attacks, and strokes, which are caused by blood clots.

Healthy Cholesterol and Triglyceride Levels

total cholesterol	less than 200 mg
LDL cholesterol	less than 130 mg
vLDL cholesterol	less than 40 mg
HDL cholesterol	greater than 35 mg
LDL to HDL ratio	less than 4.5
triglycerides	less than 150 mg

Cardiovascular function is dependent on maintaining a healthy level of cholesterol. Overproduction in the liver or getting too much from diet or both runs the risk of elevating cholesterol to dangerous levels. In managing cholesterol in our bodies, careful attention must be paid to lipoproteins and triglycerides. Even though they are very important molecules that transport cholesterol to various tissues for use in many bodily functions, low-density lipoprotein (LDL) and very low-density lipoprotein (vLDL) give rise to the label "bad cholesterol" when present in high amounts and when they become oxidized and stick to blood vessels. High-density lipoprotein (HDL) is considered "good cholesterol" because it transports cholesterol back to the liver for metabolism and excretion from the body. The ratio of LDL to HDL, known as the cardiac risk factor, tells us how much cholesterol is being taken to tissues or broken down and excreted.

Getting a proper balance of necessary fats, carbohydrates, and protein and supplementing to achieve my formulations for fundamental micronutrients (and thereby promoting xenobiotic and antioxidant detoxification and methylation) will ensure homocysteine and fibrinogen levels are within safe limits. This and adding a small amount of aspirin (80 mg/day) will help regulate fibrinogen as well as prevent the overformation of blood clots and c-reactive proteins.

The supplements in the table on page 115 will lower cholesterol and triglyceride levels and generally benefit all aspects of good cardiovascular function.

Potassium D-glucarate effectively inhibits the synthesis of cholesterol; helps lower total cholesterol, LDL, vLDL, and triglycerides; maintains high levels of HDL; stimulates its conversion, breakdown, and detoxification; and lowers blood pressure.

Cholesterol- and Triglyceride-Lowering Formulation

COMPOUNDS	AMOUNT PER DAY
potassium D-glucarate	500–2,000 mg
octacosanol	10–50 mg
gamma tocotrienol	10–50 mg
silymarin	100–300 mg
rosemary extract	100–300 mg
gamma oryzanol	100–300 mg
β-sitosterol	200–800 mg

Octacosanol, a long-chain fatty alcohol found in many plants (actually in the waxy fiber that covers the leaves and fruits), several grain oils, sugarcane, and eggs, especially caviar, and policosanol (of which octacosanol is the major component) have been found to lower LDL cholesterol and elevate HDL cholesterol. In addition, they prevent oxidation of LDL cholesterol, inflammation, and blood clots. Octacosanol and policosanol work by inhibiting the synthesis of cholesterol but the exact mechanism for this process is not known.

Gamma tocotrienol, one of the vitamin E isomers, has been found to lower total cholesterol and LDL and elevate HDL. Gamma tocotrienol appears to have a similar effect as statin drugs in inhibiting the synthesis of cholesterol, but without the many side effects.

Silymarin and rosemary extract (carnosol and related compounds) have all been found to lower total cholesterol, LDL cholesterol, and triglycerides. Increased amounts of silymarin and rosemary extracts from the recommendations in Chapter 6 can lead to an effective lowering of cholesterol and prevent LDL cholesterol oxidation.

Gamma oryzanol and β-sitosterol have been found to lower cholesterol and triglycerides as well as prevent LDL oxidation. Gamma oryzanol is an important antioxidant found in grains; it is isolated from rice bran oil. It enhances the conversion of cholesterol to bile acids, increases bile acid excretion, and inhibits the absorption of cholesterol. By increasing the conversion of cholesterol to bile acids and their excretion for detoxification purposes, circulatory cholesterol is lowered. β-sitosterol is a plant sterol, which also helps in the prevention of cholesterol absorption.

These key compounds, particularly when combined, display potent antioxidizing activity and generally support all aspects of cholesterol management and detoxification. They are effective in lowering total cholesterol, LDL cholesterol, and triglycerides; elevating the good HDL cholesterol; and preventing LDL oxidation.

Other Compounds That Promote Good Cardiovascular Health

vitamins E and C
vitamins B_6, B_{12}, folic acid, and niacin
green tea polyphenol
garlic extract
essential fats, GLA, αLA, EPA, DHA
fibers (for example, pectin)

choline, lecithin, inositol
chromium picolinate
TMG and SAMe
coenzyme Q_{10}
acetyl-L-carnitine

Preventing Inflammatory Diseases

Of the many inflammatory diseases, arthritis is the most common. The two major forms, osteoarthritis and rheumatoid arthritis, both involve inflammation in joints and loss of joint function. Rheumatoid arthritis is an autoimmune disease leading to inflammatory destruction (free radical damage) of the lining of joints whereas osteoarthritis is an inflammatory disease leading to the inability of joint cartilage to repair itself, resulting in decay of the essential cartilage. Omega-3 and omega-6 fats and many of the antioxidants are very helpful in preventing and treating arthritis and other inflammatory diseases.

Methylsulfonyl-methane (MSM) is a natural form of organic sulfur needed by all cells for many functions. MSM is present in most plants, fruits, vegetables, grains, meats, eggs, and milk. Because it is destroyed by heat and dehydration, supplementation is advisable. MSM is important for the synthesis of connective tissue, hair, nails, many proteins, enzymes, and immunoglobulin. It can counteract pain and inflammation associated with arthritis and other inflammatory disorders. It also plays a part in tissue repair. Vitamin C appears to work synergistically with MSM against inflammation and repair of joint tissue.

Glucosamine sulfate, N-acetyl glucosamine, glucuronic acid, and chondroitin sulfate work together to repair damaged joints and counteract the joint inflammation. Glucosamine sulfate and chondroitin sulfate supply the necessary building blocks to repair joint lining, especially cartilage. N-acetyl glucosamine and glucuronic acid are polymerized to make hyaluronic acid, the necessary joint lubricant. Many animal studies and clinical trials support the benefit of these compounds.

Supplements for Preventing Inflammatory Diseases	
COMPOUNDS	AMOUNT PER DAY
methylsulfonyl-methane (MSM)	400–600 mg
glucosamine sulfate	500–750 mg
N-acetyl glucosamine	500–750 mg
glucuronic acid	250–500 mg
chondroitin sulfate	500–750 mg
ginger extract	200–300 mg

Ginger is related to turmeric, which contains curcumin. Curcumin and ginger extracts containing gingerol and related compounds are potent antioxidants that counteract inflammation through their ability to inhibit cox-2 and tumor necrosis factor (TNFα), which are involved in the inflammatory reaction.

Boosting the Immune System

The immune system is extremely important in fighting bacteria, viruses, fungi, yeast, parasites, and other foreign invaders. When working at peak efficiency, it is able to destroy cancer cells that are in the process of formation. The system has a remarkable memory for this task, which obviously works to our benefit. It is a complex network of immune cells and the soluble humoral factors they release. B-lymphocytes produce antibodies in response to many antigens, and T-lymphocytes induce either humoral or cellular response from either helper cells or natural killer cells.

The immune-enhancing supplements I've selected are known for their antiviral, antibacterial, antifungal properties. Each demonstrates an ability to inhibit yeast protozoa and parasites.

High doses of D-glucarate, NAC, garlic extract, β-sitosterol, and MSM can have positive effects on immune function. Zinc D-glucarate not only supplies important zinc for its many important effects on the immune system, but it is also an effective antiviral and antibacterial agent. Antioxidant garlic extract and NAC protect the immune system from free radical damage, and inhibit the growth of bacteria and the replication of viruses. MSM appears to augment the immune system's response to bacteria, viruses, yeast, fungi, and parasites. In both animal

Immune System Boosters	
COMPOUNDS	AMOUNT PER DAY
zinc D-glucarate	500–1,000 mg
N-acetylcysteine (NAC)	500–1,000 mg
garlic extract (allyl sulfides)	500–1,000 mg
methylsulfonyl-methane (MSM)	1,000–2,000 mg
β-sitosterol	500–1,000 mg
myo-inositol hexaphosphate (1P6) and myo-inositol	1,000–2,000 mg
cranberry extract	500–1,000 mg
fructo-oligosaccharides (FOS)	1,000–2,000 mg

and human clinical trials, β-sitosterol, a phytosterol, has increased natural killer T-cell activity.

Myo-inositol hexaphosphate (1P6 or phytic acid) and myo-inositol are powerful antioxidant compounds found primarily in whole grains and soybeans. They kill tumor cells, viruses, and bacteria by increasing natural killer T-cell activity. Dr. Shamsudden at the University of Maryland School of Medicine has done extensive work in this area. 1P6 is also effective in counteracting the growth of human cancer cells in culture, especially prostate and breast cancer cells.

Cranberry extracts are very effective in preventing and treating urinary tract infection, a condition frequently found in older men and women, which is often caused by E. coli. Cranberry extract also has antiviral and antifungal activity and inhibits the growth of yeast.

Of the many beneficial bacteria that live in our gastrointestinal tract, the most important are lactobacillus acidophilus and lactobacillus bifidus. Foods fermented with lactobacilli such as yogurt, cheese, miso, and tempeh are important in healthy diets around the world. Intestinal bacteria help to create several vitamins and significantly affect immune system function. Lactobacilli inhibit or antagonize the growth of many other bad bacteria and yeast, especially Candida albicans, which is the major yeast involved in vaginal yeast infection. One way to increase the beneficial intestinal bacteria is to promote their growth with fructo-oligosaccharides (FOS). These short-chain polysaccharides are not digested by humans and therefore are available to be used by lactobacilli, especially acidophilus and bifidus that are busy reducing colonies of bad bacteria. These additional key compounds work best in combination to enhance immune function and inhibit growth of bad bacteria, viruses, and other microorganisms.

Preventing Diabetes and Obesity

Diabetes mellitus is a metabolic disease characterized by elevated blood sugar or glucose intolerance (hyperglycemia), as well as disturbances in carbohydrate, protein, and fat metabolism. Diabetics have an increased risk of heart attack, stroke, peripheral vascular disease, kidney disease, visual problems, and neurological disorders. There are two major types of diabetes: Type I (also known as insulin-dependent or juvenile-onset diabetes) and Type II (also known as non-insulin-dependent or adult-onset diabetes). Diabetes Type I is caused by a destruction of pancreatic insulin-producing cells; this type of diabetes requires patients to take insulin. Diabetes Type II is the most common form of diabetes, affecting approximately 20 million people in the United States. About 75 percent of diabetics with Type II die from a cardiovascular-related disease. Many scientists believe that eating the wrong foods, overeating, and obesity cause diabetes Type II. People with diabetes Type II often produce normal levels of insulin but their cells are effectively insulin resistant. A small percentage of people with diabetes Type II develop pancreatic problems.

Insulin helps to transport glucose from the blood to the cells where it is stored or used for energy. Years of overconsumption of refined carbohydrates (e.g., bread, pasta, and foods containing processed sugars), saturated and trans-fatty acids, and omega-6 fatty acid relative to omega-3 fatty acid cause our cells to become insulin resistant, a condition known as syndrome X. As a result, glucose has a difficult time entering our cells and blood glucose levels remain very high leading to diabetes Type II.

Glucose is a high-energy compound, which, if not used for energy, can be a major source of dangerous free radicals that work to destroy the circulatory system. Dr. Lester Packer at the University of California at Berkeley has shown that glucose can spin off large numbers of free radicals. Some of these free radicals can oxidize the large amounts of LDL cholesterol in diabetics. In addition, high levels of circulatory glucose can bind it to proteins such as hemoglobin (glycation), which also leads to rapid aging (in the same way high levels of free radical levels do). Dr. Reaven at Stanford University Medical Center has stated that insulin resistance or diabetes Type II may be a major cause of obesity as well as cardiovascular disorders. This hypothesis is gaining wide acceptance in the scientific community.

A diet emphasizing complex carbohydrates, which are broken down very slowly to glucose and therefore have much less impact on insulin release and resistance, and essential fats in proper proportion, and exercise are key to preventing and treating diabetes Type II and obesity. Complex carbohydrates are found in whole grains, seeds, fruits, and vegetables.

> ## THE CURIOUS CASE OF THE PIMA INDIANS
>
> The twelve thousand Pima Indians on the Gila River Reservation in Arizona have the highest rate of diabetes (especially Type II) in the world, and we don't know why. Half of the adults and approximately 5 percent of the children aged fifteen to eighteen have the disease. Worse still, these rates are on the rise and the age of onset appears to be falling. AMC and other researchers strongly suspect poor lifestyle factors are at work and are experimenting with dietary changes that include plenty of fruits and vegetables; whole grains and legumes; more exercise and physical activity; and vitamin and mineral supplementation.

Alpha lipoic acid helps in the uptake and breakdown of sugars for energy in cells and prevents glycation, factors that make it a major player in the prevention and treatment of diabetes. In a placebo-controlled human study, it was shown that alpha lipoic acid increased insulin sensitivity and thus increased glucose uptake in diabetes Type II. The combination of alpha lipoic acid and dihydrolipoic acid is extremely important in glucose metabolism and decreasing insulin resistance. Animal and human clinical trials support the effectiveness of alpha lipoic acid in preventing and treating diabetes Type II.

Chromium picolinate enhances insulin performance and as a consequence, it prevents syndrome X. It also decreases the amount of insulin needed. Several studies have shown that chromium can significantly increase the utilization of fat for energy and thus trigger the body to lose weight.

Green tea extract is very effective in the metabolism of glucose and fat. The polyphenols and diphenylamine in green tea extract help to lower blood glucose by inhibiting an enzyme called amylase. They also prevent glycation. The polyphenols work with caffeine to help speed up metabolism and thus have a thermogenic, or fat-burning, effect. The same can be said for coffee, by the way, but with even greater effect than

Supplements for Diabetes Type II and Weight Management

COMPOUNDS	AMOUNT PER DAY
alpha lipoic acid/dihydrolipoic acid	200–600 mg
chromium picolinate	200–400 mcg
green tea extract (80% catechins)	200–600 mg
conjugated linoleic acid (CLA)	1,000–3,000 mg
hydroxycitric acid	500–1,000 mg
soluble fiber (equal amounts of pectin, guar gum, and glucomannon)	2,000–6,000 mg

green tea. The best way, however, to increase overall metabolism is to exercise regularly. Exercise allows the body to utilize calories from fats, carbohydrates, and proteins more efficiently.

CLA supplementation has been found to decrease fat deposits and enhance muscle growth. CLA reduces body fat by enhancing the ability of insulin to cause glucose and fatty acids to enter muscle cells instead. Furthermore, CLA increases the sensitivity of insulin and thus has an effect on both obesity and diabetes Type II.

Hydroxycitric acid (HCA) is a hydroxylated version of citric acid, found in many fruits, but it is found in particularly high concentrations in the South Asian fruit *garcinia cambogia*. Several studies have shown that HCA can inhibit the conversion of carbohydrates and glucose into fat, and suppress appetite. HCA decreases fat storage by inhibiting a specific enzyme involved in fat storage, resulting in an antiobesity effect. The principle is that HCA increases the conversion of glucose into glycogen in the liver, which sends a signal to the brain telling us that the stomach is full.

Dietary fiber, which is composed of the edible plant polysaccharides that typically help form the structure of cell walls of plants, is extremely important in the prevention and management of diabetes. Although humans can't digest cellulose, it is partially digested by bacteria in the colon. This natural fermentation process breaks down some cellulose, which benefits the body by supplying some important short-chain fatty acid for the intestinal cells.

Water-soluble fiber (as opposed to water-insoluble fiber) represents the majority of plant fiber in fruits, beans, barley, oats, gum, mucilages, and pectins. It is beneficial for suppressing appetite and preventing obesity. Soluble fiber helps prevent diabetes because it decreases glucose and insulin after meals.

When taken with water (eight ounces or more) one half to one hour before meals, the water-soluble fiber in pectins, guar gum, and glucomannan, for example, swells to many times its original size, discouraging overeating by inducing the sensation of fullness. In addition, soluble fiber slows the digestion and absorption of carbohydrates. It also slows rising blood glucose and insulin levels and may decrease the number of calories the body is able to absorb. In many clinical studies this has led to significant rates of weight loss. The use of soluble fiber in the treatment of diabetes and obesity has been recommended by the National Diabetes Association of the United States, Canada, Great Britain, and Australia. For all of its positive aspects, extremely high levels of fiber can slow down or prevent absorption of important fat-soluble vitamins and essential fats, which can lead to a decrease in valuable compounds needed for detoxification. So the key to consuming fiber, as with most things in life, is moderation.

More than 70 percent of Americans are overweight (defined as at least 30 percent over ideal weight)—and the rate appears to be increasing. Of these about 25 percent are actually obese (defined as at least 100 percent over ideal weight). Diabetes Type II, which currently affects one out of every three people, is also increasing at an alarming rate. Along with much of the scientific community and good supporting data, I believe that poor diet and physical inactivity lead to diabetes Type II—and diabetes leads to obesity.

CONTROLLING THE URGE TO EAT

Try eating all or part of an apple with a large glass of water one half to one hour before each meal. Apples contain lots of fiber, which swells with water, giving a feeling of fullness. This will cause you to eat less during your meal.

Preventing Brain Degeneration and Aging

One of the most disturbing aspects of aging is a decline in overall brain function—from minor declines in cognitive ability to senile dementia and, especially, Alzheimer's disease. Circulatory disorders such as heart problems or stroke can severely restrict the pathways of oxygen and nutrients such as glucose to brain cells.

Supplements to Prevent Brain Degeneration and Aging

COMPOUND	AMOUNT PER DAY
DHA	500–1,000 mg
lecithin	500–1,000 mg
phosphatidylserine (PS)	50–200 mg
gingko biloba extract (GB)	100–250 mg
blueberry or bilberry extract	200–500 mg
gamma tocopherol	25–100 mg
ascorbyl palmitate	50–100 mg

Although DHA (docosahexaenoic acid), an essential omega-3 fatty acid derivative, plays a vital role in the development and maintenance of effective brain function throughout life, the body's ability to make DHA from alpha linolenic acid appears to decrease with age. DHA is the building block of human brain tissue and the primary structural fatty acid in the gray matter of the brain and the retina. Studies have shown that DHA deficiency and the incidence of Alzheimer's disease are closely related. This is also the case in depression, memory problems, and attention deficit disorder (ADD). DHA and the essential fats are also very important in preventing inflammatory reactions in the brain.

Lecithin contains phosphatidylcholine, phosphatidylethanolanine, and phosphatidylinositol, all of which are important phospholipids for brain function because of their critical role in cell membrane activity. These phospholipids plus phosphatidylserine have been found to correct cognitive impairment related to neurological degeneration; they also work to prevent viral damage to brain cells.

Ginkgo biloba extract has been used for several thousand years in China to enhance brain function and prevent neurological degeneration. In Chinese medicine, ginkgo biloba is used to help increase memory and age-related decline in mental performance. In many well-controlled human studies, a standardized gingko biloba extract was found effective in the treatment against Alzheimer's disease, especially in tests related to decreasing the disease's progression. Ginkgo biloba extract helps to improve cerebral circulation and prevents blood clots and radiation- and toxin-induced free radical damage. The active ingredients in ginkgo biloba are antioxidants called ginkgosides and terpenoids.

American blueberries are closely related to European bilberries. In many experimental and human clinical studies, treatment with blueberry extract provided dramatic improvement in brain function and a protective effect against neurological degeneration. In addition, both extracts have been found to increase brain and eye circulation and prevent age-related eye diseases. Overall, the flavonoids in blueberries and bilberries, because of their antioxidant activity, increase glutathione levels in the brain and eyes, decrease free radical damage, and prevent glycation.

Gamma tocopherol and ascorbyl palmitate are important fat-soluble antioxidants to prevent neurological degeneration; they also keep the lipids in the brain and aging formulation from being oxidized.

CHAPTER EIGHT

Detoxification Endgame: Avoiding Disease

———— ✿ ————

In the preceding chapters, I provided tools for ensuring a lifetime of good health by supporting your body's powerfully protective detoxification systems. But putting these words into action, given our human nature, usually requires some motivation. There is nothing like a health alarm to get things moving. So let's look beyond our discussion of the wonderful health benefits of food and supplements to what happens if our detox systems *don't* get the support they need. Let's look at the insidious world of cancer.

How Does Cancer Develop?

Cancer results from the complex interaction of many factors related to our environment, lifestyle, diet, and genetic makeup. These interactions are most often connected with what we eat and drink, use of tobacco products, exposure to sunlight and ionizing radiation, and exposure to cancer-causing agents found in our environment.

Cancer begins and flourishes in most of the tissues (organs) in our bodies where cell replication is continuously taking place. In healthy tissues a balance between cell death (apoptosis) and the formation of new cells is strictly controlled. By contrast, cancer cells divide and grow in an uncontrolled manner and the abnormal cells can spread to other tissues or organs. Carcinomas, sarcomas, myelomas, leukemia, lymphomas, neuroblastomas, and gliomas constitute the main categories of cancer. Carcinomas are the most common cancers arising in tissues of the skin, oral cavity, lung, breast, and vagina, among others; sarcomas are found in the connective tissue cells; myelomas and leukemias originate in cells of the blood-forming portion of the bone marrow; lymphomas are found in the lymphatic system; neuroblastomas arise from neuroblast cells, which are related to the sympathetic part of the nervous system; and gliomas are cancers that arise in the brain from connective tissue–like cells called glial cells and astrocytes.

Most cancers exist in the form of tumors, which are either malignant or benign. Malignant cells can spread, or metastasize, to other parts of the body through the lymphatic system or bloodstream. If they are not stopped, the malignant cells of metastatic cancer can migrate and infiltrate the brain, lungs, liver, bone marrow, and other vital organs. Benign tumors, although they are not classified as cancer because they do not invade other tissues, have been known to progress to cancer or become malignant. Typically, benign tumors are not a threat to life unless they arise in the brain or other vital organs.

In the United States, skin, lung, colon, prostate, and breast are the most common types of cancer. The number of new cases of cancer in this country is increasing each year. People of all ages get cancer. However, middle-aged and elderly people are most often affected because of the long latency period of cancer (ten to thirty years). Skin cancer is the most common type of cancer in both men and women with approximately 1.2 million cases in the year 2001. Prostate cancer is the second most common in men (198,000), and breast cancer is the second in women (194,000). Lung cancer is still the leading cause of cancer deaths in both men and women in the United States. Brain cancer and leukemia are the most common cancers in children and young adults.

Cancer development is usually a very slow process that often takes place over a period of years or even decades. The length of time (latency) to cancer formation depends on a number of factors such as genetics; the amount, type, and length of time of carcinogenic exposure; detoxification capabilities; DNA repair capacity; immune system strength; as well as diet, lifestyle, and age. The two major classes of genes critical for cancer development are oncogenes and tumor suppressor genes. Oncogenes stimulate cell growth and proliferation; tumor suppressor genes slow them down. If these genes become mutated from carcinogen exposure—or if you happen to be born with mutated forms—cancer may result.

ONCOGENES AND TUMOR SUPPRESSOR GENES

Each oncogene or tumor suppressor gene, of which there are one hundred known variations, has two alleles; one from each parent. Generally, a mutation first occurs in one of the alleles or it is inherited from one of the parents.

Some carcinogens, such as aflatoxin, require only low exposure for a short time to cause cancer. Other carcinogens, such as benzene, are relatively weaker and require higher doses for longer periods of time. People with genetically inherited high levels of detoxification enzymes obviously deal with relatively more carcinogens than those with genetically inherited lower levels. The same can be said for our DNA repair capability and immune systems, the next lines of defense: the better they function, the more they protect us. Age is also a very important factor. Animal studies have shown that because of higher levels of cell growth and turnover, younger animals are more susceptible to cancer induction than older animals, where cell growth and turnover is lower. Humans behave the same way.

Cancer development has three stages: initiation, promotion, and progression. Tumor initiation begins when DNA in skin cells, for example, is damaged by exposure to a carcinogen, such as ultraviolet light or a PAH, an event that would not likely occur in the presence of strong detoxification capabilities. However, if DNA damage does occur and it is not repaired, it can lead to a genetic mutation in either a tumor suppressor gene or an oncogene. Metaphorically speaking, the brakes fail or the accelerator sticks or both. Either way, cell proliferation increases and cancer looms. In many cancers, both oncogenes and tumor suppressor genes are mutated.

The induction of skin cancer in experimental animals provides a good illustration of the three stages of tumor formation. Over the life span of an animal, a mutation can be produced in an oncogene in skin cells from low dosages of a potent carcinogen without giving rise to cancer. However, if the animal with the mutated but dormant oncogene is exposed for a long period of time to a tumor promoter, cancer will develop. It doesn't matter if the tumor promoter is given right after the mutation occurs or months later. This example of the induction of cancer in experimental animals, in which tumor initiation is followed sequentially by tumor promotion and progression, is very important not only for the understanding of the development of cancer but also for a rational and effective prevention of cancer. Similar sequential stages are also believed to be involved in human cancer. Estrogens and androgens can act as tumor promoters by stimulating mutated cells to grow and multiply, which can lead to breast or prostate cancer. Further stimulation with low doses of other environmental toxins and carcinogens can cause the number of initiated or mutated cells, called precancerous cells, to expand and progress to true cancer cells, which can then invade surrounding tissues and metastasize.

Detoxification Strategies for Cancer

The emphasis of this book on detoxification is to prevent diseases like cancer. But that doesn't mean we scrap a detoxification strategy if cancer is diagnosed. In fact, once the stage of cancer formation is identified, it is possible, and necessary, to develop a customized intervention strategy with the appropriate protective compounds. The chart on page 129 depicts the various stages of the development of cancer and strategies that have been found to be effective in each stage.

The formulation of essential fats is also very important in cancer prevention. The sulfur compounds from cruciferous vegetables and garlic, the flavonoid compounds from fruits and vegetables, the terpenoids and curcuminoids from spices, chlorophyllin from green vegetables, and D-glucarate from fruits and vegetables are particularly potent inhibitors of the tumor initiation stage because they enhance Phase I and Phase II detoxification and DNA repair. In terms of tumor promotion and progression, the antioxidants from fruits and vegetables and critical cellular antioxidants plus essential fats and immune enhancement compounds are very effective because of inhibiting free radicals, inflammation, and cell proliferation, as well as stimulating immune function and cancer cell death.

These compounds listed in the "Breakthrough Supplements for Cancer" table on page 130 are potent inhibitors of the induction of cancer because they stimulate detoxification function. They show promise as agents for the treatment of cancer progression. Many studies have found that they inhibit the proliferation of cancer cells, stimulate apoptosis or cell death, stimulate normal differentiation in cancer cells, counteract the growth of blood vessels to tumors (antiangiogenesis),

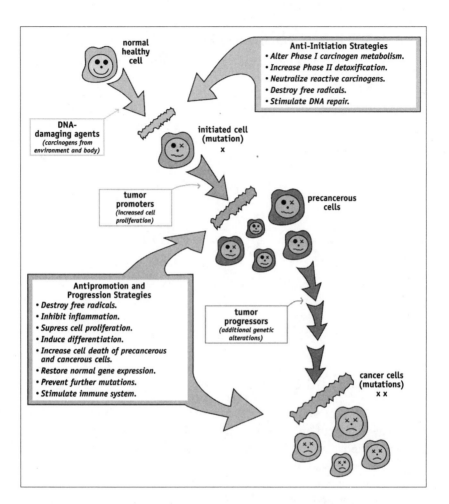

and/or stimulate the immune system to produce natural killer cells to destroy cancer cells. In some cases, curcumin, silymarin, and omega-3 fatty acids also work synergistically with certain chemotherapeutic agents such as doxorubicin (adriamycin). In addition, curcumin, silymarin (or silibinin), and omega-3 fatty acids also inhibit cox-2, a critical enzyme in cancer cell growth. Certain phytochemicals, notably green tea polyphenols, apigenin, silymarin, and genistein, are effective inhibitors of tyrosine kinases. These and other tyrosine kinase inhibitors are also starting to show promise in cancer treatment because of their ability to counteract cancer cell growth in a very selective manner without many side effects. A combination of these compounds because of their various anticancer mechanisms may be an effective approach to selectively destroying cancer cells.

Breakthrough Supplements for Cancer	
Effective Inhibitors of Cancer Cell Growth and Progression	
COMPOUNDS	AMOUNT PER DAY
silymarin or silibinin	400–1,000 mg
curcumin	1,000–2,000 mg
selenium (methyl seleninic acid)	400–600 mg
genistein (isoflavone)	400–800 mg
calcium or zinc D-glucarate	1,000–4,000 mg
N-acetylcysteine	1,000–2,000 mg
1P6 (inositol hexaphosphate)	2,000–4,000 mg
diallyl disulfide	500–2,000 mg
omega-3 fatty acid (EPA/DHA)	1,000–3,000 mg
green tea polyphenolics (catechins)	500–1,000 mg

A Cancer Diagnosis

If you or someone you know is diagnosed with cancer, it is very important to get a second opinion from an oncologist, a physician trained as a cancer specialist, and to become knowledgeable about your disease. The AMC Cancer Research Center has a free telephone service called the Cancer Information and Counseling Line (CICL) designed to help people with cancer and their families. I believe that the CICL is by far the best such service in the United States. (For contact information on CICL, see the Resource Guide at the back of the book.) For nearly twenty years, the AMC Cancer Research Center has provided valuable information by professionals well trained in all aspects of cancer treatment and counseling, including the psychosocial effects of the disease. In addition to CICL, which is in the Center for Behavioral and Community Studies, AMC has four other centers: the Center for Cancer Causation and Prevention, the Center for Nutrition in the Prevention of Disease, the Health Communication Center, and the Research Methodology and Biometrics Center. These groups are united by their goals of cancer prevention and control. The scientists at AMC are committed not only to understanding how and why cancer occurs, but also to developing effective strategies to help people counteract risk factors and reduce their chances of ever contracting the disease.

The AMC Cancer Research Center does research on three aspects of cancer prevention: primary, intervention, and postcancer prevention. Primary prevention deals with reducing cancer-causing agents through lifestyle and behavioral changes, preventing the effects of carcinogens and tumor promoters, and counteracting the activity of mutated or bad genes. Intervention prevention involves studies to decrease the cancer risk in individuals who have one or more high-risk factors for the disease. Postcancer prevention attempts to increase the length of survival and prevent recurrence of cancer, including secondary cancers that result from treatment as well as new cancers.

Recently, significant efforts have been put toward developing very specific cancer treatments that do not suppress the immune system and have few if any toxic consequences for normal cells. Together with advances in diagnostics that identify cancer at earlier stages, this is our best hope for ultimately finding a rational and effective cure for cancer. Already we have witnessed the development of some promising cancer treatments that stimulate the death of cancer cells without affecting normal cells, and inhibit the growth of blood vessels to tumors (angiogenesis). Progress will continue to be made in this area and in finding a way to keep the immune system strong throughout treatment. The AMC Cancer Research Center and other cancer centers are active participants in this research.

CHAPTER NINE

Putting It All Together: The Detox Revolution Program

$\mathcal{L}\!\mathcal{D}$

$\mathbf{I}$mplementing an effective plan to ensure the long-term optimum functioning of our detoxification systems involves first a good start and then the ability to take periodic measurements to reinforce good habits and discard bad ones. Because much of the progress made during the course of the program will go unseen and unfelt, this measurement process is one of the keys to a successful result.

Your Health Evaluation

Each of us is a unique product of our particular genetic makeup, lifestyle, and environment. Within each of these areas are risk factors for disease that scientists use to establish our individual baselines for health. A health risk assessment (HRA) questionnaire and an analysis of our blood and urine are the principle tools used to indicate the current state of our detoxification and other protective bodily functions as well as our predisposition for cancer, cardiovascular disorders, diabetes, obesity, inflammatory diseases, immune dysfunction, and neurological degenerative and other diseases.

Health risk assessments are usually tailored to an organization's purpose. For instance the National Institutes of Health has a very good diet history questionnaire. The American Cancer Society has an HRA for cancer, and the American Heart Association has one for heart disease. The American Medical Association has a health insight HRA, and several universities—including University of California at Berkeley, Harvard University, and Johns Hopkins University—have good nutrition-focused HRAs, as does the Better Life Institute.

HRAs are widely used in the health field; however, most of them are not comprehensive in terms of analyzing the various risk factors of degenerative diseases, especially cancer, heart disease, diabetes, and obesity. They often do not provide enough detailed analysis of nutritional and physical activities and, importantly, detoxification capabilities. An HRA should gather information regarding the following areas:

- family health

- personal health, including drug usage

- health screening

- occupation and workplace health

- physical activity and exercising

- family body weight

- personal body weight and weight gain, including where you gain weight

- tobacco and alcohol use

- sun exposure, including number of sunburns

- coping with stress

- amount of sleep

- diet and nutrition

- supplement use, including vitamins, minerals, phytochemicals, and other nutritional compounds

Dr. Russ Glasgow, an internationally known clinical psychologist and a specialist in changing health behaviors in cancer and diabetes patients; Dr. Cynthia Gillette Dormer, a registered dietitian and specialist in cancer, weight control, and obesity; and I have developed a comprehensive HRA at the AMC Cancer Research Center. It follows up the questionnaire with a computation of risk and individual risk reports, educational messages, and our recommendations for steps that should be taken to increase well-being. Categories include changes in lifestyle, diet, and exercise; stress control techniques; and a supplement plan. (Further information on the AMC is provided in the Resource Guide at the back of the book.)

AMC Cancer Research Test

Here is an abridged version of the AMC HRA. It is designed to provide a quick but necessarily general insight into your overall risk of cancer, cardiovascular disorders, diabetes, and obesity.

1. Do you have a family history of cancer? Yes or No

2. Do you have a family history of heart disease or stroke? Yes or No

3. Do you have a family history of diabetes? Yes or No

4. Do you have a family history of obesity? Yes or No

5. Are you overweight and do you gain weight easily? Yes or No

6. Have you consistently used tobacco products in the last five years? Yes or No

7. Are you exposed to secondhand smoke on a regular basis? Yes or No

8. Do you drink more than ten alcoholic beverages per week? Yes or No

9. Do you eat three or fewer servings of fruits and vegetables per day? Yes or No

10. Do you eat high-fat foods at least once a day? Yes or No

11. Do you eat salty foods or add salt to your foods often? Yes or No

12. Do you eat cabbage, broccoli, cauliflower, or other cruciferous foods less than two times a week? Yes or No

13. Do you eat raw and/or cooked onions and garlic less than two times a week? Yes or No

(continued)

AMC Cancer Research Test *(continued)*

14. Do you eat tomatoes or tomato products less than two times a week?   Yes or No

15. Do you eat whole-grain foods less than once a day?   Yes or No

16. Do you eat white bread or other non-whole-grain foods such as pasta, crackers, donuts, etc., more than once a day?   Yes or No

17. Do you use or eat, on a daily basis, multiple foods containing sugars and processed carbohydrates such as snacks and desserts?   Yes or No

18. Do you eat fried or charcoaled foods often (once a day)?   Yes or No

19. Do you eat well-done meats often?   Yes or No

20. Do you drink less than two glasses of water a day?   Yes or No

21. Are you exposed to sunlight without some protection for more than one hour daily on a regular basis?   Yes or No

22. Have you had more than three sunburns in your lifetime?   Yes or No

23. Do you have high blood pressure?   Yes or No

24. Do you have high cholesterol?   Yes or No

25. Do you have high blood sugar?   Yes or No

26. Do you visit a doctor because of some illness more than once a year?   Yes or No

27. Do you exercise for less than thirty minutes a day three times a week?   Yes or No

28. Are you often under stress?   Yes or No

29. Do you have a job that involves very little physical activity?   Yes or No

30. Do you take nutritional supplements infrequently?   Yes or No

If you answered yes to twenty-five or more of these questions, you are at a very-high-risk level for developing degenerative diseases because of poor genetic makeup and/or lifestyle. A yes to nineteen to twenty-four questions puts you in a high-risk level because of family history and lifestyle concerns. You reach the average risk level with a yes to thirteen to eighteen questions. Even at this level, you run a risk for chronic degenerative diseases. Only at the low-risk level, a yes to seven to twelve questions, and at the very-low-risk level, a yes to six or fewer questions, are you considered relatively safe.

A second essential component of the evaluation process involves a blood cell count and chemistry profile. In addition to the usual measurements of cholesterol—LDL, HDL, and triglyceride levels—this profile measures glucose levels, an important risk factor in Type II diabetes. Finally, the evaluation process involves urine laboratory tests and more specific laboratory tests on blood, all of which measure factors that determine whether or not an individual is on the pathway to developing cancer, cardiovascular disorders, inflammatory diseases, Type II diabetes, or obesity. The following measurements are taken.

1. overall antioxidant capacity in blood; this is a general biomarker for how effectively antioxidant enzymes are functioning and the amount of antioxidant activity from diet and supplements contributing to the body's protection against free radicals

2. level of cotinine, a breakdown product of nicotine and a biomarker for exposure to cigarettes, in the urine

3. level of creatinine in the urine, a measurement of metabolic activity

4. amount of oxidative (free radical) damage of DNA, lipids, and proteins in the blood and urine from internal and external sources; general biomarkers for all degenerative diseases, including aging

5. levels of D-glucaric acid and β-glucuronidase in both urine and blood, important biomarkers of detoxification; blood levels correlate with cancer risk

6. amount of antioxidant and Phase II detoxification enzymes in the blood; this generally determines inherited detoxification capabilities

7. amount of reduced and oxidized glutathione in the blood; this is the premier cellular antioxidant

8. amount of glycation end products in blood caused by high levels of blood glucose, which lead to diabetes and rapid aging

9. levels of homocysteine, cholesterol—LDL, HDL, and triglycerides— in the blood; this measurement relates to cardiovascular disorders

10. level of insulin-like growth factor (IGF-1) and IGF-1 binding protein levels in blood, general cancer biomarkers

11. amount of p65 level in blood, a very early biomarker of cancer, especially of the breast, prostate, lung, and colon

12. levels of fibrinogen in blood, a marker that relates to cardiovascular disorders

The evaluation can be performed in two parts. First, the detailed HRA questionnaire should be completed along with steps one through five, which involve a urine and simple blood test. From this, if it is determined that you are in a low-risk category for disease, it is not necessary to go further, unless you simply want more detailed information about your state of health. However, if you are found to be in an average- to very-high-risk category, it is very advisable to proceed with a full blood cell and chemistry profile and steps one as well as four through twelve for blood.

Implementing the Detox Revolution Program

Ensuring peak detoxification processes requires a lifelong commitment. However, the changes in diet and lifestyle required to accomplish this cannot be realistically achieved overnight; instead they must be introduced slowly, one step at a time. Trying to accomplish too much too soon can lead to discouragement and minor, short-term health issues, such as discomfort from overloading the digestive system. Part of the feedback that AMC provides in its HRA is a stepwise approach for making big changes in diet, exercise program, stress management, and supplements.

WHEN TOXINS NEED A QUICK RESPONSE

Sometimes a person's exposure to toxins is so great that it can't wait for a long-term solution. Immediate detoxification is called for, as with the anthrax infections in 2001. In most of these cases we turn to drugs for the detox work. Functioning as soft drugs, silymarin and alpha lipoic acid have been used in high doses to good effect by many physicians.

We at AMC recommend a six-month detoxification program consisting of the first month (level I), the next two months (level II), and the final three months (level III):

Six-Month Detox Program: Outline

HRA and blood and urine tests

↓

exercise program and stress control

↓

healthy diet

↓

vitamin and mineral formulation

↓

breakthrough supplements for Phase I and Phase II detoxification

↓

breakthrough supplements for antioxidant detoxification

↓

breakthrough supplements for methylation

↓

essential fats supplements

↓

immune-boosting supplements

↓

the formulation for a specific disease

↓

HRA and blood and urine tests

Level I: The First Month

Remember that the HRA and blood and urine tests should be performed before you start this program. This will give you a baseline for improvement.

Exercise and Stress Control We all need exercise to build or rebuild strength and agility, reduce stress, increase our basal metabolic rate—by which calories are utilized more efficiently—control weight, and support our detoxification systems. It's important to increase your amount of exercise gradually—both to keep your motivation and to reduce the risk of injury. Exercise should be enjoyable; this is your best chance for making it a lifelong habit. But don't overdo it: too much exercise can lead to cellular damage from the overproduction of free radicals.

Your goal for the first month of the program is to engage in some form of moderate exercise, working your way up to three days a week, for thirty minutes at a time. If you are already at this level, increase to five days, but don't go beyond. Remember the body needs downtime to prevent potential cellular damage and to recover from exercise. Remember, too, that people differ in terms of the type of exercise they need.

Walking is one of the easiest ways to stay active. Walking as well as stretching, sit-ups, push-ups, weight lifting, and running are my activities of choice. Swimming and aerobics are also good ways to get moderate exercise. Whatever you do, make sure to vary the form of exercise to ward off boredom. And never avoid the chance to incorporate additional physical activity into your daily routine. For instance, take the stairs instead of the elevator or escalator and walk, don't ride, whenever you have a choice.

Refer to Chapter 2 for recommendations for stress management. Decreasing stress is very important for good health.

STRESS REDUCTION

Exercise is very helpful in stress control. A short walk, push-ups, sit-ups, or any type of moderate exercise can help you take your mind off stressful situations. Sufficient sleep—seven to eight hours a night—is also vital in stress management.

Diet It is best to eat frequent small, nutritious meals, including breakfast, lunch, dinner, and sensible small snacks in between. Going hungry and eating later tends to put the body's metabolism in starvation mode, meaning it stores calories as fat, which can lead to weight gain.

Most Americans eat only two to three servings of fruits and vegetables, very few whole-grain foods, and only two to three glasses of water a day. Sixty percent of Americans don't eat breakfast, the most important meal of the day.

A healthy breakfast should include at least some of the following: fruits, fruit juices, whole-grain cereals and/or breads, boiled or poached eggs, yogurt, low-fat milk, and coffee or tea.

Here are the goals for level I:

- Water. Most Americans drink two to three glasses a day. Each week during the first month, add one glass a day until you reach a total of at least six glasses a day.

- Fruits and vegetables. Most Americans eat only two to three portions of vegetables and fruits a day. Each week during the first month, add one serving per day to reach a total of at least six or seven servings a day. Practice variety and emphasize those fruits and vegetables that are superfoods. My health drink mixes are an easy way to increase the number of servings per day. (See Chapter 3.)

- Whole-grain foods. Each week add one serving per day to reach a total of four to six servings.

- Refined grain foods. Each week decrease one serving per day.

- Legumes, nuts, and seeds. Every two weeks add one serving per day to reach a total of two to four servings per day.

- Cold-water fish (not fried or overcooked) and essential plant oils. Every two weeks, add one serving per day to reach a total of one to two servings per day.

- Foods containing trans-fats and saturated fats. Each week decrease one serving of these fatty foods until they are eliminated from your diet or at least eaten rarely.

- Lean meats (not fried or overcooked) as in my food pyramid. Every two weeks add one serving per day until you are eating only lean meats.

- Fatty, fried, or overcooked meat. Every two weeks decrease one serving per day until they are eliminated from your diet or at least eaten rarely.

- Spices and herbs in cooking. Each week add a beneficial spice or herb when cooking until you are using such ingredients routinely. (See Chapter 3.)

- Salt. Each day gradually decrease use of salt and consumption of foods with high salt content, such as processed foods. Instead of using salt, try pepper, which helps in the absorption of many important phytochemicals.

- Alcoholic beverages. By the end of the first month, reduce consumption of alcohol to only seven to ten drinks per week, and emphasize wines, especially red wines.

- Coffee and tea. Caffeinated or not, these beverages help with detoxification, so building up to two to four cups per day can be helpful.

- Healthy snacks. You should try this first month to replace unhealthy snacks such as potato chips and high-sugar snacks with fruits, raw vegetables, and perhaps my snack mix.

If in the course of following this program, you develop a reaction or allergy to some particular new food, try to determine what it is at an early stage. If it's a vegetable, replace it with a member of the same family or one that is closely related.

STRESS REDUCTION

Exercise is very helpful in stress control. A short walk, push-ups, sit-ups, or any type of moderate exercise can help you take your mind off stressful situations. Sufficient sleep—seven to eight hours a night—is also vital in stress management.

Supplements The multivitamin and mineral formulation (see Chapter 5) is the foundation, and the breakthrough supplements for detoxification (see Chapter 6) are the focus of the program. A regimen of these supplements must be implemented gradually so that the digestive system can adapt to them. Here are the goals for the first month:

- Multivitamin and mineral formulation. For the first two weeks take approximately one-third of the recommended dose on a daily basis. If this appears to cause some digestive problems, take one-third the amount every other day. Increase the amount by one-third for the third week and the fourth week to reach 100 percent of the recommended dose.

- Breakthrough supplements for xenobiotic Phase I and Phase II detoxification. Start with one-third of the recommended dose in the first week, phasing in the remaining two-thirds over the final three weeks.

- Breakthrough supplements for antioxidant detoxification and methylation. Start with one-third of the recommended dose and phase in the other two-thirds over the final three weeks.

HOP INTO THE SAUNA

Taking saunas can speed up the metabolic rate and increase your body's ability to detoxify and eliminate harmful substances through your pores by sweating. If possible, take a ten-minute sauna a couple of times each week.

Level II: Months Two and Three

After the first month, you should feel better and have more energy. Here is what you should achieve in the next two months.

Diet Eat a total of eight to nine servings of fruits and vegetables per day. I know this sounds difficult but if I can do it—and I do—so can you. It might be helpful to know that two glasses each of my vegetable juice and fruit juice drinks and one serving of my snack mix provides five servings per day.

Exercise and Stress Control Increase your level of exercise to at least five days a week, alternating between thirty minutes and longer, say forty-five to sixty minutes each time. Don't do the same forms of exercise on two consecutive days. You should also continue to practice stress management every day.

Supplementation You should now be actively detoxifying toxins, carcinogens, and free radicals. Because the essential fats enhance immunity, introduce the essential fatty acid formulation and the supplements for boosting the immune system at the same time, building up to the full dosage by the end of level II.

For those of you whose HRA determined that you are at a normal to high risk for cancer, cardiovascular disorders, inflammatory diseases, diabetes Type II, and/or neurological degeneration, you should introduce the various related supplements in this phase and again gradually build up to full dosage.

Level III: The Next Three-Month Period for Detoxification

After three months you will be on the way to better health and disease prevention. Level III is about maintaining and then building on success. This is the time for you to experiment with and fine-tune the different elements, to find a comfort level and then challenge yourself to go beyond it. The objective is to make the program a lifetime commitment.

At the end of the six-month period retest yourself with the comprehensive HRA and the urine and blood tests to determine how much you have improved your health. This will definitely reinforce the importance of this program, which I hope you will continue for the rest of your life.

Remember, you do have a choice—a healthy or an unhealthy lifestyle! If you choose a healthy lifestyle program to increase all aspects of your detoxification system, including your immune system, as described in this book, you will probably live a long life with a healthy body and a mind full of energy. However, if you choose an unhealthy lifestyle, you may experience the pain and suffering of some chronic degenerative disease, and more than likely you will not live a long life. Also, remember that even if you have inherited bad genes, a healthy lifestyle will improve your chances of living a long, healthy life. Furthermore, a healthy lifestyle will interact synergistically with your good genes to give you additional benefits for a longer and healthier life.

PART TWO

Detox
Recipes

CHAPTER TEN

What You Need
to Know and Have

—— ⚘ ——

When I give talks on health, the one question that comes up over and over again is "What do *you* eat?" I can understand the curiosity and the assumption that a good nutrition researcher ought to practice what he preaches. And I do. That's why the recipes, many of which are my own, make up such a large part of this book. The recipes are divided into sections such as soups and pasta dishes.

We'll begin with the recipes for the first meal of the day.

Breakfast Is Still the Most Important Meal

At AMC we don't believe in skipping meals and this is particularly important when it comes to breakfast. The fact is we need a continual supply of nutrients to help break down and eliminate toxins and to support the genes that protect against disease. Eating smaller portions of food throughout the day starting with breakfast gives your body the life-saving nutrition it needs. The toxins to which you may have been exposed on your drive home from work have a better chance of being detoxified if you replenish your system with the nutrients it needs starting at breakfast the following day. Do not confuse skipping a meal—especially the first meal of the day—with some form of fasting. Skipping meals is not a good thing for cleansing the body. We need nutrients to properly do that job. In addition to the breakfast recipes in the next chapter, here are some simple suggestions for a complete breakfast:

fruit
yogurt
Dr. Slaga's Healthy Mix (see Chapter 3 for recipe)

whole-grain pancakes with blueberries and walnuts
grapefruit juice
mixed fresh fruit

poached egg (range fed)
Canadian bacon
whole-grain toast
Dr. Slaga's Healthy Mix (see Chapter 3 for recipe) or grapefruit
Dr. Slaga's Vegetable Drink (see Chapter 3 for recipe)

hard- or soft-boiled eggs (range fed)
whole-grain toast
fruit
Dr. Slaga's Vegetable Drink (see Chapter 3 for recipe)

Wheat

Wheat is not a big part of the recipes in *The Detox Revolution*. The gluten found in wheat is one of the most common causes of allergic responses in people. Its use is minimized here so that you can benefit from the detoxifying properties of food without also having to deal with the distraction of food allergies.

A Well-Stocked Kitchen

This chapter opens the door, so to speak, to my kitchen. The foods in my pantry and refrigerator contain the vitamins, minerals, and micronutrients intrinsic to the process of detoxification.

Spices

curry	lemon peel (dehydrated)	red pepper
garlic	mint	rosemary
ginger	paprika	turmeric

Nuts and Seeds

almonds	milk thistle	soybeans (roasted)
flax	walnuts	

Grains and Dry Cereal

barley	puffed brown rice	rice (brown)
buckwheat	puffed buckwheat	teff
oatmeal	quinoa	

Oils

canola	olive	walnut
flax		

Dried Fruit

apricots	raisins

Teas

black	green	herbal

Canned Goods

fruit juice	tomato juice	olives
salmon	tuna	

Frozen Foods

blueberries	cranberries	strawberries

Refrigerated Foods

eggs	lean meat	low-fat yogurt
egg whites		

Produce

apples	fresh garlic, onions,	grapefruit
asparagus	and shallots	strawberries
blueberries	fresh herbs (basil,	watercress
crucifers	rosemary, oregano, etc.)	watermelon

Legumes

garbanzo	lentils	soybeans
kidney	lima	

Cooking Glossary

I've included a brief glossary in order for you to understand some of the more esoteric items used in the recipes.

arame Wiry black sea vegetable, rich in minerals.

daikon Long, white radish that is a member of the cruciferous family. Can be eaten raw, in salads, or steamed as a side dish.

hijiki A black sea vegetable that grows off the coast of Maine, rich in minerals.

mirin Sweet cooking wine made from rice; available in Asian markets or in the macrobiotic section of health-food stores.

miso Fermented soybeans and sea salt made into a paste and used as a seasoning in soups and stews.

shiitake A mushroom from Japan used fresh or dried for soups and other dishes.

soba Noodles made from buckwheat flour or a combination of buckwheat and whole-wheat flour.

suribachi An earthenware bowl with a serrated bottom used for grinding herbs and pureeing.

sweet rice vinegar A type of vinegar made from rice that is less harsh than other vinegars.

tahini Paste made from ground sesame seeds and used as seasoning for sauces, dips, and spreads. High in calcium.

tamari Traditional naturally made soy sauce that is not processed in the same way as the ordinary variety.

umeboshi vinegar Salty-sour type vinegar that is made from a type of Japanese plum. Used in recipes for salads, vegetables, and dressings.

wakame A deep green, edible seaweed popular in Asian countries; used in soups, stews, and salads.

CHAPTER ELEVEN

The Recipes

T he following recipes feature the detoxification superfoods discussed in this book. Where required for cooking, recipes include only healthy sources of fat, including flax, olive, canola, and sesame oils. Frying or charcoal broiling methods are discouraged and therefore do not appear in these recipes. In addition, these recipes help you avoid the dangers of overheating food while cooking, particularly meat, which as you now know can be the source of strong carcinogens. *The Detox Revolution* suggests sautéing at gentle temperatures. In some recipes you will learn the trick of adding a little water in the pan first, before oil is added, to effectively reduce the cooking temperature. This prevents the oil from becoming heat damaged.

Some unusual foods are also featured in the recipes—foods that may not be familiar to you. I hope you will enjoy the wonderfully protective foods and new cooking techniques. Remember to select organic ingredients and low-sodium products whenever possible, wash all fruits and vegetables, and keep portions small. Enjoy!

Breakfasts

BLUEBERRY OAT MUFFINS
TWELVE SERVINGS

1¼ cups rolled oats
1¼ cups whole-wheat flour
1 teaspoon baking powder
2 cups fresh or frozen (thawed) blueberries
¼ cup canola oil
⅓ cup honey
3 tablespoons water
1 large egg or ¼ cup egg substitute
1 teaspoon fresh lemon or lime rind (optional)*
2 tablespoons lemon or lime juice

*Wash the fruit before grating.

Preheat the oven to 375°F. Spray a twelve-cup muffin tin with nonstick cooking spray or line the cups with paper liners. In a large mixing bowl, mix oats, flour, and baking powder. Make a well in the center. In a separate bowl, mix the remaining wet ingredients. Pour the wet ingredients into the dry ingredients and stir until just blended; add the lemon or lime rind. Divide the batter evenly among the prepared muffin cups.
Bake eighteen minutes.

MUFFINS

Muffin making is a great kitchen activity for kids. Be sure to use egg substitute when baking with children so they can lick bowls and spoons without fear of salmonella.

- If you leave extra muffins sitting around, they will call your name and you will eat too many of them. Put extra muffins in the freezer. Thaw and serve them another time—perhaps with soup for a quick wholesome meal.

- Muffins make a healthy, inexpensive, portable snack for kids, hikers, and skiers.

- Muffins are also a great way to get healthy plant nutrients into vegetable-phobic people. Pumpkin, shredded carrot, shredded zucchini, and even leftover winter squash puree can be baked into muffins, making them just as nutritious as they are delicious.

- To make low-fat or nonfat muffins, use egg substitute instead of whole egg, and applesauce instead of oil.

CHOCOLATE CHIP PUMPKIN MUFFINS

TWELVE SERVINGS

1 cup rolled oats
1 cup whole-wheat flour
2 teaspoons baking powder
$^3/_4$ cup miniature, dark, semisweet chocolate chips
1 15-ounce can (2 cups) pumpkin puree
$^1/_4$ cup canola oil
$^1/_3$ cup honey
1 large egg or $^1/_4$ cup egg substitute

Preheat oven to 375°F. Spray a twelve-cup muffin tin with nonstick cooking spray or line the cups with paper liners. Mix oats, flour, baking powder, and chocolate chips in a large mixing bowl. Make a well in the center. Mix remaining wet ingredients in a separate bowl. Pour the wet ingredients into the dry ingredients and stir until just blended. Divide the batter evenly among the prepared muffin cups. Bake eighteen minutes.

CORNBREAD MUFFINS

TWELVE SERVINGS

1 cup yellow cornmeal
1 cup whole-wheat flour
1 teaspoon baking powder
1 15-ounce can (2 cups) cream-style corn
$^1/_4$ cup canola oil
$^1/_3$ cup honey
1 large egg or $^1/_4$ cup egg substitute
$^1/_4$ cup unsulfured molasses

Preheat oven to 375°F. Spray a twelve-cup muffin tin with nonstick cooking spray or line the cups with paper liners. In a large bowl, mix the cornmeal, flour, and baking powder. Make a well in the center. In a separate bowl, thoroughly mix the wet ingredients. Pour the wet ingredients into the dry ingredients and stir until just blended. Divide the batter evenly among the prepared muffin cups. Bake eighteen minutes.

FRUIT GRANOLA

TEN SERVINGS

4 cups rolled oats
$1^3/_4$ cups rolled wheat flakes
1 cup sunflower seeds
1 cup chopped nuts, such as almonds, walnuts, or pecans
$^1/_3$ cup toasted sesame seeds
$^1/_3$ cup sunflower oil
$^1/_4$ cup honey
$^1/_2$ cup raisins
$^1/_2$ cup chopped dried apricots
$^1/_2$ cup chopped dried peaches
$^1/_2$ cup chopped dried apples

Fruit Granola *(continued)*

Preheat the oven to 400°F. In a large bowl, blend the oats, wheat flakes, sunflower seeds, nuts, sesame seeds, oil, and honey. Transfer to a large roasting pan and spread evenly. Bake until lightly browned at the edges, stirring occasionally about fifteen minutes. Let cool completely. Stir in fruit. Store in an airtight container.

NUTTY FRUIT MUFFINS

TWELVE SERVINGS

1³/₄ cups whole-grain pastry flour
1¹/₂ teaspoons baking powder
1¹/₂ teaspoons ground cinnamon
¹/₂ teaspoon baking soda
¹/₄ teaspoon salt
1 cup fat-free vanilla yogurt
¹/₂ cup packed brown sugar
1 large egg or ¹/₄ cup egg substitute
2 tablespoons canola oil
1 teaspoon vanilla extract
¹/₂ cup finely shredded carrots
¹/₂ cup drained crushed pineapple
¹/₃ cup currants or raisins
¹/₂ cup toasted chopped walnuts

Preheat the oven to 400°F. Coat a twelve-cup muffin pan with nonstick cooking spray. In a large bowl, combine the flour, baking powder, cinnamon, baking soda, and salt. In a separate bowl, combine the yogurt, brown sugar, egg, oil, and vanilla extract. Pour the wet ingredients into the flour mixture. Mix well. Stir in the carrots, pineapple, currants or raisins, and walnuts. Divide the batter evenly among the prepared muffin cups. Bake twenty minutes, or until a wooden toothpick inserted in the center of a muffin comes out clean. Cool on a rack.

ORANGE PECAN MUFFINS

TWELVE SERVINGS

1 cup rolled oats
1 cup whole-wheat flour
2 teaspoons baking powder
$^3/_4$ cup chopped pecans
1 medium seedless orange, washed
$^1/_3$ cup water
$^1/_4$ cup canola oil
$^1/_3$ cup honey
1 large egg or $^1/_4$ cup egg substitute
$^3/_4$ cup chopped pecans

Preheat the oven to 375°F. Spray a twelve-cup muffin tin with nonstick cooking spray or line the cups with paper liners. In a large bowl, mix the oats, flour, baking powder, and pecans. Make a well in the center and set the bowl aside. Cut the orange into quarters and place it, peel and all, in a blender. Add the water and blend on high until smooth. Add the oil, honey, and egg to the blender and continue to blend until thoroughly mixed. Pour the wet ingredients into the dry ingredients and stir until just mixed. Stir in the pecans. Divide the batter evenly among the prepared muffin cups. Bake eighteen minutes.

_&_

ORANGE YOGURT PANCAKES WITH FRUIT

FOUR SERVINGS

grated rind of 1 orange*
¹/₃ cup orange juice
1–2 tablespoons sugar
³/₄ cup plain yogurt + ¹/₄ cup for garnish
1 large egg or ¹/₄ cup egg substitute
2 tablespoons canola oil
1 cup whole-wheat flour
1 teaspoon baking soda
¹/₂ teaspoon double-acting baking powder
¹/₄ teaspoon salt
1 pint fresh or frozen (thawed) strawberries

*Wash the fruit before grating.

In a small bowl combine grated rind, juice, and sugar, stirring to dissolve sugar. Add the yogurt, egg, and oil, and mix well. In another bowl, sift together flour, baking soda, baking power, and salt. Add yogurt mixture to the dry ingredients and stir to form a thick batter. Heat a griddle to medium and spoon out batter to form three-inch round pancakes. Cook until the edges are golden; then carefully turn them over and cook for approximately four minutes. Top with fresh fruit and dollop of yogurt. Serve immediately.

Soups

&

BEEF AND BARLEY SOUP

EIGHT SERVINGS

Pearl Barley
3 cups water
1 cup uncooked pearl barley

Soup
2 pounds lean ground beef
2 tablespoons extra-virgin olive oil
2 cups sliced carrots
2 cups chopped onion
2 cups sliced celery
2 cloves garlic, chopped fine
8 cups beef broth
2 14.5-ounce cans Italian-style stewed tomatoes
$\frac{1}{2}$ cup red wine
1 teaspoon dried thyme
1 bay leaf
Salt to taste
Freshly ground black pepper to taste
$\frac{1}{4}$ cup finely chopped fresh parsley
Croutons and/or sour cream (optional)

TO MAKE THE PEARL BARLEY

In medium saucepan, bring to boil three cups of water. Add one cup pearl barley and return to boil. Reduce heat to low, cover, and cook forty-five minutes or until the barley is tender and the liquid is absorbed. You may cook the barley ahead of time, place it in an airtight container, and refrigerate or freeze it for up to one week. For best results, bring refrigerated or frozen barley to room temperature before using.

Beef and Barley Soup *(continued)*

TO MAKE THE SOUP

In a large lidded pot, cook the ground beef over medium-high heat until browned, breaking the meat up with a fork. Remove the meat from the pot and set aside. Heat olive oil in the pot. Add carrots, onion, celery, and garlic; cook about five minutes or until the vegetables are tender-crisp. Add the cooked beef, cooked pearl barley, broth, tomatoes, red wine, thyme, and bay leaf. Season with salt and pepper. Bring soup to a boil. Reduce heat, cover, and cook twenty minutes. Stir in parsley and serve. Garnish each serving with toasted croutons or a dollop of sour cream, if desired.

CREAM OF CARROT SOUP

SIX SERVINGS

1 tablespoon canola oil
2 medium onions, chopped fine
$1/2$ teaspoon sea salt
1 pound carrots, peeled and chopped
6 cups filtered water
1 teaspoon roasted sesame tahini

In a medium skillet heat the oil and then sauté the onions for about four minutes. Add half the salt and sauté another minute. Add the carrots and water and bring to a boil. Add the remaining salt. Reduce the heat and simmer for about twenty-five to thirty minutes. Pour the soup into a blender, add the tahini, and puree until smooth. Transfer the contents back to the skillet and reheat. Serve with chopped fresh herbs or leeks.

This departure from ordinary split pea soup has subtle undertones of the exotic spices from Thailand. I especially like the taste of freshly ground spices from whole seeds. Freshly ground mustard, cardamom, and allspice seeds taste powerfully different from the stale preground and packaged spices available in most stores.

SPLIT PEA SOUP—THAI STYLE

TEN SERVINGS

1-inch piece of Kombu sea vegetable
3 tablespoons + 8 cups filtered water
3 shallots, chopped
$^1/_2$ cup chopped onion
1 medium stalk celery, chopped
1 cup chopped carrot
1–2 teaspoons sea salt
1 cup split peas
$^1/_2$ teaspoon mustard seed
$^3/_4$ teaspoon cardamom seed
$^1/_4$ teaspoon allspice seed
$^1/_4$ teaspoon ground cumin
4 cups cubed buttercup squash
1 stalk lemon grass, peeled and minced
Freshly ground black pepper to taste
Sesame oil to taste

Lightly wipe the Kombu with a clean damp cloth and let it soak in a little water to reconstitute. Set the Kombu aside. In a large, heavy soup kettle gently sauté in two to three tablespoons of filtered water, the shallots, onion, celery, and carrot for about fifteen minutes. Season moderately with several pinches of salt and cook until tender.

Split Pea Soup—Thai Style *(continued)*

When the Kombu has softened (about ten minutes), chop it into little pieces and add to sautéed vegetables. Clean the split peas and add them to the ingredients in the pot. Add eight cups of water and bring to a slow boil. After the soup begins to boil, gently skim the foam with a large spoon. Turn down to medium, and cook, stirring occasionally, for about two hours.

In a little nut/seed grinder, grind together the mustard, cardamom, and allspice seeds for two minutes; mix in the cumin. Add to soup the spice mixture, buttercup squash, lemon grass, and salt and pepper to taste and continue cooking thirty minutes, stirring occasionally. Serve with a drizzle of sesame oil and enjoy.

> Kombu sea vegetable was the original source for natural MSG, before the modern synthetic version. Kombu was commonly known in Asia as a flavor enhancer, but it also is a rich source of minerals and aids in the softening of dried beans and peas during the cooking process.
>
> When making soups, don't add salt, tomatoes, vinegar, citrus juices, miso, or tamari until the end, when beans are practically cooked. Acidic foods and condiments, as well as salt, prevent beans from softening and should not be used until the end of cooking.

TURKEY AND BLACK BEAN CHILI

SIX SERVINGS

2 teaspoons extra-virgin olive oil
1/2 cup chopped onion
1/2 pound ground turkey breast
1 8-ounce package black beans and seasoned rice
1 teaspoon chili powder
1/2 teaspoon ground cumin
1 14.5-ounce can diced tomatoes (no salt added)
1/4 cup chopped scallions

Heat the oil in a large saucepan over medium heat. Add the onion and sauté two minutes. Add the turkey and cook two to three minutes until browned, breaking up the meat as it cooks. Add the beans-and-rice mixture, chili powder, and cumin and toss to coat rice. Carefully add water according to package instructions. Add tomatoes and bring to a boil. Reduce the heat to low, cover, and simmer for the amount of time indicated on the package, stirring occasionally, until the liquid is absorbed and the rice is tender. Top individual servings with chopped scallions.

Dressings, Sauces, and Dips

> The French are believed to enjoy good health despite a relatively high-fat diet because of the daily consumption of antioxidant-rich red wine and a variety of fruits and vegetables. Asparagus is one of their favorite foods. It contains protective plant compounds for which the olive oil and pepper in this recipe act as carriers.

ASPARAGUS VINAIGRETTE

FOUR SERVINGS

1 pound asparagus, cleaned and trimmed
Juice from $1/3$ lemon
1 tablespoon extra-virgin olive oil
Salt to taste
Freshly ground black pepper to taste

Place the asparagus in lightly boiling salted water and cook for four to five minutes until just tender. Remove, drain, and arrange on a plate. When the asparagus has cooled a bit, dress it with lemon juice, olive oil, salt, and pepper.

AVOCADO GREEN GODDESS DRESSING

SIX SERVINGS

5 tablespoons mirin
³/₄ cup filtered or spring water
12 slices sun-dried tomatoes
1 large very ripe avocado
2 cloves garlic, minced
Juice of 2 limes
³/₄ cup oil (half extra-virgin olive oil, half flax oil)
3 tablespoons soy sauce
1 tablespoon balsamic vinegar
3 tablespoons minced cilantro
3 pinches cumin
3 pinches cayenne pepper
Salt to taste

Bring mirin to a gentle boil (boiling mirin brings out its sweetness and evaporates the alcohol). Set aside to cool for thirty minutes. Heat water to a low boil. Pour over the tomatoes. In about twenty minutes they will be reconstituted. Put the tomatoes, along with the soaking water and remaining ingredients, into a blender and puree. Serve over your favorite tossed salad or with very fresh, quickly cooked shrimp, tomatoes, and butter lettuce.

CREAMY ROASTED RED PEPPER DIP

SIX SERVINGS

2 large red bell peppers
1 tablespoon minced garlic
1 teaspoon extra-virgin olive oil
1 cup yogurt
1 teaspoon wine vinegar
1¹/₂ tablespoons finely chopped basil
Salt to taste
Freshly ground pepper to taste

Creamy Roasted Red Pepper Dip *(continued)*

Roast the peppers under the broiler. When charred, place in a bowl covered with a dishtowel for fifteen minutes. After the peppers have cooled, peel them and chop. In a large pan over medium heat, sauté minced garlic in olive oil. Add the peppers and cook over medium-low heat for ten minutes. Transfer to a bowl to cool. Add the yogurt, vinegar, basil, and salt and pepper to taste. Serve with julienned raw vegetables such as celery, fennel, carrots, or daikon radish.

⸎

HONEY ROSEMARY MARINADE
FOUR SERVINGS

½ cup lemon juice
½ cup lime juice
3–4 tablespoons honey
¼ cup fresh rosemary
Pinch of salt
Pinch of red pepper flakes

Puree all ingredients together in a blender for thirty seconds. Use as a marinade for poultry, fish, or vegetables. Do not baste with used marinade and do not serve as a sauce later. Discard all unused marinade.

Rosemary is rich in carnosol and ursolic acid, which may help protect against breast cancer by detoxifying chemicals that may initiate the cancer process. Carnosol and ursolic acid may also provide added protection against lung and skin cancer.

ℓℓℓ

LEMON MUSTARD VINAIGRETTE

FOUR SERVINGS

1 scallion, minced
1¹/₂ tablespoons extra-virgin olive oil
2 tablespoons flaxseed oil
1 tablespoon mirin
5 tablespoons fresh lemon juice (2–3 large lemons)
1 tablespoon Dijon mustard
1 teaspoon minced garlic
1 teaspoon dried oregano
2 pinches sea salt

Combine all ingredients in a high-speed food processor or blender until mixed. Serve over salad or cooked vegetables. For a thicker consistency, you can add one tablespoon of any light miso such as sweet, mellow, or chickpea.

Try this twist on pesto sauce by substituting basil with parsley, a rich source of glutathione, a potent detoxification agent. Although pesto is usually served over pasta, this delicious sauce also works well over fish, tofu, or tempeh. Simply add sauce to fish or soy food about two-thirds of the way through the cooking process. It's most flavorful when not overcooked. For pasta recipes, simply prepare pasta and serve with pesto sauce.

ℓℓℓ

PESTO SAUCE

THREE TO FOUR SERVINGS

3–4 tablespoons water
³/₄ cup loosely packed basil or flat leaf parsley
3 tablespoons extra-virgin olive oil
2 tablespoons flaxseed oil
5 cloves garlic, minced
2 tablespoons light miso
¹/₂ cup pine nuts

Pesto Sauce *(continued)*

Wash the basil or parsley and pat it dry. Chop fine. Combine all ingredients in blender and blend on low speed until creamy.

ℓℓ

SAVORY CILANTRO SAUCE

SIX SERVINGS

1 onion, chopped
2 ribs celery, chopped
2 carrots, chopped
1 teaspoon minced fresh ginger
1 tablespoon extra-virgin olive oil
1 14.5-ounce can low-sodium fat-free chicken broth
Salt to taste
Freshly ground black pepper to taste
$1/_2$ cup chopped cilantro

In a medium pan over low heat, sauté onion, celery, carrots, and ginger in olive oil for ten minutes. Add chicken broth. Simmer, partially covered, until the vegetables are tender—about ten minutes. Season to taste. Puree in a blender. Add the cilantro and stir to mix. Serve over bean and whole-grain dishes.

Coriander, also known as cilantro or Chinese parsley, has powerful aroma and flavor. It is rich in coriandrol, which scientists believe may help protect against skin, liver, and breast cancer.

SPICY ROASTED RED PEPPER DIP
EIGHT SERVINGS

4 medium red bell peppers
$1/2$ teaspoon ground cumin
$1/2$ cup toasted walnuts
2 slices firm whole wheat bread, torn into pieces
2 tablespoons vinegar, preferably raspberry
1 tablespoon extra-virgin olive oil
$1/2$ teaspoon salt
$1/8$ teaspoon ground cayenne pepper

Roast the peppers under the broiler. When charred, place in a bowl covered with a dishtowel for fifteen minutes. After the peppers have cooled, cut them into large pieces. In a small skillet, toast the cumin over low heat, stirring constantly, until very fragrant, about one or two minutes. In a food processor with knife blade attached, process the walnuts until they are thoroughly ground. Add peppers, cumin, bread, vinegar, oil, salt, and cayenne. Puree until smooth. Transfer to a bowl. If you do not plan to serve it right away, cover the dip and refrigerate it for up to four hours. Serve with toasted pita bread wedges.

SPICY TOFU DIP
SIX SERVINGS

6 cups filtered water
1 pound extra-firm tofu
10 radishes, washed, trimmed, and chopped
3 tablespoons grated fresh horseradish
2 scallions, minced
2 tablespoons umeboshi vinegar
2 tablespoons extra-virgin olive oil
3 tablespoons minced fresh dill

Spicy Tofu Dip *(continued)*

Bring water to a boil. Quickly submerge tofu for ten seconds. Remove and let cool. Clean and chop radishes. Grate horseradish after first removing skin. Use small holes for grating. (To avoid watery eyes, keep face away from grater.) Combine all ingredients, except the dill, in a blender. Puree. Add dill, mix thoroughly, and serve. Garnish with additional fresh dill.

TROPICAL MINT SALSA

FOUR SERVINGS

2 medium tomatoes, diced
1 mango, diced
1 small red onion, minced
²/₃ cup chopped fresh mint
Juice of 1 lime
¹/₈ teaspoon cayenne pepper or 1 jalapeño pepper, seeded and minced
Salt to taste

Mix all ingredients together in a bowl. Serve over fish, poultry, or tofu.

Mint contains two important phytochemicals. One is luteolin, which may help prevent certain types of cancer. The other is limonene, an anticancer agent that may help block the development of breast tumors.

Salads

ꬑ

CELERY ROOT AND DAIKON SALAD WITH MINT
THREE TO FOUR SERVINGS

Salad Ingredients
1 medium celery root
1 small daikon radish
$1/4$ teaspoon sea salt
Freshly ground black pepper to taste
$1/2$ cup chopped fresh mint

Dressing Ingredients
$3/4$ teaspoon sea salt
1 clove garlic, minced
1 shallot, minced
$1/5$ cup extra-virgin olive oil
$1/2$ cup orange juice
1 teaspoon lemon juice
Freshly ground black pepper to taste

TO MAKE THE SALAD

Trim and peel the celery root, slice it in half, and cut into julienne strips.
You should have about two cups. After scrubbing the daikon radish with a
natural bristle brush, cut it into julienne strips. You will have approximately
$1^1/3$ cups of daikon. Combine celery root and daikon in a serving bowl.
Season with salt and ground pepper. Add mint leaves and toss.

TO MAKE THE DRESSING

In a suribachi or food processor, add the salt and garlic. Puree. Slowly add
the shallots and olive oil. Continue to grind ingredients together. Combine
the rest of the dressing ingredients. Toss the dressing with the salad;
marinate for an hour. Adjust seasonings to taste and serve.

⤷ℓℓ

BLACK-EYED PEAS WITH CILANTRO SALAD

FOUR SERVINGS

*1 3-inch strip of Kombu, wiped with a damp cloth and soaked until soft,
approximately 30 minutes*
1 cup black-eyed peas, soaked overnight
5–6 cups filtered water
2 teaspoons dry mustard
3 tablespoons lime juice
1/2 teaspoon sea salt
2 tablespoons extra-virgin olive oil
2 tablespoons filtered water
3 cloves garlic, minced
1/3 cup minced cilantro

Place the Kombu in bottom of saucepan. Discard soaking water from beans. Add beans and filtered water. Bring to a boil. Reduce heat and simmer for ten minutes, periodically skimming off the foam. Cover with a bamboo mat and continue to simmer until beans are just about soft, another forty to fifty minutes. Remove the pan from the heat, drain, transfer the beans to a bowl, and let cool. Crush the beans a little to break skin. This will help the dressing's flavors to adhere to the beans. Whisk together mustard, lime juice, oil, water, and sea salt. In a suribachi, grind and press garlic into the other sauce ingredients. Slowly add the cilantro and mix well. Toss the dressing with the peas. Serve on lettuce leaves or radicchio.

Recent studies of cruciferous vegetables show that raw broccoli has stronger abilities to detoxify carcinogenic chemicals than cooked broccoli. To make a wonderfully simple detox treat, slice raw broccoli very thin, toss it with salt, and add it to lettuce, tomato, and carrots. Drizzle with your favorite low-fat dressing.

❧

DETOX CHEF'S SALAD

FOUR TO SIX SERVINGS

1 head romaine lettuce, coarsely shredded
¼ cup chopped watercress or parsley
1 3-ounce container broccoli sprouts
1 red onion, chopped
1 15-ounce can chickpeas
6 radishes, sliced
1 carrot, sliced
1 tomato, sliced
1 pound poached salmon or lean cooked turkey or chicken, sliced

In a large bowl combine the vegetables and then evenly distribute on plates. Top with equal portions of salmon, turkey, or chicken and drizzle with Avocado Green Goddess Dressing (page 164) or Lemon Mustard Vinaigrette (page 166).

❧

LIGHTLY BLANCHED SALAD

ONE SERVING*

Asparagus
Brussels sprouts
Carrots
Cauliflower
Collard greens
Green peas
Leeks
Onions
Summer squash
Juice from lemon to taste
Soy sauce to taste
Flaxseed or olive oil to taste

*You may choose varying amounts and any combination of vegetables. Number of servings will vary depending on your selection.

Lightly Blanched Salad *(continued)*

Place several inches of water and a pinch of salt in a pot and bring to a boil. Drop in the vegetable(s) requiring the longest cooking time. A minute or two later add the rest of the vegetables. Remove the vegetables quickly and place into a strainer. Season with lemon, soy sauce, and oil and serve.

> When boiling vegetables lightly, or blanching as it is called, add the vegetables that need the most cooking first. For example, when preparing the Lightly Blanched Salad, you would add carrots to the pot before the collard greens.

ℓℓ

PAILLARDS OF TURKEY WITH PEA, HERB, AND CHILI SALAD

FOUR SERVINGS

3 cups shelled peas or 1 package frozen peas
2 teaspoons chopped fresh parsley
1½ tablespoons chopped fresh cilantro + extra for garnish
3 tablespoons chopped fresh mint
1 hot chili pepper, stemmed, seeded, and minced
3 scallions (green part only), sliced thin
½ teaspoon sea salt
1 teaspoon canola oil
1 pound skinless turkey breast, sliced into four pieces
2 cups mixed butter lettuce and arugula, cleaned
Juice of 1 lime

Blanch the peas in boiling salted water for one minute. Drain and rinse under cold running water. If using frozen peas, cook according to instructions, *but don't overcook*. Toss the peas with parsley, cilantro, mint, chili, and scallions. Salt lightly. Set aside. Heat oil in a heavy iron skillet. Salt the turkey slices and sauté until done, about 1½ to 2 minutes on each side, depending on the thickness. On each of four plates, arrange arugula and lettuce. Add the pea mixture on top of lettuce and arugula. Place a piece of turkey on each serving and top with a generous squeeze of lime juice. Garnish with fresh chopped cilantro.

Ellagic acid, which helps to detoxify tobacco smoke and other air pollutants, is contained in grapes, raspberries, and strawberries. Grapes also contain resveratrol, which encourages detoxification.

POWER THREE-FRUIT SALAD
FOUR SERVINGS

1 cup grapes, sliced in halves
1 cup raspberries
1 cup sliced strawberries
$1/2$ cup chopped mint

Toss the fruit, and garnish with chopped mint. This salad makes an excellent breakfast. Try it with a small serving of yogurt or low-fat cheese.

PRESSED SALAD
SIX SERVINGS

4 cups chopped Chinese cabbage or lettuce
$1/2$ cup sliced daikon radish
$1/2$ cup chopped scallions
$1/2$ cup chopped cilantro
2 teaspoons umeboshi vinegar
1 teaspoon brown rice vinegar
Sea salt to taste

Combine vegetables and spread thinly and evenly on large platter. Sprinkle vegetables with umeboshi and brown rice vinegar. Add sea salt. Cover with an equal-sized platter, right side up. Place a heavy weight on top of the platter. Press for ten to forty-five minutes. Liquid should appear at bottom of platter.

Savoy cabbage is richer in protective plant chemicals than ordinary purple or green cabbage.

⟨leaf ornament⟩

SAFFRON CHICKEN AND WILD RICE SALAD
WITH RAISINS AND PINE NUTS

FOUR SERVINGS

Chicken

1 cup wild rice

2 cups + 1/4 cup water

5 cloves garlic, minced

1/2 teaspoon + 1/3 teaspoon sea salt

2 1/3 tablespoons extra-virgin olive oil

1 1/2 tablespoons saffron threads

2 tablespoons chopped cilantro

2 serrano chilies, minced

5 skinless chicken thighs

3/4 cup pine nuts

3/4 cup chopped purple onion

1/2 tablespoon honey

1/2 tablespoon balsamic vinegar

3/4 cup raisins

1 cup shelled green peas

2 1/2 tablespoons lemon zest

Blood Orange Sauce

1 clove garlic, minced

1/2 teaspoon sea salt

Juice from 3 blood oranges

2 tablespoons extra-virgin olive oil

1 1/2 tablespoons chopped cilantro

1 1/2 tablespoons chopped flat leaf parsley

1/4 teaspoon paprika

1/2 teaspoon red pepper flakes

Garnish

1 1/2 tablespoons minced cilantro

1 1/2 tablespoons minced flat leaf parsley

2 blood oranges, sliced

(continued)

**Saffron Chicken and Wild Rice Salad
with Raisins and Pine Nuts** *(continued)*

TO MAKE THE CHICKEN

Rinse the rice and soak it in two cups of water overnight. Prepare a marinade by crushing together garlic and ½ teaspoon of salt (using a mortar and pestle). Add the olive oil, saffron, and cilantro. Puree ingredients together. Add minced chilies and continue to puree. (Be sure to wear rubber gloves to protect your hands when mincing the chilies.) Wash and dry the chicken. Put it in a baking dish and coat it with the saffron marinade. Cover and refrigerate for a couple of hours. In a 325°F oven, roast chicken (tightly covered in foil) for two hours. Remove chicken from baking dish immediately and put on a plate to cool.

In a covered pot, bring rice, soaking water, and a couple of pinches of salt to boil. Reduce heat to simmer and cook for forty-five minutes. Put the rice into a large bowl and cover with a clean dishtowel. (Fabric helps to absorb water in rice to ensure a fluffy texture.)

In a pan over medium-high heat roast pine nuts, stirring to prevent burning, for eight to ten minutes until golden. Stir the pine nuts into the rice.

In a small pan over medium heat, sauté the onion in honey and balsamic vinegar for about eight minutes. Add a pinch or two of salt, stir, and add sautéed onions to the rice.

Once the chicken has sufficiently cooled, remove from the bone, cut into bite-size pieces, and add to rice mixture.

Cover raisins in ¼ cup of heated water. Mix together well. Allow raisins to plump (approximately twenty minutes). In a small pot, bring water to a boil. Add the peas, and boil gently for three to four minutes until just tender. Remove peas immediately from cooking water and strain. Remove the raisins from the soaking water and pat dry. Add the raisins, lemon zest, and peas to the rice mixture. Sprinkle approximately ⅓ teaspoon of salt and mix gently.

**Saffron Chicken and Wild Rice Salad
with Raisins and Pine Nuts** *(continued)*

TO MAKE THE SAUCE

Using a mortar and pestle, combine the sauce ingredients as follows: Puree the garlic and sea salt. Add juice, olive oil, cilantro, parsley, and the rest of the ingredients. Continue to puree.

Place the wild rice and chicken salad on a large serving plate. Garnish with minced cilantro and parsley, and surround with slices of blood orange. Serve with sauce on the side.

&ℓℓ

SOUTHWESTERN BEAN SALAD

SIX SERVINGS

2 15-ounce cans soybeans, drained*
1 cup frozen yellow corn, cooked and drained
2 plum tomatoes, seeded and diced
1 small red pepper, diced
$\frac{1}{2}$ cup minced red onion
2 tablespoons minced cilantro
2 teaspoons minced parsley
2 tablespoons extra-virgin olive oil
1 tablespoon red wine vinegar
2–3 teaspoons fresh lemon juice
2 garlic cloves, minced
$\frac{1}{8}$ teaspoon cayenne pepper
Salt to taste
Freshly ground black pepper to taste
Romaine lettuce leaves, for garnish

*Most health-food stores have canned soybeans. Other beans may be substituted if soybeans are not available.

In a large salad bowl, combine the soybeans, corn, tomatoes, red pepper, onion, cilantro, and parsley. In a separate bowl, whisk together oil, vinegar, lemon juice, garlic, cayenne pepper, salt, and black pepper. Pour the mixture over the salad. Cover and refrigerate at least one hour. Serve salad over romaine lettuce leaves.

SPICY PURPLE CABBAGE SALAD

FOUR TO SIX SERVINGS

4 cups shredded purple cabbage
1 cup sliced tomatoes
1 cup thinly sliced radishes
$1/4$ teaspoon cayenne pepper
2 tablespoons Bragg Liquid Aminos
Juice from $1/2$ large lemon
1 tablespoon grated lemon peel*
2–3 pinches of sea salt
2 scallions, minced

*Wash the fruit before grating.

Combine all ingredients, except for scallions. Marinate for thirty minutes.
Garnish with scallions.

WAKAME CUCUMBER SALAD AND ORANGE DRESSING

FOUR SERVINGS

$1/2$ cup wakame
1 medium cucumber
$1/4$ teaspoon sea salt
Pulp of one blood orange or regular orange
$1/8$ cup umeboshi vinegar

Soak the wakame in enough water to cover for thirty minutes. Remove the
center stem. Cut the leaves into half-inch squares. Boil water and dip in
wakame for one minute. Cool. Peel and slice the cucumber and sprinkle
with sea salt. Let stand for twenty minutes and drain. Combine the
wakame, cucumber, and orange pulp in a bowl. Add umeboshi vinegar, toss
well, and serve.

WATERCRESS SALAD

SIX SERVINGS

Salad

1 bunch watercress, chopped
³/₄ cup chopped butter lettuce
¹/₂ cucumber, peeled, quartered, and sliced thin
5 radishes, sliced thin
¹/₂ carrot, shredded

Vinaigrette

3 tablespoons flaxseed oil
1 tablespoon lemon juice
¹/₂ cup filtered water
3 tablespoons rice vinegar
3 tablespoons tamari
2 tablespoons mirin

Toss the vegetables together in a bowl. Whisk vinaigrette ingredients and drizzle over the salad. Lightly toss the ingredients. Let stand for thirty minutes and serve.

WATERCRESS AND CUCUMBER SALAD

FOUR SERVINGS

2 cups watercress, stems removed
2 cucumbers, peeled, halved, seeded, and julienned
4 teaspoons lemon juice
3 teaspoons extra-virgin olive oil
¹/₄ teaspoon salt
Freshly ground black pepper to taste

Toss the watercress and cucumbers together in a bowl. Add lemon juice, oil, salt, and pepper (if desired). Toss to coat and serve.

Vegetarian Dishes

ARAME SEA VEGETABLE WITH SNOW PEAS
FOUR TO SIX SERVINGS

1 cup arame
1 cup snow peas
4 dried shiitake mushrooms
1–2 teaspoons sesame oil
1 tablespoon tamari or soy sauce
2 tablespoons grated ginger
2 tablespoons roasted sesame seeds

Rinse the arame in water and drain. Clean and rinse the snow peas. Wash the mushrooms and soak them in water until they are soft. To speed up the process, you can use boiling water. After the mushrooms are reconstituted, trim off the stems (save them for stock) and slice.

Put sesame oil in a sauté pan. Add the sliced mushrooms and sauté them for five minutes. Add the arame, and just enough water (filtered) to cover the mushrooms. Cover, bring to a boil, and cook for fifteen minutes. Add snow peas and cook for three to five minutes, until snow peas are just tender. Do not overcook. Carefully drain excess liquid, put the mixture into a bowl, and season with soy sauce and ginger. Garnish with sesame seeds.

CURRIED WHOLE-WHEAT COUSCOUS WITH PINE NUTS
FOUR SERVINGS

2 tablespoons pine nuts
1 cup whole-wheat couscous
2 tablespoons curry powder
1¼ cups vegetable broth
1 cup fresh or frozen (thawed) cauliflower florets
1 cup baby carrots, cut into ¼-inch diagonal slices
¼ cup chopped fresh cilantro

In a medium saucepan over medium-high heat, roast pine nuts until golden brown, about one minute, shaking the pan constantly to prevent burning. Add couscous and curry powder and stir to coat couscous. Add broth, cauliflower, and carrots and bring to a boil. Reduce heat to low, cover, and cook two minutes. Remove from heat and let stand five minutes. Add cilantro and fluff with a fork. Serve warm or at room temperature.

FIFTEEN-MINUTE TEX-MEX RICE CASSEROLE
FOUR SERVINGS

2 cups cooked brown rice
1½ cups tomato salsa
1 teaspoon chili pepper
1 15-ounce can black beans, not drained
1 7-ounce can whole-kernel corn or 1 cup frozen whole-kernel corn
2 ounces reduced-fat sharp cheddar cheese, sliced ¼-inch thick
2 tablespoons chopped black or green olives (optional)

In a large mixing bowl, combine the brown rice, salsa, chili pepper, beans, and corn. Spoon into a six-inch square shallow casserole dish. Top with sliced cheese and olives. Microwave on high for twelve minutes, until the ingredients are heated through and the cheese is melted.

GOAT CHEESE AND AVOCADO PITA POCKETS

TWO TO FOUR SERVINGS

2 whole-grain pitas, sliced in half
1 tablespoon miso mustard
1 cup chopped avocado
4 tablespoons crumbled goat cheese
8 black olives, pitted and sliced
$^1/_3$ cup broccoli sprouts
$^1/_2$ cup shredded lettuce
$^1/_4$ cup chopped purple onion

Spread the inside of each pita pocket with mustard. Fill each pocket with equal amounts of the remaining ingredients.

MILLET AND CAULIFLOWER

FOUR SERVINGS

1 cup millet
3 cups water
2 cups coarsely chopped cauliflower
Pinch of sea salt

Wash and drain millet. Dry roast in pan for about three minutes on stovetop over medium heat. Add water, cauliflower, and salt. Cover and bring to a boil. Reduce heat and simmer for about thirty minutes.

> Potatoes contain detoxifying plant compounds such as protease
> inhibitors that protect against harmful fumes from cars and
> trucks as well as radiation.

NEW-WAY POTATOES

FOUR SERVINGS

1 pound Idaho, Yukon gold, or red potatoes, peeled and sliced
$1/2$ teaspoon salt
$1/4$ cup flaxseed oil
$1/4$ cup extra-virgin olive oil

Combine ingredients and spread evenly in baking dish. Bake until soft in a
400-degree oven for approximately sixty minutes. This is a delicious
addition to almost any meal.

QUINOA WITH ROASTED FENNEL

FOUR SERVINGS

1 teaspoon extra-virgin olive oil
2 cups coarsely chopped fennel
2 pinches of sea salt
2 cups filtered water
1 cup uncooked quinoa, rinsed thoroughly
Pinch of whole cloves
Umeboshi vinegar (optional)

Preheat the oven to 400°F. Lightly rub Pyrex dish with half of the oil. Add
fennel and pour the remaining oil over it to coat. Sprinkle with a pinch of
salt. Cover and roast for thirty to forty minutes. Combine water, quinoa,
cloves, and the remaining pinch of salt in a pot. Bring to a boil. Reduce
heat and cover. Simmer until the grain is fluffy and water is fully absorbed,
about fifteen minutes. Remove from heat and remove cloves. Combine with
the roasted fennel. As an option, add a few drops of umeboshi vinegar.

SAVORY TOFU SANDWICH SLICES
WITH MINCED LEEKS

THREE TO FOUR SERVINGS

1 tablespoon light miso
2 tablespoons tahini
2–3 tablespoons filtered water
1 small leek
1 16-ounce package extra-firm tofu
Mesclun greens, for garnish
Grated carrots, for garnish

Preheat the oven to 375°F. In a suribachi or small bowl, combine miso, tahini, and water until blended. Clean the leek by cutting off the dark green top (save it for vegetable stock) and discarding the root. Cut the leek in half lengthwise. Rinse thoroughly in a bowl of water to remove sand, pat dry, and mince. You will have about ⅓ cup minced leek to combine in the suribachi. Crush the minced leek gently with the rest of the ingredients.

Cut the tofu into twelve slices and arrange on a Pyrex dish. Spread the miso-tahini-leek mixture over the tofu, and roast in the oven for twenty minutes. Remove, cool thoroughly, and garnish with mesclun greens and carrots.

STUFFED CABBAGE ROLLS WITH WILD RICE

EIGHT SERVINGS

1 cup wild rice
5 cups water
$\frac{1}{2}$ cup diced onion
2 tablespoons extra-virgin olive oil
$\frac{1}{2}$ cup grated carrots
$\frac{1}{2}$ cup currants or raisins
$\frac{1}{2}$ cup finely chopped mushrooms
$\frac{1}{3}$ cup pine nuts
1 tablespoon finely chopped fresh rosemary
2 tablespoons fresh lemon juice
Salt to taste
Freshly ground black pepper to taste
8 large cabbage leaves
3–4 cups prepared chunky tomato sauce

Rinse and drain the rice. In a small saucepan, bring four cups of water to a boil. Add rice. Reduce heat to low. Cover and simmer for one hour. If any water remains, drain rice. Meanwhile, in a pan over medium heat, sauté the onion in oil for five minutes. Add carrots, currants or raisins, mushrooms, pine nuts, and rosemary, and sauté six to eight minutes more, until the vegetables are tender. Place cooked rice and vegetables in large bowl and mix well. Season with lemon juice, salt, and pepper. (Filling can be refrigerated up to two days.) In a large pan, steam cabbage leaves and remaining water three to four minutes or until leaves are tender but still bright green. Drain and blot dry on clean kitchen towel. Cut away and discard any tough inner stems or leaves. Place $\frac{2}{3}$ cup of the stuffing mixture in the center of a cabbage leaf. Fold sides in toward center, and roll to form neat packages. Repeat with the remaining cabbage leaves. In a large baking dish, pour two cups tomato sauce. Place cabbage rolls on top in a single layer. Spoon another cup or two of sauce over the rolls and cover the baking dish with foil, shiny side down. These can be refrigerated for up to six hours before baking. When you are ready to bake, preheat oven to 350°F. Bake twenty to thirty minutes, until piping hot.

TABBOULEH WITH WHITE BEANS AND FETA

FOUR SERVINGS

1 5.25-ounce box tabbouleh salad mix
1 19-ounce can cannellini beans, rinsed and drained
2 tablespoons fresh lemon juice
1 teaspoon dried oregano
1 cup diced tomato
1 cup frozen green peas, thawed
2 tablespoons crumbled feta cheese

Prepare the tabbouleh according to package instructions, omitting any oil and adding white beans, lemon, and oregano. Once the liquid is absorbed, add the tomato and peas and toss. Divide into four servings and top each with feta cheese.

WILD RICE

TWO SERVINGS

2 cups filtered water
1 cup wild rice
2 pinches sea salt

For fluffy rice, bring water, rice, and salt to a boil. When boiling resumes, reduce heat to low. Cook for about one hour. Fluff with a fork before serving.

Seafood Dishes

BRAISED GINGER SHRIMP

FOUR SERVINGS

3 cloves garlic, minced
¼ cup Bragg Liquid Aminos
Juice of 1 lemon
1 pound large shrimp, peeled and cleaned
1 large onion, cut into 1-inch chunks
1 cup chopped celery
2 teaspoons extra-virgin olive oil
1 cup chopped carrots
2 sprigs minced parsley + chopped parsley for garnish
3 tablespoons minced ginger
⅓ teaspoon cloves
2 cups filtered water or vegetable stock
1 pound asparagus, trimmed and cleaned

In a suribachi, grind and press two of the garlic cloves into Bragg Aminos and lemon juice. Marinade shrimp in this mixture for one to two hours. In a pot over medium heat, sauté the remaining garlic clove, onion, and celery in olive oil until mixture begins to brown, about two minutes. Add the carrots, parsley, two tablespoons of the ginger, the cloves, and the vegetable stock or water. Bring to a boil. Place the asparagus in a steamer basket with shrimp. Add the remaining tablespoon of ginger. Place in the same pot, cover, and steam until shrimp is cooked, about five minutes. Serve shrimp over asparagus and ladle broth from bottom of pot onto each serving. Garnish with fresh chopped parsley.

EAST-WEST STEAMED CHILEAN SEA BASS WITH MISO SAUCE

THREE TO FOUR SERVINGS

1¹/₃ pounds Chilean sea bass, with the skin on, cut into 3–4 pieces

Rub

³/₄ teaspoon ground cumin seeds
2 pinches of salt
1 tablespoon extra-virgin olive oil
1 teaspoon lemon juice
2 tablespoons light miso

Sauce

12 cherry tomatoes
6 cloves garlic
¹/₂ lemon
¹/₄ teaspoon red pepper flakes
Several large kale or romaine lettuce leaves

Rinse fish and pat dry. Using a suribachi or mortar and pestle, crush the cumin seeds and mix with salt. Add the olive oil, lemon juice, and miso. Massage the mixture into fish. Place fish in a covered container and refrigerate for two to three hours.

Rinse tomatoes and put them into a bowl. Bring water (enough to cover the tomatoes) to a boil. Pour the water over the tomatoes and let stand for about seven minutes. Strain the tomatoes, cool, and peel. Cut peeled tomatoes in half and lightly squeeze out seeds. Using a food processor combine the tomatoes, garlic, lemon, and red pepper.

Line the bottom of a steamer with cleaned (and dried) kale or lettuce leaves. Place fish on top of leaves. Cover with sauce, and steam for fifteen minutes.

Wooden skewers need to be soaked in water for thirty minutes to prevent burning while grilling. Assemble the skewers ahead of time and baste them with marinade.

MIDDLE EASTERN FISH KABOBS
FOUR SERVINGS

Marinade
2 tablespoons extra-virgin olive oil
4 tablespoons lemon juice
$\frac{1}{4}$ teaspoon cumin
1 teaspoon turmeric
3 bay leaves
Sea salt to taste
Freshly ground black pepper to taste
6 cloves garlic, minced

Skewers
$\frac{1}{2}$ pound cubed salmon
$\frac{1}{2}$ pound large sea scallops
1 pound cubed tomatoes or halved cherry tomatoes
2 medium onions, chopped
Lemon wedges, for garnish
2–3 sprigs fresh rosemary or mint

Combine the olive oil, lemon juice, cumin, turmeric, bay leaves, salt, pepper, and garlic and mix well. Pour this over the fish and scallops and marinate for two hours. Skewer the fish and vegetables. Place under the broiler. Cook for about three minutes. Turn and baste with marinade and continue to cook for another three or four minutes. Garnish with lemon wedges and rosemary (or mint) and serve over long-grain brown rice.

ORANGE GLAZED SALMON
FOUR SERVINGS

$1/2$ cup orange juice
1 tablespoon grated fresh ginger
2 teaspoons sesame oil
2 tablespoons soy sauce
1 pound center-cut salmon fillets, cut into 4 pieces
1 tablespoon cornstarch
1 tablespoon filtered water

In a medium bowl, combine the orange juice, ginger, sesame oil, and soy sauce. Add salmon. Cover and refrigerate for thirty minutes. Drain the fish and reserve the marinade. Place salmon fillets on a broiler pan lined with foil and oiled. Broil salmon ten to fifteen minutes or until it is opaque in the center. Put the reserved marinade in a saucepan and bring to a boil. In a separate small bowl, mix the cornstarch with the water. Add to the sauce and cook one minute until the mixture has thickened. Serve the salmon with orange sauce on the side.

SALMON WITH PECAN CRUNCH COATING
FOUR SERVINGS

4 6-ounce salmon fillets
Salt to taste
Freshly ground black pepper to taste
2 tablespoons Dijon mustard
2 tablespoons extra-virgin olive oil
$1^1/_2$ tablespoons honey
$1/4$ cup bread crumbs
$1/4$ cup chopped pecans
2 teaspoons chopped fresh parsley

Preheat the oven to 450°F. Sprinkle salmon liberally with salt and pepper. Place fillets, skin side down, in a lightly greased baking dish. In a small mixing bowl, combine mustard, butter, and honey. Brush this mixture on fillets. Combine bread crumbs, pecans, and parsley and sprinkle the mixture evenly on top of each fillet. Bake ten minutes or until fish flakes easily.

-ℓℓℓ

SALMON TERIYAKI OVER SOBA NOODLES

TWO SERVINGS

3 cloves garlic, minced
$1/3$ cup + 2 tablespoons barbecue sauce
$3/4$–1 pound salmon steaks
1 large leek
4 tablespoons filtered water
$1/3$ pound thin soba noodles
$3/4$ cup carrots, cut into matchsticks
$3/4$ cup sliced onion
1 teaspoon sea salt
$2 1/3$ tablespoons soy sauce
$1 1/2$ tablespoons sesame oil
3–4 tablespoons freshly grated ginger

Preheat the oven to 325°F. In a suribachi (or with a mortar and pestle), grind minced garlic and barbecue sauce together. Clean salmon and pat it dry. Rub garlic-barbecue sauce all over salmon. Clean the leek and cut in half lengthwise and then in half again horizontally. Prepare the salmon for cooking by placing it atop the cut leek in a Pyrex dish. The leek provides flavor as well as serves as a roasting rack. Make sure the sauce coats the salmon. Combine two tablespoons of the water with an additional two tablespoons of barbecue sauce and mix. Add the mixture around the edge of the leeks. Cover the baking dish with foil, and place it in the oven. Roast the salmon for twenty-five minutes. Turn the oven up to 400°F, remove foil, and continue to cook for another five to seven minutes. The fish should be succulent but not overcooked.

In a large pot of rapidly boiling water, cook the soba noodles for six to eight minutes. Meanwhile, sauté the carrots in the remaining two tablespoons of filtered water for seven minutes over medium heat. Add the sliced onions, and continue to sauté for another seven minutes. Add salt and $1/3$ tablespoon of the soy sauce. When noodles have finished cooking, drain and toss them with the remaining two tablespoons of soy sauce and sesame oil. Add fresh ginger. Combine the sautéed carrots and onions with the soba noodles. Toss well. Serve the salmon on a bed of soba noodles.

SHRIMP JAMBALAYA

SIX SERVINGS

1½ pounds large fresh shrimp, peeled and cleaned
3 cups cooked basmati rice
2 tablespoons extra-virgin olive oil
12 ounces shiitake mushrooms, sliced
6 cloves garlic, minced
4 shallots, minced
1 medium onion, diced
3 pinches salt
1 red pepper, diced
1 large carrot, diced
1 cup diced celery
½ teaspoon chopped fresh oregano
2 cups reconstituted sun-dried tomatoes
¼ cup red miso
1 cup filtered water
Bottled hot sauce to taste
3 teaspoons turmeric
1 cup blanched green peas
½ cup chopped flat leaf parsley

Preheat the oven to 350°F. Combine the shrimp and rice in a large casserole dish. In a saucepan, heat one tablespoon of the olive oil and sauté the mushrooms, garlic, shallots, and onion with a pinch or two of salt for approximately five minutes. In another pan, sauté the pepper, carrot, celery, oregano, and a pinch of salt in the remaining tablespoon of olive oil until tender. Combine in a blender the tomatoes, miso, water, hot sauce, and turmeric. Puree. Add the sautéed red pepper, carrot, and celery into the shrimp and rice mixture. Pour the sauce over the mixture and stir gently to combine. Cover and bake for thirty minutes. Remove from oven and fluff with a fork. Add the peas, parsley, and more salt and hot sauce if desired. Serve immediately.

SOUTH-OF-THE-BORDER CHILI GREY SOLE

TWO TO THREE SERVINGS

1 pound grey sole
2 tablespoons lemon juice
$1/4$ teaspoon chili powder
$1/4$ teaspoon chili pepper flakes
Several pinches of sea salt
2 cloves garlic, minced
$3/4$ cup chopped onion
2 tablespoons filtered water
$1 1/2$ cups canned diced tomatoes and green chilies
1–2 tablespoons extra-virgin olive oil

Preheat the oven to 400°F. Clean and dry the fish. In a small bowl, mix lemon juice, chili powder, chili pepper flakes, a pinch of salt, and garlic. Pour this mixture over the fish and set it aside to marinate. In a small saucepan, sauté the onion in the water until just tender. Add a pinch or two of salt. Combine with the diced tomatoes and green chilies in a Pyrex dish. Add the fish on top. Bake the fish uncovered for seven minutes. Turn the fish and tomato-onion mixture out onto a serving plate. Lightly drizzle each serving with olive oil. Serve immediately.

STEAMED SALMON AND ROSEMARY IN MISO GARLIC SAUCE

TWO SERVINGS

6 cloves garlic, minced
Juice of 1 lemon
2 teaspoons barley miso
2 salmon steaks ($1/2$ pound each), cleaned and dried
Handful of rosemary leaves

In a suribachi, grind and press the garlic into the lemon juice and miso until thoroughly combined. Place the salmon in a steamer basket, pour on sauce, and sprinkle with rosemary. Steam over medium heat for about seven to ten minutes or until done. Don't overcook. Garnish with fresh rosemary.

SZECHUAN SEA BASS

TWO SERVINGS

2 serrano chilies
3 cloves garlic, minced
³/₄ cup chopped tomatoes
3 tablespoons lemon juice
1¹/₂ tablespoons light miso
³/₄ pound Chilean sea bass
2 tablespoons chopped cilantro

Preheat the oven to 425°F. Rinse and dry the chilies. Then mince them and put them into a suribachi. Wear rubber gloves to protect your hands from fiery serrano seeds. Add the minced garlic. Combine the tomatoes, lemon juice, and miso with the ingredients in the suribachi. You will have a chunky sauce of mayonnaise-like consistency. Rinse the fish and pat it dry. Put it into a Pyrex dish and top with the sauce. Cover tightly with foil. Roast in the oven for twenty minutes. Turn the fish out onto a large plate. Pour the remaining sauce over it. Garnish it with chopped cilantro. Serve with roasted sweet potatoes or over light udon noodles flecked with cilantro for an aromatic, richly flavorful meal.

ℓℓ

VEGETABLE AND FISH STIR-FRY

FOUR SERVINGS

1½ tablespoons canola or extra-virgin olive oil
1½ pounds orange roughy, skin removed and cut into 1½-inch pieces
1 clove garlic, minced
1 shallot, minced
1 cup chopped red pepper
1 cup sliced celery
1 cup fresh snow peas, trimmed
1 cup sliced water chestnuts
½ cup orange juice
2 teaspoons cornstarch
1 teaspoon sesame oil
1 teaspoon rice vinegar
1 teaspoon soy sauce
Chopped scallions for garnish
2 cups hot cooked brown rice

Heat one tablespoon of the oil in heavy skillet over medium-high heat. Add fish and stir-fry gently for two or three minutes until the fish is opaque. Remove the fish from skillet and set aside. Add the remaining oil to the skillet and stir-fry the garlic and shallot for one minute. Add the red pepper, celery, snow peas, and water chestnuts. Cover the pan and steam for two minutes. Meanwhile, in a measuring cup or small dish, combine the orange juice, cornstarch, sesame oil, rice vinegar, and soy sauce. Add this mixture to the skillet and cook until the sauce thickens, about one minute. Return the fish to pan and cook one minute. Garnish with chopped scallions. Serve with rice.

Pasta Dishes

PASTA WITH RAISINS, CAPERS, AND PINE NUTS

FOUR SERVINGS

$1/2$ cup raisins
1 pound ziti or other tubular pasta
$1/2$ cup extra-virgin olive oil
$1/3$ cup dry bread crumbs
2 tablespoons butter
3 tablespoons pine nuts
3 tablespoons drained capers
6 anchovy fillets, mashed
$1/4$ cup reserved pasta cooking water
Salt to taste
Freshly ground black pepper to taste

Place the raisins in a small bowl and cover them with water. Set aside. Cook the pasta in lightly salted water until it is *al dente* (firm to the bite). While the pasta is cooking, heat one tablespoon of the olive oil in a small pan. Add the bread crumbs and cook, stirring frequently, over moderate heat for four minutes or until the bread crumbs are browned. Set aside. Drain the pasta; reserve ¼ cup of the cooking water. Drain the raisins; set aside. In a large sauté pan, heat the butter plus one tablespoon of the olive oil. Add the pine nuts and cook for three to four minutes over moderate heat until lightly browned. Add the capers, raisins, and anchovy fillets. Cook, stirring frequently, for about two minutes. Add the drained pasta and the remaining olive oil and cook, stirring constantly to break up the pieces and coat the pasta with the sauce. Pour in the reserved cooking water and sprinkle with salt and pepper. Continue to cook for another minute or so, until the pasta is thoroughly glazed. Sprinkle the bread crumbs over the pasta and toss a few times to coat the pasta thoroughly. Serve immediately.

PASTA WITH VEGETARIAN SAUSAGE AND ROASTED TOMATOES

FOUR SERVINGS

6 ripe tomatoes
2 tablespoons extra-virgin olive oil
3 tablespoons chopped fresh rosemary
6 cloves garlic, minced
3 pinches dried oregano
Sea salt to taste
Freshly ground black pepper to taste
1/2 cup basil leaves
1/4 cup extra-virgin olive oil
8 vegetarian Italian sausages
1 1-pound package wild yam soba noodles
2 cloves garlic, minced fine
2 chili peppers, seeded and chopped

Preheat the oven to 250°F. Slice the tomatoes and arrange them in a Pyrex baking dish with the oil, rosemary, garlic, oregano, salt, and pepper. Roast approximately sixty minutes until very tender. Remove from the oven and set aside to cool. When the tomatoes cool enough to handle, remove skins and transfer to large bowl. Chop the tomatoes and set aside with juices.

In a food processor, chop the basil leaves. Add two tablespoons of the olive oil and puree. Transfer the mixture from the food processor to a bowl. Set aside. Meanwhile, cut the sausage into bite-size pieces. In an iron skillet over low heat, cook the sausage approximately fifteen minutes, turning every four or five minutes. Turn up to medium heat for the last couple of minutes to achieve a light browning. Remove sausage from pan and set aside.

Cook pasta according to instructions. Set pasta aside to drain.

In the same skillet you used to cook the sausage, put in about three tablespoons olive oil, the garlic, and peppers. Cook gently over low heat to release aroma. Sauté in this way for about four minutes. Add tomatoes with juices. Heat for two minutes, then add the sausage. Transfer the pasta to a serving bowl. Pour the sauce over the pasta and drizzle with the basil puree. Toss thoroughly and serve.

ℓℓ

PIQUANT PAN-SAUTÉED SOBA
TWO SERVINGS

4 ounces (half an 8-ounce package) soba noodles
¼ pound firm tofu
½ bunch watercress or 1 cup chopped scallions
1 clove garlic, minced
1 teaspoon extra-virgin olive oil
½ teaspoon tamari
1 teaspoon miso mustard

Cook the noodles and drain. Cut the tofu into small cubes and pat dry. Wash watercress (or scallions) and chop into one-inch pieces. In a skillet over medium heat, sauté the garlic in oil. Gently add the tofu and continue to sauté. Add the watercress or scallions and continue to sauté for another minute. Toss in noodles and cook for two to three minutes. In a small bowl, whisk together tamari and mustard and add to them to the contents of skillet. Remove from heat after one minute and serve.

ℓℓ

ROASTED GARLIC AND RED LENTIL SAUCE OVER PASTA
FOUR SERVINGS

3–4 cloves of unpeeled elephant garlic, washed
1 teaspoon extra-virgin olive oil
1 cup red lentils, washed
1 3-inch strip of Kombu, wiped and soaked
5 cups filtered water
3 tablespoons fresh minced cilantro
2–3 pinches of sea salt
2 tablespoons minced parsley
1 pound pasta, cooked*

*Use low-wheat or wheat-free pastas made from Jerusalem artichoke, brown rice, kamut, or quinoa. Any shape pasta may be used.

Roasted Garlic and Red Lentil Sauce over Pasta *(continued)*

Preheat the oven to 350°F. Coat the inside of a Pyrex baking dish and the cloves of garlic with olive oil. Roast the garlic, uncovered, about one hour until soft. Test with sharp knife. Remove from the oven and let cool. Place the lentils and Kombu in a pot. Add the water and bring to a low boil. Reduce heat and cook for about twenty minutes. After ten minutes salt the lentils to taste. Continue to cook, removing the residue periodically. Peel garlic and combine it with the lentils and cilantro in a blender. Puree. Serve over pasta. Garnish with minced parsley.

ℓℓ

SOBA NOODLES AL PESTO
FOUR TO SIX SERVINGS

1 pound buckwheat soba noodles
$1/3$ cup pine nuts, rinsed
$2^1/2$ cups chopped cilantro
$2^1/2$ cups chopped parsley
$1/4$ cup Bragg Liquid Aminos
2 tablespoons extra-virgin olive oil
3–4 cloves garlic, chopped
3 shallots, minced
$1/3$ cup filtered water

Cook noodles according to package directions. Drain and set aside. In a cast-iron or stainless steel skillet over low heat, roast the pine nuts, stirring constantly. Watch closely to avoid burning. Combine all ingredients except noodles in blender and process until smooth. Serve over soba noodles.

ℒ

TASTY MUSHROOM LASAGNA
NINE SERVINGS

12 lasagna noodles
16 ounces soft tofu
³/₄ cup low-fat ricotta cheese
¹/₂ cup low-fat cottage cheese
³/₄ cup shredded part-skim mozzarella cheese
1 teaspoon dried basil
1 teaspoon dried oregano
¹/₄ teaspoon freshly ground black pepper
¹/₄ teaspoon salt
2 teaspoons extra-virgin olive oil
1 8-ounce package mushrooms, cut into ¹/₄-inch slices
3 cups low-fat marinara sauce
¹/₄ cup grated Parmesan cheese or grated soy Parmesan

Boil noodles according to package directions. Drain and set aside. Preheat
the oven to 375°F. In medium bowl, mash the tofu with a fork. Add
ricotta, cottage and mozzarella cheeses, basil, oregano, pepper, and salt.
Mix until smooth. In a medium skillet, heat oil over medium-high heat.
Add mushrooms and sauté until browned, about five to six minutes. Drain
any excess moisture.

Pour about half a cup of marinara sauce on the bottom of a large baking
pan. Add four lasagna noodles. Spread some tofu filling on top of noodles.
Sprinkle with some mushrooms. Add more marinara sauce to cover
mushrooms, then add four more lasagna noodles. Repeat layers until all
ingredients are used—you will have three layers of noodles—ending with
sauce. Sprinkle Parmesan cheese liberally over the top of the lasagna.
Bake, covered, for about thirty minutes. Uncover and continue baking ten
more minutes or until the cheese is bubbly. Remove from the oven and let
stand about twenty minutes before slicing.

UDON NOODLES WITH UMEBOSHI DRESSING

FOUR SERVINGS

1 pound udon rice noodles
1¹/₂ tablespoons umeboshi paste
1 tablespoon sesame tahini
¹/₂ cup water
3 scallions, chopped fine
2 tablespoons black sesame seeds

Boil water for the noodles. In a suribachi, blend umeboshi paste and tahini. Slowly add water. Blend well. Add chopped scallions and blend again. If consistency is too thick, add a little more water. Cook the udon until tender, about eight to ten minutes. Drain. Mix in sauce. Top with sesame seeds.

Chicken Dishes

❧

BROWN AND WILD RICE WITH CHICKEN AND MUSHROOMS
TWO SERVINGS

1 4.5-ounce box brown and wild rice mix with mushrooms
1 teaspoon extra-virgin olive oil
1 teaspoon dried thyme
2 cups fresh or frozen (thawed) broccoli florets
1 cup cubed cooked chicken
2 tablespoons chopped fresh parsley

Cook the rice according to package instructions, using half or more of the seasoning packet, according to taste. Add olive oil and thyme. Meanwhile, steam fresh broccoli or cook frozen broccoli according to package directions. Add broccoli to rice mixture one minute before the rice is done. Toss rice with chicken and parsley. Serve warm.

❧

CHICKEN WITH LEMON, OLIVES, CAPERS, AND ROSEMARY
FOUR SERVINGS

2 tablespoons extra-virgin olive oil
1 whole chicken, cut up
1 onion, chopped
2 cloves garlic, chopped
2 lemons, sliced
1 tablespoon capers, rinsed
3 sprigs fresh rosemary
1/2 cup sliced green olives
1/2 cup sliced black olives

Chicken with Lemon, Olives, Capers, and Rosemary *(continued)*

Heat the olive oil in a sauté pan. Add the chicken and brown over moderate heat approximately ten minutes. Remove the chicken and set aside. Discard excess fat from the pan, leaving only a film on the bottom. Add the onion and cook over moderate heat two to three minutes. Add the garlic and cook briefly. Return the chicken to the pan and add lemon, capers, rosemary, and olives. Cover and cook about twenty-five minutes or until chicken is cooked through. Baste occasionally.

EASY ROASTED CHICKEN AND THYME IN PARCHMENT
FOUR SERVINGS

1 tablespoon minced garlic
$1/2$ cup Bragg Liquid Aminos
Juice of 2 lemons
3 tablespoons minced fresh thyme
2 chicken breasts, skinned, split, washed, and patted dry
4 pieces of 15-inch-long parchment paper
1 leek, chopped
1 large clove of elephant garlic, sliced, or 2 shallots, sliced

Preheat the oven to 350°F. In a suribachi (or using a mortar and pestle), press the minced garlic into a small amount of the Bragg Aminos. Add the remainder of the Bragg Aminos as well as lemon juice, continuing to grind and press the garlic into the liquids. Add one tablespoon of the minced thyme and mix well. Place chicken breasts in a Pyrex dish. Cover with the garlic-Bragg-lemon mixture and marinate for about one hour, turning the meat over occasionally.

Place each split chicken breast in the center of a piece of parchment paper and add the leek and sliced garlic or shallots. Bring short sides of paper together over the chicken and secure, through a combination of rolling and folding. Close the other ends in the same way. Proficiency will improve with practice. Make sure to leave a space between the parchment and the top of the meat. Bake approximately twenty minutes.

HERBED COUSCOUS WITH CHICKEN

FOUR SERVINGS

2 tablespoons extra-virgin olive oil
1 cup sliced leeks
3 cloves garlic, minced
1 cup quartered Brussels sprouts
2 cups peeled, bite-size cubes of butternut squash
1 pound skinless, boneless chicken breasts, cut into bite-size chunks
1½ cups fat-free chicken broth, divided
Salt to taste
Freshly ground black pepper to taste
1 cup whole-wheat couscous
2–4 tablespoons minced herb blend of fresh sage, thyme, and marjoram
¼ cup minced parsley

In a large pan heat olive oil and sauté leeks, garlic, Brussels sprouts, and butternut squash for five minutes. Add chicken and ¼ cup of the broth. Season with salt and pepper. Cover and simmer five to ten minutes or until chicken is cooked and vegetables are tender. Stir in the couscous. Add remaining chicken broth and the herb blend. Cover and simmer five more minutes or until liquid is absorbed. Adjust the seasonings to taste. Stir in parsley.

Desserts

CARROT CAKE WITH CREAM CHEESE FROSTING
TEN SERVINGS

Cake
2 cups whole-grain pastry flour

2 teaspoons baking powder

2 teaspoons baking soda

1 teaspoon ground cinnamon

$1/4$ teaspoon salt

$1/4$ cup granulated sugar

2 eggs

2 egg whites

$1/3$ cup canola oil

2 teaspoons vanilla extract

1 cup buttermilk or fat-free plain yogurt

2 cups finely shredded carrots

$1/2$ cup golden raisins

$1/2$ cup well-drained crushed pineapple

Frosting
2 ounces reduced-fat cream cheese, softened

2 tablespoons unsalted butter, softened

$3/4$ cup confectioners' sugar

$1/2$ teaspoon vanilla extract

3 tablespoons chopped walnuts or pecans

(continued)

Carrot Cake with Cream Cheese Frosting *(continued)*

TO MAKE THE CAKE

Preheat the oven to 350°F. Coat two eight-inch round cake pans with cooking spray. In a medium bowl, combine the flour, baking powder, baking soda, cinnamon, and salt. In a separate large bowl, beat the granulated sugar, eggs, egg whites, oil, and vanilla extract with a wire whisk until well blended and frothy. Whisk in the buttermilk or yogurt. Stir in the carrots, raisins, and pineapple. Add the flour mixture and stir just until blended. Evenly divide the batter between the prepared cake pans. Bake twenty-five minutes, or until a wooden pick inserted into the center comes out clean. Cool the cakes in the pans on a rack for thirty minutes. Loosen the edges and turn the cakes out onto racks to cool completely.

TO MAKE THE FROSTING

In a medium bowl, with an electric mixer on medium-high speed, beat the cream cheese and butter just until blended. Beat in the confectioners' sugar and vanilla extract until the texture of the frosting is light and fluffy. Frost cooled cake and sprinkle with walnuts or pecans.

CHOCOLATE LOVER'S CAKE WITH RASPBERRY SAUCE

TEN SERVINGS

Cake
    1¹/₂ cups semisweet dark chocolate chips
    1 19-ounce can (2 cups) cooked chickpeas, drained and rinsed*
    4 eggs or 1 cup egg substitute
    ¹/₂ cup sugar
    ¹/₂ teaspoon baking powder
    1 tablespoon powdered sugar

Raspberry Sauce
    ¹/₂ cup seedless raspberry jam
    2 teaspoons fresh lemon juice
    1 pint fresh raspberries

    *Using legumes instead of flour adds fiber and protein and reduces unhealthful spikes in blood sugar.

Chocolate Lover's Cake with Raspberry Sauce *(continued)*

TO MAKE THE CAKE

Preheat oven to 350°F. In small bowl, melt chocolate chips in the microwave two minutes on medium power. In a blender or food processor, combine the beans, eggs, sugar, baking powder, and the melted chocolate, and process until smooth. Pour the batter into nonstick nine-inch round cake pan. Bake forty-five minutes or until a knife inserted in the center comes out clean. Cool thoroughly. Sprinkle with powdered sugar.

TO MAKE THE RASPBERRY SAUCE

In a small bowl, microwave jam until it is completely melted, about one minute. Stir in the lemon juice and berries. Serve over cake wedges.

le

GINGER PUMPKIN PIE

EIGHT SERVINGS

Dough

$1^1/_4$ cups whole-grain pastry flour
$^1/_4$ teaspoon salt
3 tablespoons canola oil
2 tablespoons cold butter, cut into small pieces
2–4 tablespoons ice water

Filling

$^1/_2$ cup packed brown sugar
1 egg
2 egg whites
$1^1/_2$ teaspoons vanilla extract
$^1/_2$ teaspoon ground cinnamon
$^1/_2$ teaspoon ground ginger
$^1/_4$ teaspoon ground nutmeg
$^1/_8$ teaspoon salt
1 15-ounce can plain pumpkin
1 cup fat-free evaporated milk

(continued)

Ginger Pumpkin Pie *(continued)*

TO MAKE THE DOUGH

In a food processor, combine the flour and salt. Pulse until blended. Add
the oil and butter. Pulse until the mixture resembles a fine meal. Add the
water, one tablespoon at a time, as needed, and pulse just until the dough
forms large clumps. Form the dough into a rough ball and flatten into a
disk. Cover and refrigerate for at least one hour, or until well chilled. Coat
a nine-inch pie pan with cooking spray. Place the dough between two
pieces of waxed paper and, with a floured rolling pin, roll it into a twelve-
inch circle. Lift off the top sheet of waxed paper and quickly invert the
dough into the prepared pie pan. Peel off the second piece of waxed paper.
Press the dough into the pan and up onto the rim, patching it where
necessary. Turn under the rim and flute as desired. Refrigerate the crust
while you prepare the filling.

TO MAKE THE FILLING

In a large bowl, with a wire whisk, beat the brown sugar, egg, egg whites,
vanilla extract, cinnamon, ginger, nutmeg, and salt until well blended.
Whisk in the pumpkin and evaporated milk.

Preheat the oven to 425°F. Pour the filling into the chilled crust. Bake
fifteen minutes. Reduce the oven temperature to 350°F. Bake for twenty-
five minutes longer, or until a knife inserted into the center comes out
clean. Cool on a rack before slicing.

OATMEAL COOKIES WITH CRANBERRIES AND CHOCOLATE CHIPS

EIGHTEEN SERVINGS

2 cups rolled oats
1/2 cup whole-grain pastry flour
3/4 teaspoon baking soda
1/2 teaspoon ground cinnamon
1/4 teaspoon salt
1/2 cup packed brown sugar
1/3 cup canola oil
3 egg whites
2 teaspoons vanilla extract
3/4 cup dried sweetened cranberries
1/2 cup semisweet chocolate chips

Preheat the oven to 350°F. Coat two large baking sheets with cooking spray. In a large bowl, combine the oats, flour, baking soda, cinnamon, and salt. In a separate medium bowl, beat the brown sugar, oil, egg whites, and vanilla extract with a wire whisk until smooth. Stir in the cranberries and chocolate chips. Stir the brown sugar mixture into the flour mixture just until blended. Drop the batter by scant tablespoons onto the prepared baking sheets. Bake for ten minutes, or until the cookies are golden brown. Place the cookies on racks and allow them to cool completely. Store in an airtight container.

RESOURCE GUIDE

Organizations

Agency for Toxic Substances and Disease Registry
(A division of the Centers for Disease Control)
Phone: (888) 42-ATSDR or (888) 422-8737
Fax: (404) 498-0057
E-mail: ATSDRIC@cdc.gov
Website: www.atsdr.cdc.gov
(Up-to-date listing of chemical toxins specific to region)

Alive Academy of Nutrition
7436 Fraser Park Drive
Burnaby, BC V5J 5B9
Canada
Phone: (604) 435-1919

Allergy and Environmental Health Association
85 Walmsley Boulevard
Toronto, ON M4V 1X7
Canada
Phone: (613) 860-2342 or (819) 777-5848
(Information clearinghouse for people with environmental sensitivities)

AMC Cancer Research Center
1600 Pierce Street
Denver, CO 80214
Phone: (303) 239-3422 (information and counseling)
(800) 321-1557 (research and foundation information)
Website: www.cicl.amc.org

American Academy of Pediatrics
Phone: (202) 347-8600

American College for the Advancement of Medicine
23121 Verdugo Drive #204
Laguna Hills, CA 92653
Phone: (714) 583-7666
(Resource for chelation therapy)

American College of Occupational and Environmental Medicine
55 West Seegers Road
Arlington Heights, IL 60005-3919
Phone: (847) 632-0402
Fax: (847) 228-1856

American Environmental Health Foundation
8345 Walnut Hill Lane, Suite 225
Dallas, TX 75231
Phone: (800) 428-2343
Website: www.aehf.com
(Environmentally safe products catalog)

American Industrial Hygiene Association
2700 Prosperity Avenue, Suite 250
Fairfax, VA 22031
Phone: (703) 849-8888
Fax: (703) 207-3561
Website: www.aiha.org
(Listing of laboratories that will test for pesticide residue)

American Lung Association
1740 Broadway
New York, NY 10019
Phone: (212) 315-8700
E-mail: info@lungusa.org
Website: www.lungusa.org

Beyond Pesticides
701 E Street SE, Suite 200
Washington, DC 20003
Phone: (202) 543-5450
Fax: (202) 543-4791
Website: www.beyondpesticides.org
(Up-to-date information on legislation regarding pesticides)

Bio-Integral Resource Center (BIRC)
P.O. Box 7414
Berkeley, CA 94707
Phone: (510) 524-2567
Fax: (510) 524-1758
E-mail: birc@igc.org
Website: www.birc.org
(Safer alternatives to toxic pest management)

Bristol Cancer Help Centre
Grove House, Cornwallis Grove
Clifton, Bristol B28 4PG
England
Phone: 011-44-1179-743216

British Columbia Naturopathic Association
409 Granville Street, #218
Vancouver, BC V6C 1T2
Canada
Phone: (604) 688-8336

CambridgeSoft
100 Cambridge Park Drive
Cambridge, MA 02140
Phone: (617) 588-9100
Fax: (617) 588-9190
E-mail: info@cambridgesoft.com
Website: www.chemfinder.com

Canadian College of Naturopathic Medicine
2300 Yonge Street, 18th Floor, Box 2431
Toronto, ON M4P 1E4
Canada
Phone: (416) 436-8585

Center for Science in the Public Interest
1875 Connecticut Avenue NW, #300
Washington, DC 20009-5728
Phone: (202) 332-9110
Fax: (202) 265-4954
Website: www.cspinet.org

Consumer Health Organization of Canada
1220 Sheppard Avenue East, #412
Toronto, ON M2K 2S5
Canada
Phone: (416) 498-0986

Dental Amalgam Toxicity Removal
Ronald W. Niklaus, D.M.D.
Camp Hill, PA 17011
Phone: (717) 737-3353

Doctor's Data, Inc.
170 West Roosevelt Road
Chicago, IL 60185
Phone: (800) 323-2784

Environmental Health Center of Dallas
8345 Walnut Hill Lane, Suite 220
Dallas, TX 75231
Phone: (214) 368-4132
Website: www.ehcd.com

Environmental Protection Agency
Ariel Rios Building
1200 Pennsylvania Avenue NW
Washington, DC 20460
Phone: (202) 260-2090
Websites: www.epa.gov
www.epa.gov/pesticides
(Information regarding the status of registered pesticides)

Environmental Protection Agency's Safe Drinking Water Hotline
Phone: (800) 426-4791

Food and Nutrition Information Center
Agricultural Research Service, USDA
National Agricultural Library, Room 105
10301 Baltimore Avenue
Beltsville, MD 20705-2351
Phone: (301) 504-5719
Fax: (301) 504-6856
E-mail: fnic@nal.usda.gov
Website: www.nal.usda.gov/fnic

Foundation for Advancements in Science and Education
4801 Wilshire Boulevard, Suite 215
Los Angeles, CA 90010
Phone: (323) 937-9911
Websites: www.fafemet.org
www.futurechannels.com

Genetic Alliance, Inc.
4301 Connecticut Avenue NW, Suite 404
Washington, DC 20008-2304
Phone: (202) 966-5557
Fax: (202) 966-8553
E-mail: info@geneticalliance.org
Website: www.geneticalliance.org

Great Smokies Diagnostic Laboratory
63 Zillicoa Street
Asheville, NC 28801
Phone: (800) 522-4762
Website: www.gsdl.com

Greater Boston Physicians for Social Responsibility
Phone: (617) 497-7440

Healthfinder
P.O. Box 1133
Washington, DC 20013-1133
E-mail: healthfinder@nhic.org
Website: www.healthfinder.gov

Immuno Diagnostic Lab
10930 Bigge Street
San Leandro, CA 94577
Phone: (800) 888-1113

International Academy of Oral Medicine and Toxicology
P.O. Box 608531
Orlando, FL 32860
Phone: (407) 298-2450
Fax: (407) 298-3075
Website: www.iaomt.org
(Health-care professionals and scientists for nontoxic dentistry)

Life Extension Foundation
P.O. Box 229120
Hollywood, FL 33022
Phone: (954) 766-8433
(800) 544-4440 (orders)
(800) 678-8989 (customer service)
Fax: (954) 761-9199
Website: www.lef.org

Metamatrix Medical Laboratory
#110-5000 Peachtree Industrial Boulevard
Norcross, GA 30071
Phone: (800) 221-4640

National Alliance to End Childhood Lead Poisoning
227 Massachusetts Avenue NE, #200
Washington, DC 20002
Phone: (202) 543-1147

The National Cancer Institute
Cancer Information Service
Phone: (800) 422-6237

National Center for Human Genome Research
NCI Public Inquiries Office
6116 Executive Boulevard, Suite 3036A
Bethesda, MD 20892-8322
Phone: (800) 422-6237
Website: www.nci.nih.gov/index.html

National College of Naturopathic Medicine
11231 Southeast Market Street
Portland, OR 97216
Phone: (503) 255-4860

National Institute of Dental and Craniofacial Research
NIDCR Public Information and Liaison Branch
45 Center Drive, MSC 6400
Bethesda, MD 20892-6400
Phone: (301) 496-4261
Website: www.nidr.nih.gov

National Medical Services
3701 Welsh Road
Willow Grove, PA 19090
Phone: (800) 522-6671

National Pesticide Information Center Oregon State University
333 Weniger
Corvallis, OR 97331-6502
Phone: (800) 858-7378
Fax: (541) 737-0761
Website: www.npic.orst.edu/index.html
E-mail: npic@ace.orst.edu
(Information on the toxicity of pesticides)

Natural Resources Defense Council
1200 New York Avenue NW, #400
Washington, DC 20005
Phone: (202) 289-6868
Website: www.nrdc.org

NSF International
789 North Dixboro Road
Ann Arbor, MI 48113
Phone: (800) NSF-MARK
Website: www.nsf.org
(Independent organization that evaluates water filters)

Ontario Naturopathic Association
4195 Dundas Street West, Suite 213
West Toronto, ON M9X 1X8
Canada
Phone: (416) 233-2001

Pesticide Action Network (North America)
49 Powell Street, Suite 500
San Francisco, CA 94102
Phone: (415) 981-6205, ext. 316
Fax: (415) 981-1991
Website: www.pesticideinfo.org
(Database of registered pesticides)

Radon Office
Phone: (800) 644-6999

Vitamin Information Program
Hoffman-La Roche Ltd.
P.O. Box 877
Cambridge, ON N1R 5X9
Canada
Phone: (519) 624-2792
(Free research studies on vitamins and antioxidants for environmental
professionals)

Worldwatch Institute
1776 Massachusetts Avenue NW
Washington, DC 20036
Phone: (202) 452-1999
Website: www.worldwatch.org
(International nonprofit environmental research organization providing
information on children, the environment, and health)

Publications for Physicians, Nutritionists, and Natural Pharmacists

Alternative and Complementary Therapies
Phone: (914) 834-3100

Alternative Medicine Review
Phone: (800) 228-1966

Berkeley Wellness Newsletter
Phone: (386) 447-6328
Website: www.berkeleywellness.com

Harvard Health Letter
Harvard Health Publications
10 Shattuck Street, Suite 612
Boston, MA 02115
Website: www.health.harvard.edu

Herbgram
Phone: (512) 926-4900

Internal Medicine Alert
Phone: (800) 688-2421

International Journal of Integrative Medicine
Phone: (800) 477-2995

Journal of the American Nutraceutical Association
Phone: (205) 833-1750

Life Extension Foundation
P.O. Bcx 229120
Hollywood, FL 33022
Phone: (800) 544-4440 (orders)

Natural Pharmacy Magazine
Phone: (914) 834-3100

The Townsend Letter for Doctors
911 Tyler Street
Port Townsend, WA 98368
Phone: (360) 385-6021

Products

Fresh Alternatives™
Phone: (800) 551-8989
(Source for broccoli sprouts and green tea with optimum levels of sulferophane GS)

Health from the Sun
Division of Arkopharma
19 Crosby Drive, Suite 300
Bedford, MA 01730
Phone: (800) 458-8471
Website: www.healthfromthesun.com
(Omega 3 and 6 essential fatty acid products)

Misto Spray Olive Oil Dispenser
Phone: (888) 645-7772
Website: www.misto.com
(For nonstick cooking)

Natural Vitality, Inc.
217 Flume Street, Suite 130
Chico, CA 95928
Phone: (530) 894-0900
Website: www.naturalvitality.net
(Herbs, vitamins, and minerals, nutritional support for hot flashes and PMS, and breast, bone, and heart health)

Nature's Gate Natural Suncare SPF 15
Phone: (800) 327-2012
(Oil-free sunblock with vitamin E and aloe)

Sun Chlorella
Phone: (800) 829-2828
Website: www.sunwellness.com
(Dietary chlorella supplements)

Whole Foods, Inc.
6015 Executive Boulevard
Rockville, MD 20852
Phone: (301) 984-4874
(Located throughout the United States and offering an extensive selection of foods and health products)

Xavier Natural Flea Control Products for Your Pets
Phone: (800) 543-4379
(Collars, sprays, and shampoo containing flea-resistant natural limonene from citrus oils)

BIBLIOGRAPHY

Chapter One

Adamson, R. H., et al., eds. *Heterocyclic Amines in Cooked Food: Possible Human Carcinogens.* Princeton, N.J.: Princeton Scientific Publishing Co., 1995.

Alworth, W. L., et al. "Potent Inhibitory Effects of Suicide Inhibitors of 7, 12-Dimethylbenz[a]anthracene and Benzo[a]pyrene Initiated Skin Tumors." *Carcinogenesis* 12 (7): 1209–15 (1991).

Diet, Nutrition, and Cancer. Washington, D.C.: National Academy of Sciences Press, 1982.

Doll, R., and R. Peto. "The Cause of Cancer: Quantitative Estimates of Available Risks of Cancer in the United States Today." *Journal of the National Cancer Institute* 66: 1192–1308 (1981).

Dutton, G. J. *Glucuronidation of Drugs and Other Compounds.* Boca Raton, Fla.: CRC Press, 1980.

Fisbein, L., ed. *ILSI Monographs: Biological Effects of Dietary Restriction.* Berlin, Germany: Springer-Verlag, 1991.

Huang, M. T., et al., eds. "Food Phytochemicals for Cancer Prevention I: Fruits and Vegetables." American Chemical Society Symposium Series 546, Washington, D.C., 1994.

Hursting, S. D., and F. W. Kari. "Inhibition of Tumorigenesis by Calorie Restriction." *Perspectives in Prevention, The Cancer Bulletin* 47: 505–10 (1995).

Hursting, S. D., et al. "Mechanism-Based Cancer Prevention Approaches: Targets, Examples, and the Use of Transgenic Mice." *Journal of the National Cancer Institute* 91 (3): 215–25 (1999).

Mitchell, T. "Methylation: A Little Known but Essential Process." *Life Extension*, August 1998.

Pascale, R. M., et al. "Chemoprevention of Rat Liver Carcinogenesis by S-Adenosyl-L-Methione: A Long-Term Study." *Cancer Research* 52: 4979–86 (1992).

Pryor, W. A. "Antioxidants in the Prevention of Human Atherosclerosis." *Circulation* 85: 2337–44 (1992).

Reddy, B. S., et al. "Fecal Bacterial B-Glucuronidase: Control by Diet." *Science* 183: 416–17 (1974).

Slaga, T. J. "Antioxidants and Cancer Prevention." Report of the Thirteenth Ross Conference on Medical Research, Columbus, Ohio, 1994.

———. "Cancer: Etiology, Mechanisms and Prevention—A Summary." In *Carcinogenesis: A Comprehensive Survey*. New York: Raven Press, 1980.

———. "Inhibition of the Induction of Cancer by Antioxidants." *Advances: Experimental Medicine and Biology* 369: 167–74.

Slaga, T. J., and J. DiGiovanni. "Inhibition of Chemical Carcinogenesis." In *Chemical Carcinogens*. 2nd ed. In *ACS Monograph # 182*: 21, 1279–1321 (1984).

Slaga, T. J., and J. Quilici-Timmcke, eds. *A New Breakthrough in Cancer Research: D-Glucarate Helps Remove Toxins and Carcinogens from the Body*. New York: Keats Publishing Company, 1999.

Slaga, T. J., et al. "The Effects of Benzoflavones on Polycyclic Hydrocarbon Metabolism and Skin Tumor Initiation." *Chemico-Biological Interactions* 17: 297–312 (1977).

Walaszek, Z. "Chemopreventive Properties of D-Glucarate Acid Derivatives." *Cancer Bulletin* 45: 453–57 (1993).

———. "Potential Use of D-Glucaric Acid Derivatives in Cancer Prevention." *Cancer Letters* 54: 1–8 (1990).

Walford, R. L. "Caloric Restriction." *Life Extension*, February 1998.

Wattenberg, L. W. "Inhibition of Carcinogenesis by Minor Dietary Constituents." *Cancer Research* 52: 2085–91 (1992).

Weitzman, S. A., et al. "Free Radical Adduct Induce Alterations in DNA Cytosine Methylation." *Proceedings of the National Academy of Science* 9: 1261–64 (1994).

Chapter Two

Adamson, R. H., et al., eds. *Heterocyclic Amines in Cooked Food: Possible Human Carcinogens*. Princeton, N.J.: Princeton Scientific Publishing Co., 1995.

Brody, J. "On Tap or Bottled, Pursuing Purer Water." *The New York Times*, July 18, 2000.

"Dangerous Nail Polish? A Cosmetic Ingredient Is at the Center of Alarming Reports." *Natural Health Magazine*, March 2001.

DiGiovanni, J., and T. J. Slaga. "Modification of Polycyclic Aromatic Hydrocarbon Carcinogenesis." *Polycyclic Hydrocarbons and Cancer* 3: 259–92. Academic Press, New York, 1981.

DiGiovanni, J., et al. "Inhibitory Effects of Environmental Chemicals on Polycyclic Aromatic Hydrocarbon Carcinogenesis." In *Carcinogenesis: A Comprehensive Survey*. New York: Raven Press, 1980.

"FDA Warns Women Not to Eat Some Fish." *The New York Times*, January 14, 2001.

Fisbein, L., ed. *ILSI Monographs: Biological Effects of Dietary Restriction.* Berlin, Germany: Springer-Verlag, 1991.

"The Great Indoors." *Berkeley Wellness Letter*, February 1999.

Hursting, S. D., and F. W. Kari. "Inhibition of Tumorigenesis by Calorie Restriction." *Perspectives in Prevention, The Cancer Bulletin* 47 (1995).

IARC Monographs on the Evaluation of the Carcinogenic Risk of Chemicals to Humans: Tobacco Habits Other than Smoking. Vol. 37. Lyon, France: IARC Press, 1985.

IARC Monographs on the Evaluation of the Carcinogenic Risk of Chemicals to Humans: Tobacco Smoking. Vol. 38. Lyon, France: IARC Press, 1986.

"In the Air That They Breathe: Lead Poisoning Remains a Major Health Hazard for America's Children." *US News Online*, December 20, 1999.

"Kids at Risk: Chemicals in the Environment Come Under Scrutiny as the Number of Childhood Problems Soar." *US News Online*, June 19, 2000.

Lipinski, E. R. "The Battle Against Mold." *The New York Times*, September 12, 1999.

Nagourney, E. "Vital Signs: A Good Word for the Maligned Oxidant." *The New York Times*, March 9, 2000.

"Now the Hard Part: Putting the Genome to Work." *Science Times*, June 27, 2000.

"Science and Ideas: Assessing Children's Toxic Risks." *US News Online*, October 18, 1999.

Searle, Charles E., ed. *Chemical Carcinogens.* 2nd ed. *ACS Monograph # 182*: (1984).

Slaga, T. J. "Critical Events and Determinants in Multistage Skin Carcinogenesis." *Carcinogenicity and Pesticides: ACS Symposium Series* 414: 78–93 (1989).

———. "Food Additives and Contaminants as Modifying Factors in Cancer Induction." In *Nutrition and Cancer.* New York: Raven Press, 1980.

———. "Potential for Preventing Cancer by Chemical Inhibitors." *Cancer Bulletin* 36 (1): 61–64 (1984).

Slaga, T. J., and J. DiGiovanni. "Inhibition of Chemical Carcinogenesis." *Chemical Carcinogens* 2 (182): 1279–1321 (1984).

Wagner, E. "The Lowdown on Leftover." *Natural Health Magazine*, October 1999.

Walford, R. L. "Caloric Restriction." *Life Extension*, February 1998.

Weisel, C. P., et al. "Ingestion, Inhalation, and Dermal Exposure to Chloroform and Trichloroethene from Tap Water." *Environmental Health Perspectives* 104: 48–51 (1996).

Chapter Three

Brown, A. L., ed. *Present Knowledge in Nutrition.* 6th ed. Washington, D.C.: International Life Science Foundation, 1990.

Cadenas, E., and L. Packer, eds. *Handbook of Antioxidants.* New York: Marcel Dekker, Inc., 1996.

Fenwick, C. R., and J. N. Mullin. "Glucosinolates and Their Breakdown Products in Food and Food Plants." *CRC Critical Reviews in Food Science and Nutrition* 8: 123–201 (1982).

Fischer, S. M., et al. "Differential Effects of Dietary Linoleic Acid on Mouse Skin-Tumor Promotion and Mammary Carcinogenesis." *Cancer Research* (Supplement) 52: 2049s–54s (1992).

Fischer, S. M., et al. "The Effect of Dietary Fat on the Rapid Development of Mammary Tumors Induced by 7, 12-Dimethylbenz(a)anthracene in Sencar Mice." *Cancer Research* 52: 662–66 (1992).

Frei B., ed. *Natural Antioxidants in Human Health and Disease.* San Diego, Calif.: Academic Press, 1994.

Hayaski, Y., et al., eds. *Diet, Nutrition, and Cancer.* Tokyo, Japan: Japan Scientific Society Press, 1985.

Ho, C. T., et al., eds. "Phenolic Compounds in Food and Their Effects on Health I: Analysis, Occurrence and Chemistry." American Chemical Symposium Series 506, Washington, D.C., 1992.

Huang, M. T., et al., eds. "Food Phytochemicals for Cancer Prevention I: Fruits and Vegetables." American Chemical Society Symposium Series 546, Washington, D.C., 1994.

Huang, M. T., et al., eds. "Food Phytochemicals for Cancer Prevention II: Teas, Spices, and Herbs." American Chemical Symposium Series 546, Washington, D.C., 1994.

Huang, M. T., et al., eds. "Phenolic Compounds in Food and Their Effects on Health II: Antioxidants and Cancer Prevention." American Chemical Society Symposium Series 507, Washington, D.C., 1992.

Jordan, J. G. "Fats for Life." *Life Extension*, July 2001.

MacLeod, M., and T. J. Slaga. "Multiple Strategies for the Inhibition of Cancer Induction." *Cancer Bulletin* 47: 492–98 (1995).

Pryor, W. A. "Antioxidants in the Prevention of Human Atherosclerosis." *Circulation* 85: 2337–44 (1992).

Raloff, J. "Chocolate Hearts." *Science News Online*, March 18, 2000.

Reddy, B. S., and L. A. Cohen, eds. *Diet, Nutrition, and Cancer: A Critical Evaluation*. Vols. I and II. Boca Raton, Fla.: CRC Press, 1986.

Rice-Evans, C. A., and L. Packer, eds. *Flavonoids in Health and Disease*. New York: Marcel Dekker, Inc., 1998.

Rosenberg, J. H., ed. "The Nutritional Role of Fat: Fourteenth Marabon Symposium." *Nutrition Reviews* 50: 1–74 (1992).

Slaga, T. J. "Food Additives and Contaminants as Modifying Factors in Cancer Induction." In *Nutrition and Cancer*. New York: Raven Press, 1980.

Steinmetz, K., and J. D. Potter. "A Review of Vegetables, Fruit and Cancer." *Epidemiology, Cancer Causes and Control* 2: 325–57 (1991).

————. "Vegetables, Fruits and Cancer Prevention: A Review." *Journal of the American Diet Association* 96: 1027–37 (1996).

Thompson, H., et al. "Effect of Increased Vegetable and Fruit Consumption on Markers of Oxidative Cellular Damage." *Carcinogenesis* 20: 2261–66 (1999).

Walaszek, Z. "Potential Use of D-Glucaric Acid Derivatives in Cancer Prevention." *Cancer Letters* 54: 1–8 (1990).

Wattenberg, L. W. "Inhibition of Carcinogenesis by Minor Dietary Constituents." *Cancer Research* 52: 2085–91 (1992).

Yeager, S., et al., eds. *Prevention's New Foods for Healing*. Emmaus, Pa.: Rodale Press, 1998.

Chapter Four

Alworth, W. L., and T. J. Slaga. "Effects of Ellipticine, Flavone and 7, 8-Benzoflavone upon 7, 12-Dimethylbenz-[a]Anthracene, 7, 14-Dimethyldibenzo[a,h] Anthracene and Dibenzo [a,h] Anthracene Initiated Skin Tumors in Mice." *Carcinogenesis* 6: 487–93 (1985).

Brown, A. L., ed. *Present Knowledge in Nutrition.* 6th ed. Washington, D.C.: International Life Science Foundation, 1990.

Diet and Health: Implications for Reducing Chronic Disease Risk. Washington, D.C.: National Academy of Sciences Press, 1989.

Diet, Nutrition, and Cancer. Washington, D.C.: National Academy of Sciences Press, 1982.

DiGiovanni, J., and T. J. Slaga. "Modification of Polycyclic Aromatic Hydrocarbon Carcinogenesis." In *Polycyclic Hydrocarbons and Cancer.* Academic Press 3: 259–92 (1981).

Gardner, C. D. "The Role of Plant-Based Diets in the Treatment and Prevention of Coronary Artery Disease." *Coronary Artery Disease* 12 (7): 553–59 (2001).

Gardner, C. D., and H. C. Kraemer. "Monounsaturated Versus Polyunsaturated Dietary Fat and Serum Lipids: A Meta-Analysis." *Arteriosclerosis Thrombosis Vascular Biology* 12 (11): 1917–27 (1995).

Hirayama, T. "Epidemiology of Stomach Cancer in Japan with Special Reference to the Strategy for the Primary Prevention." *Japanese Journal of Clinical Oncology* 14 (2): 159–68 (1984).

Ho, C. T., et al., eds. "Phenolic Compounds in Food and Their Effects on Health I: Analysis, Occurrence, and Chemistry." American Chemical Symposium Series 506, Washington, D.C., 1992.

Huang, M. T., et al., eds. "Food Phytochemicals for Cancer Prevention I: Fruits and Vegetables." American Chemical Society Symposium Series 546, Washington, D.C., 1994.

Huang, M. T., et al., eds. "Food Phytochemicals for Cancer Prevention II: Teas, Spices and Herbs." American Chemical Symposium Series 546, Washington, D.C., 1994.

Huang, M. T., et al., eds. "Phenolic Compounds in Food and Their Effects on Health II: Antioxidants and Cancer Prevention." American Chemical Society Symposium Series 507, Washington, D.C., 1992.

Reddy, B. S., and L. A. Cohen, eds. *Diet, Nutrition, and Cancer: A Critical Evaluation.* Vols. I and II. Boca Raton, Fla.: CRC Press, 1986.

Rice-Evans, C. A., and L. Packer, eds. *Flavonoids in Health and Disease.* New York: Marcel Dekker, Inc., 1998.

Rotstein, J. B., and T. J. Slaga. "Effect of Exogenous Glutathione on Tumor Progression in the Murine Skin Multistage Carcinogenesis Model." *Carcinogenesis* 9 (9): 1547–51 (1988).

Slaga, T. J. "Inhibition of Skin Tumor Initiation, Promotion and Progression by Antioxidants and Related Compounds." *Critical Reviews in Food Science and Nutrition* 35 (1–2): 51–57 (1995).

Slaga, T. J., ed. *Modifiers of Chemical Carcinogenesis: An Approach to the Biochemical Mechanisms and Cancer Prevention.* New York: Raven Press, 1980.

Slaga, T. J., and W. M. Bracken. "The Effects of Antioxidants on Skin Tumor Initiation and Aryl Hydrocarbon Hydroylase." *Cancer Research* 37: 1631–35 (1977).

Slaga, T. J., et al. "The Effects of Benzoflavones on Polycyclic Hydrocarbon Metabolism and Skin Tumor Initiation." *Chemico-Biological Interactions* 17: 297–312 (1977).

Steinmetz, K., and J. D. Potter. "A Review of Vegetables, Fruit and Cancer." *Epidemiology, Cancer Causes and Control* 2: 325–57 (1991).

———. "Vegetables, Fruits and Cancer Prevention: A Review." *Journal of the American Diet Association* 96: 1027–37 (1996).

Suzuki, M., et al. "Implications from and for Food Cultures for Cardiovascular Disease: Longevity." *Asia Pacific Journal of Clinical Nutrition* 10 (2): 165–71 (2001).

Yeager, S., et al., eds. *Prevention's New Foods for Healing.* Emmaus, Pa.: Rodale Press, 1998.

Chapter Five

Berkson, B., ed. *The Alpha Lipoic Acid Breakthrough.* Rocklin, Calif.: Prima Publishing Company, 1998.

DeLuca, H. F., and J. W. Sultie, eds. *The Fat-Soluble Vitamins.* Madison, Wis.: The University of Wisconsin Press, 1969.

Griffith, H. W. *Complete Guide to Vitamins and Minerals and Supplements.* Tucson, Ariz.: Fisher Books, 1998.

Hendler, S. S. *The Doctors' Vitamin and Mineral Encyclopedia: The Most Comprehensive and Authoritative Guide to Food Supplements Ever Published.* New York: Simon and Schuster, 1990.

Kronhausen, E., et al., eds. *Formula for Life: The Antioxidant Free-Radical Detoxification Program.* New York: William Morrow and Company, 1989.

Levy, J., and P. Bach-y-Rita, eds. *Vitamins: Their Use and Abuse.* New York: Lweright, 1976.

Lieberman, S., and N. Bruning. *The Real Vitamin and Mineral Book: Going Beyond the RDA for Optimum Health.* New York: Avery Publishing, 1990.

Marks, J., ed. *A Guide to the Vitamins: Their Role on Health and Disease.* Baltimore, Md.: University Park Press, 1975.

Mertz, W., et al., eds. *Risk Assessment of Essential Elements.* Washington, D.C.: ILSI Press, 1994.

Murray, M. T., ed. *Encyclopedia of Nutritional Supplements.* Rocklin, Calif.: Prima Publishing Company, 1996.

Packer, L., and J. Fuchs, eds. *Vitamin C in Health and Disease.* New York: Marcel Dekker, Inc., 1997.

———. *Vitamin E in Health and Disease.* New York: Marcel Dekker, Inc., 1993.

Prasad, A. S., and D. Oberleas, eds. *Trace Elements in Human Health and Disease.* Vols. 1 and 2. New York: Academic Press, 1976.

Quillin, P., ed. *Healing Nutrients.* New York: Vintage Books, 1987.

Veris Vitamin E Newsletter. LaGrange, Ill.: Vitamin E Research and Information Service, 1996–2002.

Zifferblatt, S. M. *Antioxidants and Your Health.* Grand Rapids, Mich.: Better Life Institute, 1992.

Chapter Six

Abou-Issa, H. "Relative Efficacy of Glucarate on the Initiation and Promotion Phases of Rat Mammary Carcinogenesis." *Anticancer Research* 15 (3): 805–10 (1995).

Agarwal, C., et al. "A Polyphenolic Fraction from Grape Seeds Causes Irreversible Growth Inhibition of Breast Carcinoma MDA-MB468 Cells by Inhibiting Mitogen-Activated Protein Kinases Activation and Inducing G_1 Arrest and Differentiation." *Clinical Cancer Research* 6: 2921–30 (2000).

Ames, B. N., et al. "Oxidants, Antioxidants, and the Degenerative Diseases of Aging." *Proceedings of the National Academy of Science* 90: 7915–22 (1993).

Berkson, B., ed. *The Alpha Lipoic Acid Breakthrough.* Rocklin, Calif.: Prima Publishing Company, 1998.

Brienholt, V., et al. "Dietary Chlorophyllin Is a Potent Inhibitor of Aflatoxin B₁ Heptocarcinogenesis." *Cancer Research* 55: 57–62 (1995).

Brown, M. L., ed. *Present Knowledge in Nutrition.* 6th ed. Washington, D.C.: International Life Sciences Foundation, 1990.

Cadenas, E., and L. Packer, eds. *Handbook of Antioxidants.* New York: Marcel Dekker, Inc., 1996.

Dashwood, R. H. "Chlorophylls as Anticarcinogens (Review)." *International Journal of Oncology* 10: 721–27 (1997).

DeLuca, H. F., and J. W. Sultie, eds. *The Fat-Soluble Vitamins.* Madison, Wis.: The University of Wisconsin Press, 1969.

"Diet, Nutrition, and Cancer." The Committee on Diet, Nutrition, and Cancer. National Academy of Sciences, National Academy Press, Washington, D.C., 1982.

Dwivedi C., et al. "Effect of Calcium Glucarate on Beta-Glucuronidase Activity and Glucarate Content of Certain Vegetables and Fruits." *Biochemistry and Medical Metabolic Biology* 43 (2): 83–92 (1990).

Dwivedi, C., et al. "Effects of the Experimental Chemopreventive Agent, Glucarate, on Intestinal Carcinogenesis in Rats." *Carcinogenesis* 10: 1539–41 (1989).

Frei, B., ed. *Natural Antioxidants in Human Health and Disease.* San Diego, Calif.: Academic Press, 1994.

Greenwell, I. "Green Tea. Part I: Anti-Carcinogenic Properties of Green Tea." *Life Extension*, June 1999.

———. "Green Tea. Part II: Cardio-Protective Properties of Green Tea." *Life Extension*, June 1999.

———. "Very Berry—and Grape Too! Benefits Abound: An Update on Blueberries, Bilberry Extract, Cranberry Extract and Grape Seed Extract." *Life Extension*, March 2001.

Groopman, J. D., et al. "Molecular Epidemiology: Aflatoxin, p53 Mutations and Liver Cancer." Aspen Cancer Conference, Aspen Colo., July 2001.

Hecht, S. S. "Chemoprevention by Isothiocyanates." *Journal of Cellular Biochemistry* (Supplement) 22: 195–209 (1995).

Heerdt, A. S., et al. "Calcium D-Glucarate as a Chemopreventive Agent in Breast Cancer." *Journal of Medical Science* 31: 101–5 (1995).

Hendler, S. S. *The Doctors' Vitamin and Mineral Encyclopedia: The Most Comprehensive and Authoritative Guide to Food Supplements Ever Published.* New York: Simon and Schuster, 1990.

Ho, C. T., et al. "Phytochemicals in Teas and Rosemary and Their Cancer-Preventive Properties." American Chemical Society, 1994.

Ho, C. T., et al., eds. "Phenolic Compounds in Food and Their Effects on Health I: Analysis, Occurrence, and Chemistry." American Chemical Society Symposium Series 506, Washington, D.C., 1992.

Huang, M. T., et al. "Inhibition of Skin Tumorigenesis by Rosemary and Its Constituents Carnosol and Ursolic Acid." *Cancer Research* 54: 701–8 (1994).

Huang, M. T., et al., eds. "Food Phytochemicals for Cancer Prevention I: Fruits and Vegetables." American Chemical Society Symposium Series 546, Washington, D.C., 1994.

Huang, M. T., et al., eds. "Food Phytochemicals for Cancer Prevention II: Teas, Spices and Herbs." American Chemical Society Symposium Series 546, Washington, D.C., 1994.

Huang, M. T., et al., eds. "Phenolic Compounds in Food and Their Effects on Health II: Antioxidants and Cancer Prevention." American Chemical Society Symposium Series 507, Washington, D.C., 1992.

Jordan, K. G. "Osteoarthritis and Rheumatoid Arthritis." *Life Extension*, October 1999.

Kensler, T. W., and K. J. Helzlsourer. "Oltipraz: Clinical Opportunities for Cancer Prevention." *Journal of Cellular Biochemistry* (Supplement) 22: 101–7 (1995).

Kensler, T. W., et al. "Oltipraz Chemoprevention Trial in Qidong P.R.C." *Cancer Epidemiology, Biomarkers and Prevention* 7: 127–34 (1998).

Khachik, F., et al. "Lutein, Lycopene and Their Oxidative Metabolites in Chemoprevention of Cancer." *Journal of Cellular Biochemistry* (Supplement) 22: 236–46 (1995).

Levy, J., and P. Bach-y-Rita, eds. *Vitamins: Their Use and Abuse.* New York: Lweright, 1976.

Longenecker, J. B., et al., eds. *Advances in Experimental Medicine and Biology.* Vol. 369, *Nutrition and Biotechnology in Heart Disease and Cancer.* New York: Plenium Press, 1995.

Marks, J., ed. *A Guide to the Vitamins: Their Role on Health and Disease.* Baltimore, Md.: University Park Press, 1975.

Murray, M. T., ed. *Encyclopedia of Nutritional Supplements.* Rocklin, Calif.: Prima Publishing Company, 1996.

Nishino, H. "Cancer Chemoprevention by Natural Carotenoids and Their Related Compounds." *Journal of Cellular Biochemistry* (Supplement) 22: 231–35 (1995).

Oredipe, O. A., et al. "Dietary D-Glucarate Mediated Inhibition of Initiation of Diethylnitrosamine-Induced Hepatocarcinogenesis." *Toxicity* 74 (2–3): 209–22 (1992).

Packer, L., and E. Cadenas, eds. *Biothiols in Health and Disease.* New York: Marcel Dekker, Inc., 1995.

Page, M. "Vegetables Without Vitamins." *Life Extension*, March 2001.

Prasad, A. S., and D. Oberleas, eds. *Trace Elements in Human Health and Disease.* Vols. 1 and 2. New York: Academic Press, 1976.

Pryor, W. A. "Antioxidants in the Prevention of Human Atherosclerosis." *Circulation* 85: 2337–44 (1992).

Rice-Evans, C. A., and L. Packer, eds. *Flavonoids in Health and Disease.* New York: Marcel Dekker, Inc., 1998.

Slaga, T. J., and J. DiGiovanni. "Inhibition of Chemical Carcinogenesis." In *Chemical Carcinogens.* 2nd ed. In *ACS Monograph # 182*: 21, 1279–1321, (1984).

Slaga, T. J., and J. Quilici-Timmcke, eds. *A New Breakthrough in Cancer Research: D-Glucarate Helps Remove Toxins and Carcinogens from the Body.* New York: Keats Publishing Company, 1999.

Stoner, G. D., and H. Mukhtar. "Polyphenols as Cancer Chemopreventive Agents." *Journal of Cellular Biochemistry* (Supplement) 22: 169–80 (1995).

Van Zandwijk, N. "N-Acetylcysteine (NAC) and Glutathione (GSH): Antioxidant and Chemopreventive Properties." *Journal of Cellular Biochemistry* (Supplement) 22: 24–32 (1995).

Walaszek Z. "Potential Use of D-Glucaric Acid Derivatives in Cancer Prevention." *Cancer Letters* 54: 1–8 (1990).

Walaszek, Z., et al. "Antiproliferative Effect of Dietary Glucarate on the Sprague-Dawley Rat Mammary Gland." *Cancer Letters* 49 (1): 51–57 (1990).

Walaszek, Z., et al. "Dietary Glucarate as Anti-Promoter of 7, 12-Dimethylbenz[a]anthracene-Induced Mammary Tumorigenesis." *Carcinogenesis* 7 (9): 1463–66 (1986).

Walaszek, Z., et al. "Effect of Dietary Glucarate on Estrogen Receptors and Growth of 7, 12-Dimethylbenz(a)anthracene-Induced Rat Mammary Carcinomas." *Breast Cancer Research* 12: 128 (1988).

Walaszek, Z., et al. "Metabolism, Uptake, and Excretion of a D-Glucaric Acid Salt and Its Potential Use in Cancer Prevention." *Cancer Detection and Prevention* 21 (2): 178–90 (1997).

Wattenberg, L. W. "Inhibition of Carcinogenesis by Minor Dietary Constituents." *Cancer Research* 52: 2085–91 (1992).

Webb, T., et al. "Mechanism of Growth Inhibition of Mammary Carcinomas by D-Glucarate and the Glucarate-Retinoid Combination." *Anticancer Research* 13: 2095–2100 (1993).

Webb, T., et al. "Pharmacokinetics Relevant to the Anti-Carcinogenic and Anti-Tumor Activities of Glucarate and the Synergistic Combination of Glucarate-Retinoid in the Rat." *Biochemical Pharmacology* 347 (9): 1655 (1994).

Yang, C. S., and J. M. Landau. "Effects of Tea Consumption on Nutrition and Health." *Recent Advances in Nutritional Sciences, American Society for Nutritional Sciences* 2409–12 (2000).

Yoshimi, N., et al. "Inhibition of Azoxymethane-Induced Rat Colon Carcinogenesis by Potassium Hydrogen D-Glucarate." *International Journal of Oncology* 16: 43–48 (2000).

Chapter Seven

Abrabam, A. S., et al. "The Effects of Chromium Supplementation on Serum Glucose and Lipids in Patients with and Without Non-Insulin-Dependent Diabetes." *Metabolism* 41: 768–71 (1992).

Bracco, U., ed. *ILSI Monographs: Oxidants, Antioxidants and Disease Prevention*. Brussels, Belgium, 1995.

Brown, M. L., ed. *Present Knowledge in Nutrition*. 6th ed. Washington, D.C.: International Life Sciences Foundation, 1990.

Cadenas, E., and L. Packer, eds. *Handbook of Antioxidants*. New York: Marcel Dekker, Inc., 1996.

Diet and Health: Implications for Reducing Chronic Disease Risk. Washington, D.C.: National Academy Press, 1989.

Drovani, A., et al. "Therapeutic Activity of Oral Glycosamine Sulfate in Osteoarthritis: A Placebo Controlled Double Blind Investigation." *Clinical Therapy* 3 (4): 280 (1980).

Faloon, W. "Arthritis and Aging." *Life Extension*, July 2000.

Frei, B., ed. *Natural Antioxidants in Human Health and Disease*. San Diego, Calif.: Academic Press, 1994.

Greenwell, I. "Antioxidant Power." *Life Extension*, March 2000.

———. "Very Berry—and Grape Too! Benefits Abound: An Update on Blueberries, Bilberry Extract, Cranberry Extract, and Grape Seed Extract." *Life Extension*, March 2001.

Jordan, K. G. "Osteoarthritis and Rheumatoid Arthritis." *Life Extension*, October 1999.

Longenecker, J. B., et al., eds. *Advances in Experimental Medicine and Biology.* Vol. 369, *Nutrition and Biotechnology in Heart Disease and Cancer.* New York: Plenium Press, 1995.

Mertz, W., and E. E. Roginski. "Chromium Metabolism: The Glucose Tolerance Factor." In *Newer Trace Elements in Nutrition.* New York: Marcel Kedder, 1971.

Montagnier, L., et al., eds. *Oxidative Stress in Cancer, AIDS, and Neurodegenerative Diseases.* New York: Marcel Dekker, Inc., 1998.

Pujalte, J. M., et al. "Double Blind Clinical Evaluation of Oral Glucosamine Sulfate and the Basic Treatment of Osteoarthritis." *Curt Research Medical Opinion* 7 (2): 110 (1984).

Rabinowitz, M. B., et al. "Clinical Trial of Chromium and Yeast Supplements on Carbohydrate and Lipid Metabolism in Diabetic Men." *Biological Trace Element Research* 5: 449–66 (1983).

Rice-Evans, C. A., and L. Packer, eds. *Flavonoids in Health and Disease.* New York: Marcel Dekker, Inc., 1998.

"Veris Research Summary: The Neurological Role of Antioxidants." December 1997.

"Veris Research Summary: The Role of Antioxidants in Diabetes." May 1998.

Walaszek, Z., et al. "D-Glucarate Acid Content of Various Fruits and Vegetables and Cholesterol-Lowering Effects of Dietary D-Glucarate in the Rat." *Nutrition Research* 16 (4): 673–81 (1996).

Walaszek, Z., et al. "Hypocholesterolemic and Antiproliferative Effects of Glucarate." *Federated American Society of Experimental Biology Journal* 5: A930 (1991).

Chapter Eight

Bracco, U., ed. *ILSI Monographs, Oxidants, Antioxidants, and Disease Prevention.* Brussels, Belgium, 1995.

Diet, Nutrition and Cancer. Washington, D.C.: National Academy of Sciences Press, 1982.

Doll, R., and R. Peto. "The Cause of Cancer: Quantitative Estimates of Available Risks of Cancer in the United States Today." *Journal of National Cancer Institute* 66: 1192–1308 (1981).

Fishman, J., et al. "Low Urinary Estrogen Glucuronides in Women at Risk for Familial Breast Cancer." *Science* 204 (4397): 1089–91 (1979).

Greenwell, I. "Antioxidant Power." *Life Extension*, March 2000.

Hursting, S. D., et al. "Mechanism-Based Cancer Prevention Approaches: Targets, Examples, and the Use of Transgenic Mice." *Journal of the National Cancer Institute* 91 (3): 215–25 (1999).

MacLeod, M., and T. J. Slaga. "Multiple Strategies for the Inhibition of Cancer Induction." *Cancer Bulletin* 47: 492–98 (1995).

Minton, J. P., et al. "B-Glucuronidase Levels in Patients with Fibrocystic Breast Disease." *Breast Cancer Research and Treatment* 8: 217–22. Boston: Martinus Nijoff Publishers, 1986.

Rotstein, J. B., et. al. *A Possible Role for Free Radicals in Tumor Progression, Radioprotectors and Anticarcinogenesis: Anticarcinogenesis and Radiation Protection*. Plenum Publishing Corp., 1987.

Simon, L., and A. Figus. "Diagnostic Value of Determination of Lactate Dehydrogenase and B-Glucuronidase Activity in Gastric Juice." *Digestion* 7: 174 (1972).

Slaga, T. J. "Cancer: Etiology, Mechanisms, and Prevention—A Summary." In *Carcinogenesis: A Comprehensive Survey*. New York: Raven Press, 1980.

———. "Inhibition of Skin Tumor Initiation, Promotion, and Progression by Antioxidants and Related Compounds." *Critical Reviews in Food Science and Nutrition* 35 (1–2): 51–57 (1995).

———. "Overview of Chemical Carcinogenesis and Anti-Carcinogenesis." In *Radioprotectors and Anticarcinogens*. New York: Academic Press, 1983.

Walaszek, Z., et al. "D-Glucaric Acid as a Prospective Tumor Marker." In *Methods in Molecular Medicine*. Vol. XX, *Tumor Marker Protocols*. Totowa, N.J.: Humana Press, 1997.

"What You Need to Know About Cancer." *NIH Publication* No. 90: 1566 (1988).

Chapter Nine

Bracco, U., ed. *ILSI Monographs, Oxidants, Antioxidants and Disease Prevention*. Brussels, Belgium, 1995.

Brown, M. L., ed. *Present Knowledge in Nutrition*. 6th ed. Washington, D.C.: International Life Sciences Foundation, 1990.

Cadenas, E., and L. Packer, eds. *Handbook of Antioxidants*. New York: Marcel Dekker, Inc., 1996.

Diet and Health: Implications for Reducing Chronic Disease Risk. Washington, D.C.: National Academy Press, 1989.

Ditschuneit, H. H., et al. "Metabolic and Weight-Loss Effects of a Long-Term Dietary Intervention in Obese Patients." *American Journal of Clinical Nutrition* 69: 198–204 (1999).

Frei, B., ed. *Natural Antioxidants in Human Health and Disease.* San Diego, Calif.: Academic Press, 1994.

Gurr, M., ed. *ILSI Monographs, Healthy Lifestyles Nutrition and Physical Activity.* Brussels, Belgium, 1998.

Hyner, G. C. "Strategy for Planning and Evaluating Health Risk Appraisal and Screening Interventions." *Journal of Health Education* 26 (6): 345–52, (1995).

Loft, S., et al. "Energy Restriction and Oxidative DNA Damage in Humans." *Cancer, Epidemiology, Biomarkers, and Prevention* 4: 515–19 (1995).

Longenecker, J. B., et al., eds. *Advances in Experimental Medicine and Biology.* Vol. 369, *Nutrition and Biotechnology in Heart Disease and Cancer.* New York: Plenium Press, 1995.

Martin, K., et al. "Healthy Lifestyle Check: A Computerized Health Screening Program." *Computers in Nursing* 15 (2): 77–81 (1997).

Meeker, W. C. "A Review of the Validity and Efficacy of the Health Risk Appraisal Instrument." *Journal of Manipulative and Physiological Therapeutics* 11 (2): 108–13 (1988).

Montagnier, L., et al., eds. *Oxidative Stress in Cancer, AIDS, and Neurodegenerative Diseases.* New York: Marcel Dekker, Inc., 1998.

Reilly, M., et al. "Modulation of Oxidant Stress in Vivo in Chronic Cigarette Smokers." *Circulation* 94 (1): 19–25 (1996).

Schoenbach, V. J., et al. "Health Risk Appraisal: Review of Evidence for Effectiveness." *Health Services Research* 22 (4): 553–80 (1987).

Simon, L., and A. Figus. "Diagnostic Value of Determination of Lactate Dehydrogenase and B-Glucuronidase Activity in Gastric Juice." *Digestion* 7: 174 (1972).

Walaszek, Z., et al. "D-Glucaric Acid as a Prospective Tumor Marker." In *Methods in Molecular Medicine.* Vol. XX, *Tumor Marker Protocols.* Totowa, N.J.: Humana Press, 1997.

INDEX

A

A vitamins, 77–78
Acetyl-l-carnitine, 103, 104–5
Actinidiaceae, 42
Adenosine triphosphate (ATP), 16
Aflatoxin, 102
Agaricaceae, 42
Agarwal, Dr., 96
Agency for Toxic Substances, 20, 211
Aging, 122–24
Air fresheners, 32
Air pollution
  in home, 29
  household dust, 30
Alcohol, 142
Alive Academy of Nutrition, 211
Allergy and Environmental Health
  Association, 211
Allium, 42, 45–46
Allyl sulfides, 100
Almonds, 59
Alpha lipoic acid, 103, 104, 120
Alternative and Complementary
  Therapies, 217
Alternative Medicine Review, 217
Alzheimer's disease, 122
AMC Cancer Research Center, v, 3,
  60, 74, 131–32, 211
American Academy of Pediatrics, 211
American Cancer Society, 23, 134
American College for the
  Advancement of Medicine, 211
American College of Occupational
  and Environmental Medicine,
  211
American Environmental Health
  Foundation, 212
American Health Foundation, 30
American Heart Association, 134
American Industrial Hygiene
  Association, 212

American Lung Association, 212
American Medical Association, 134
Amino acids, 88–89
Anacardiaceae, 42
Androgens, 6
Animals, grain-fed, 66–67
Animals, range-fed, 66–67
Annonaceae, 42
Anthocyanin, 103, 105–7
Anthrax, 139
Antioxidant detoxification system,
  vii, 3, 12–14, 94. *See also*
  Detoxification
  antioxidants working together, 88
  supplements for, 103–9
Apigenin, 94, 98–99
Apples, 57
Arame, 150
Arthritis, 116
Ascorbyl palmitate, 123, 124
Atherosclerosis, 97
Attention deficit disorder (ADD), 33

B

B vitamins, 16, 51, 80–82
Berkeley Wellness Newsletter, 217
Better Life Institute, 134
Beyond Pesticides, 212
β-glucuronidase, 10–11, 96
Bilberries, 123, 124
Bio-Integral Resource Center
  (BIRC), 212
Biotin. *See* B vitamins
Birt, Dr., 98
Bladder cancer, 99
Blood cell count, 137
Blueberries, 56, 123, 124
  blueberry oat muffins, 152
Boron, 86
Brain degeneration, 122–24